Praise for Developmental Environmentalism

'Climate change remains the greatest moral challenge of our generation. And this is a novel, compelling and accessible account of East Asia's ambitious green energy transformation, and the major economic and environmental payoffs that our region and the world are already reaping as a result. Essential reading for policymakers and scholars alike.'

Kevin Rudd, former Prime Minister of Australia
and Global President of the Asia Society

'Impressive scholarship, with fresh insights accessible to the general reader on why the transformation to clean energy is bound to continue in Northeast Asia, despite current setbacks, as well as on the opportunities this presents for Australia and others if we understand the dynamics.'

Howard Bamsey, Honorary Professor, REGNET, ANU.
Chair of the Global Water Partnership.
Former Director General of the Global Green Growth Institute.
Former Executive Director of the Green Climate Fund

'This important book provides fresh insights into a critical question: why some countries—particularly China—appear more willing and able to accelerate green energy technologies than phase out fossil fuels. The authors nonetheless make a compelling case that the dedicated greening efforts of East Asian countries, especially in light of escalating geostrategic competition, represent a fundamental transformation with profound consequences for the battle to curb climate change.'

Barbara Finamore, Oxford Institute for Energy Studies and Founder of the
Natural Resources Defense Council (NDRC) China Program

'Northeast Asia is centrally important in humanity's struggle with climate change—biggest user of fossil and renewable energy, world factory for energy transition goods. This valuable book explains where China and Korea are at and where they are going.'

Ross Garnaut, Professor Emeritus of Business and Politics, University of
Melbourne. Author of Superpower: Australia's Low Carbon Opportunity

'China and South Korea are global leaders in state sponsored green energy transitions. Under the banner of "developmental environmentalism" this innovative new book argues that such transitions need to be understood from a Schumpeterian perspective of creative destruction, involving the creation of new green energy sources together with the winding back of older fossil fuel energy sources. These transitions are well under way in China and South Korea and this insightful and carefully researched book has important comparative lessons and is a must read for those interested in the future of the planet.'

Stephen Bell, Professor of Political Economy, School of Political Science and International Studies, University of Queensland

'A massive techno-economic transformation may be needed to save the planet from climate change. In this extraordinary book, Thurbon and her colleagues show how it may result as much from interstate economic and geostrategic rivalry as from well-meaning international cooperation. That, at least, is the lesson they draw from China's and Korea's remarkably rapid and ambitious state-led initiatives to build green technology and industry, including the world's largest renewable energy system. Empirically and theoretically rich, this beautifully written analysis is one of the most interesting and important works of political economy I have read in recent years. Its analysis of "developmental environmentalism" may also provide a small ray of hope for weary environmentalists.'

Eric Helleiner, Professor of International Political Economy, University of Waterloo

'This book breaks new ground in showing how East Asia's approach to the green energy shift is different from its Western counterpart. To do this, it develops and utilizes a powerful new theoretical framework of "developmental environmentalism." The authors focus on the delicate mix and sequence of creation versus destruction, namely, between creation of new green energy industries versus the destruction of fossil-fuel incumbencies. They arrive at this insightful comparison as they consider green energy shift as Schumpeterian "creative destruction," beyond the simple dichotomy of growth vs. de-growth. The book shows persuasively that it is possible for us to both "green" and "grow" our economy.'

Keun Lee, Winner of the 2014 Schumpeter Prize; Distinguished Professor, Seoul National University

'The world is grappling with the largest transformation since the industrial revolution: transforming energy systems to renewable energy to avert dangerous climate change. This book is a must-read for understanding the international political economy of such a process. *Developmental Environmentalism* examines how China and Korea are driving the transition to green technology through an elite mindset, a process of political legitimation, and state-led industrial policy sequencing, while struggling to engage in the creative destruction of the fossil fuel industry necessary for a transformation to occur. This meticulous, forceful account of China's and Korea's green technology ambitions provides a detailed assessment of how these countries are seeking a greater alignment of both creative and destructive aspects of the shift to clean energy. A valuable resource for all scholars of international and comparative political economy, and global environmental politics, as we enter the critical phase of mitigating climate change.'

Susan Park, Professor of International Relations,
University of Sydney

'Scholars and policymakers have increasingly noticed and discussed the central importance and dynamism of East Asia in relation to the necessary global energy transition to address climate change. And they have fiercely debated if China in particular is "saviour" or "disaster" in this regard. Thurbon and colleagues magisterially navigate these debates and provide us with both the most expansive evidence to debate, and a compelling overall framework—developmental environmentalism—for understanding what exactly is going on in the region regarding the energy transition. They show the crucial importance of understanding the difference between creating new green energy systems, and destroying old fossil-fueled ones, and that while China and South Korea in particular have been spectacularly good at the former, they (like many other countries) have struggled with the latter. This is a must read for those of us wanting to understand whether and how we might get to a successful energy transition.'

Matthew Paterson, Professor of International Politics,
University of Manchester

Developmental Environmentalism

Developmental Environmentalism

State Ambition and Creative Destruction in East Asia's Green Energy Transition

ELIZABETH THURBON
SUNG-YOUNG KIM
HAO TAN
JOHN MATHEWS

OXFORD
UNIVERSITY PRESS

OXFORD
UNIVERSITY PRESS

Great Clarendon Street, Oxford, OX2 6DP,
United Kingdom

Oxford University Press is a department of the University of Oxford.
It furthers the University's objective of excellence in research, scholarship,
and education by publishing worldwide. Oxford is a registered trade mark of
Oxford University Press in the UK and in certain other countries

Published in the United States of America by Oxford University Press
198 Madison Avenue, New York, NY 10016, United States of America

British Library Cataloguing in Publication Data
Data available

Library of Congress Control Number: 2022948744

ISBN 978–0–19–289779–4
ISBN 978–0–19–289850–0 (pbk.,)

DOI: 10.1093/oso/9780192897794.001.0001

Printed and bound by
CPI Group (UK) Ltd, Croydon, CR0 4YY

Acknowledgements

When we began work on this book in 2019, we could not have imagined the chaotic circumstances under which we would eventually be required to research, write, and bring it to conclusion. However, if the Covid-19 pandemic has taught us anything, it is that the seemingly impossible can be made possible—and even enjoyable—with the steadfast support of wonderful colleagues, friends, and family. We are thus eternally grateful to the many people who have supported and encouraged us along the way.

In writing this book, we have drawn inspiration from the work, insights, and feedback of many great scholars, including Steve Bell, Andrew De Wit, Alexander Korolev, Keun Lee, Susan Park, Linda Weiss, and Fengshi Wu.

Our brilliant team of research assistants have provided invaluable support and input over the past four years. Our heartfelt thanks go out to Caitlin Biddolph, Carol Huang, Christopher Khatouki, Alexander Mitchell-Hynd, Amila Withanaarachchi, and Mengying Yang. All have the brightest of careers in research ahead of them.

We have enjoyed outstanding support from our institutions—UNSW Sydney, Macquarie University, and University of Newcastle, and from our Heads of School Jan Breckenridge (UNSW School of Social Sciences), Professor Chris Dixon and Professor Greg Downey (Macquarie School of Social Sciences), Professor Steven Grover (MQ Business School), and Professor Abul Shamsuddin (University of Newcastle).

A special thanks to The Asia Society for giving ET a platform to share our teams' work with policymakers in Australia and around the globe under their fellowship program, in collaboration with the Australian Department of Foreign Affairs and Trade.

To the Oxford University Press Team, especially Adam Swallow and Ryan Morris, who have supported this project from the outset—thank you for your wonderful editorial guidance from start to finish!

We could not have completed this project without the invaluable financial support of the Australian Research Council under Discovery Project DP190103669.

And finally, we've been fortunate to have been wrapped in the love and support of our families who have extended us much understanding and kindness throughout this process, especially as we wrestled with writing during a series of extended lockdowns: Linda, Ken, Xander, Amélie, Jae Hyun, Seo-jin, So-ul, Carol, Kepei, and James—we dedicate this book to you.

Contents

List of Figures

List of Tables

List of Acronyms and Abbreviations

AC	Alternating current
ADB	Asian Development Bank
AESC	Automotive Energy Supply Corporation
AI	Artificial intelligence
AICBM	Artificial intelligence, IoT, Cloud, Big Data and Mobile
AMI	Advanced metering infrastructure
B-EMS	Buildings—Energy Management Systems
BEV	Battery electric vehicle
BMW	Bayerische Motoren Werke
BNEF	Bloomberg New Energy Finance
BV	Battery vehicle
CAGR	Compound annual growth rate
CALB	China Aviation Lithium Battery
CATL	Contemporary Amperex Technology Limited
CCP	Chinese Communist Party
CD	Creative-destruction
CDMA	Code-division multiple access
CDB	China Development Bank
C-EMS	Cloud—Energy Management Systems
CET	Clean energy transition
c/kWh	Cents per kilowatt hour
CNG	Compressed natural gas
CNY	Chinese Yuan
CO_2	Carbon dioxide
DARPA	Defense Advanced Research Projects Agency, United States
DC	Direct current
DE	Developmental environmentalism or developmental-environmental
DEC	Dongfang Electrical Corporation
DEWA	Dubai Electricity and Water Authority
DS	Developmental State
EA	East Asia/East Asian
EMS	Energy management systems
EPB	Economic Planning Board (Korea)
EPSIS	Electric Power Statistics Information System
ESS	Energy storage systems
EU	European Union
EV	Electric vehicle
FAW	First Auto Works, PR China

FC	Fuel cell
FCV	Fuel cell vehicle
FCEV	Fuel cell electric vehicle
F-EMS	Factories—Energy Management Systems
FEPC	Federation of Power Companies (Japan)
FF	Fossil fuel
FPDs	Flat panel displays
FYP	Five-Year Plan (PR China)
FYPGG	Five-Year Plan for Green Growth (Korea)
G7	Group of Seven
GDP	Gross domestic product
GE	General Electric
GEI	Global Energy Interconnection
GEP	Global Environmental Politics
GET	Green energy transition
GFC	Global financial crisis
GG	Green growth
GHG	Greenhouse gas
Gt	Giga tonne
GW	Gigawatt
HEV	Hybrid electric vehicle
HIE	Hybridized industrial ecosystem
HMC	Hyundai Motor Company
HSR	High-speed rail
HVDC	High-voltage direct current
HyNet	Hydrogen Energy Network
IC	Integrated circuit
ICCT	International Council on Clean Transportation
ICE	Internal combustion engine
ICEV	Internal combustion engine vehicle
ICT	Information and communications technology
IEA	International Energy Agency
IEEE	Institute of Electrical and Electronic Engineers
IETF	Internet Engineering Task Force
IoT	Internet-of-Things
IPE	International Political Economy
ISGAN	International Smart Grid Action Network
IT	Information technology
JV	Joint venture
KAIA	Korea Agency for Infrastructure Technology Advancement
KAIST	Korea Advanced Institute of Science and Technology
KAPES	KEPCO-Alstom Power Electronic Systems
KEPCO	Korea Electric Power Corporation
km	Kilometres
K-MEG	Korea Micro Energy Grid

koe	Kilogram of oil equivalent
KOGAS	Korean Gas Corporation
KPIs	Key performance indicators
KPX	Korea Power Exchange
KRW	South Korean Won
kV	Kilovolt
LCGG	Low-Carbon, Green Growth strategy, South Korea
LIB	Lithium-ion battery
LNG	Liquefied natural gas
LPG	Liquefied petroleum gas
MEE	Ministry of Ecology and Environment, PR China
MEST	Ministry of Education, Science and Technology, South Korea
MIC	Ministry of Information and Communication. South Korea
MIIT	Ministry of Industry and Information Technology, PR China
MKE	Ministry of Knowledge Economy, South Korea
ML	Machine learning
MLP for S&T	Medium to Long-Term Plan for Science and Technology, PR China
MOCIE	Ministry of Commerce, Industry and Energy, South Korea
MOEF	Ministry of Economy and Finance, South Korea
MOIS	Ministry of the Interior and Safety, South Korea
MOLIT	Ministry of Land, Infrastructure and Transport, South Korea
MOSF	Ministry of Strategy and Finance, South Korea
MOST	Ministry of Science and Technology, South Korea
MoST	Ministry of Science and Technology, PR China
MOTIE	Ministry of Trade, Industry and Energy, South Korea
MOU	Memorandum of Understanding
MSIT	Ministry of Science and ICT, South Korea
MVA	Megavolt ampere
MW	Megawatt
MWh	Megawatt hour
NASA	National Aeronautics and Space Administration, United States
NBoS	National Bureau of Statistic, PR China
NCCA	National Council on Climate and Air Quality, South Korea
NDRC	National Development and Reform Commission, PR China
NEA	Northeast Asia/Northeast Asian
NEV	New energy vehicle (term used in China)
NIEs	Newly industrializing economies
NPOPSS	National Planning Office of Philosophy and Social Sciences, PR China
OECD	Organization for Economic Co-operation and Development
PCFIR	Presidential Committee on the Fourth Industrial Revolution, South Korea
PCGG	Presidential Committee on Green Growth, South Korea
PC	Personal computer
PCS	Power Conversion Systems
PEVE	Prim Earth EV Energy

PHEV	Plug-in hybrid electric vehicle
PM	Particulate matter
PMDD	Permanent magnet direct drive
PPCA	Powering Past Coal Alliance
PPP	Purchasing power parity
PV	Photovoltaic
RD&C	Research, development and commercialization
R&D	Research and development
RE	Renewable energy
RMB	People's renminbi (Chinese currency)
SAIC	Shanghai Auto Industry Corporation
SAW	Second Auto Works, PR China
SGCC	State Grid Corporation of China
SMEs	Small- and medium-sized enterprises
SMR	*Sloan Management Review*
SoEs	State-owned enterprises
SPC	Special purpose company
S&T	Science and technology
TSMC	Taiwan Semiconductor Manufacturing Company Ltd
TWh	Terawatt-hour
U-Cities	Ubiquitous Cities
UHV	Ultra-high voltage
UHV-AC	Ultra-high voltage alternating-current
UHV-DC	Ultra-high voltage direct-current
UK	United Kingdom
UN	United Nations
UNEP	United Nations Environmental Program
UNFCCC	United Nations Framework Convention on Climate Change
US	United States
USD	US dollar
V	Volts
V2G	Vehicle-to-Grid
VAT	Value-added tax
VPP	Virtual power plant
VW	Volkswagen
WTI	West Texas Intermediate (oil)
WTO	World Trade Organization
WWII	World War II
WWS	Water, wind, and solar
xGrids	Extensible power grid management platforms with intelligence
XJ	Xuji Electric

1

Cutting through the Conflicting Images of East Asia's Green Energy Shift

For the past decade, the topic of Northeast Asia's green energy shift has sparked fierce controversy in both scholarly and public debate. In some quarters, Northeast Asian (NEA) countries are commended for their dedicated greening efforts. Proponents of this view observe that since the mid-2000s, the governments of China, South Korea, Japan, and more recently Taiwan, have released a series of ambitious national greening strategies and poured billions of dollars into developing, commercializing, and scaling green energy technologies and related industries.[1] These dedicated planning and investment efforts have seen NEA emerge—within the space of just a decade—as the epicentre of global green energy gravity. For example, China's renewable energy (RE) system involving energy generated from water, wind, and solar (WWS) now reaches a generating capacity of 906 gigawatts (GW) and dwarfs that of both the United States (US) (296 GW) and Germany (127 GW).[2] For their part, Korea and Japan have achieved global leadership in some of the most important green energy-related technologies and industries including smartgrids, lithium-ion batteries, and hydrogen fuel cells. For example, Japan, China, and Korea now effectively monopolize the global market for electric vehicle (EV) batteries, accounting for approximately 16, 47, and 37 per cent of the global market respectively in December 2020.[3]

Yet in other quarters, despite these achievements, NEA states are heavily criticized for their lack of progress towards the green energy shift. While critics acknowledge these states' significant investments in green energy industries, they note that the emissions reduction benefits have failed to materialize because governments continue to support fossil fuel (FF) energy expansion, for example by subsidising FF imports and building new coal and gas-fired power plants at home and abroad.[4] At the same time, critics censure NEA governments for dragging their feet in international climate negotiations, for failing to set more ambitious

---

[1] See for example Dent (2018), De Wit (2015, 2020), Jaffe (2018), Malcomson (2020).

[2] See 2021 *BP Statistical Review of World Energy* and 2021 Hydropower Status Report. Also the 2020 statistical report by the China Electricity Council.

[3] See M. Kane, 'SNE Research: Global xEV Battery Market—142.8 GWh In 2020', *Insideevs*, 18 February 2021, https://insideevs.com/news/488274/sne-research-global-xev-battery-market-2020/ (xEV captures the Battery, Plug-in Hybrid and Hybrid Electric Vehicle markets combined).

[4] Examples of scholarly critiques include Sonnenschein and Mundaca (2016), Ha and Byrne (2019), Chen et al. (2020), Ohta (2021).

Developmental Environmentalism. Elizabeth Thurbon et al., Oxford University Press. © Elizabeth Thurbon, Sung-Young Kim, Hao Tan, and John Mathews (2023). DOI: 10.1093/oso/9780192897794.003.0001

renewable energy and emissions reduction targets, and for missing those targets they do set. Thanks to this foot-dragging, to take Korea as an example, per capita emissions have continued to increase since 2008 while the uptake of renewables has lagged well behind its Organisation for Economic Co-operation and Development (OECD) counterparts, reaching only around 7.1 per cent of total energy generation in 2020.[5] Since the COVID-19 crisis, governments across the region have sought to turbocharge their green energy shifts by directing massive government stimulus packages to the further development and deployment of green energy technologies, and by announcing ambitious new green energy targets and zero emission goals, while setting their sights on coal-exit. Nevertheless, on the basis of past performance, these announcements have been met with significant scepticism, with some commentators suggesting that these states—especially China—are more likely to shirk than shoulder their new carbon reduction commitments (Erickson and Gabriel 2021). This scepticism is likely to swell since Russia's brutal invasion of Ukraine in early 2022 sent gas prices sky-rocketing, leading some East Asian countries to ramp up their use of coal—a story just starting to unfold as this book went to press.[6]

These conflicting images of Northeast Asia's progress towards the green energy shift are striking. In highlighting them here, our purpose is not to defend one image as more accurate than the other. Indeed, we believe both images to be at least partially true, insofar as over the past decade NEA's performance in the green energy shift has been decidedly mixed. Rather, we draw attention to these conflicting images because in our view, they reveal three important realities about the *nature of the green energy shift* and the *potential role of the state in expediting that shift*—not only in East Asia but also more broadly.

The first reality we observe relates to the fundamental nature of the green energy shift—and thus the principal policy challenges it involves. At its core, the green energy shift that we are grappling with today is a major techno-economic paradigm shift, the kind of shift that has characterized the evolutionary system of industrial capitalism since the early 1800s. In this sense, the green energy shift is no different from the techno-economic shifts that have preceded it, such as that from canals to railways in the early nineteenth century, from steam to electric power in the late nineteenth century, and from quill and ink to information technology (IT) in office automation in the twentieth century. And as economic theory tells us—and economic history confirms—in a capitalist system, all major techno-economic shifts involve a process of 'creative-destruction' (Schumpeter 2003). Specifically, as the Northeast Asian experience to date reveals, the green energy shift demands not only the *creation* of new green energy industries, but the

---

[5] See 2021 *BP Statistical Review of World Energy*
[6] While the data presented in our case studies covers the 2000–2021 period, the 2022 Russia crisis does not change our argument; we canvas the most likely implications of this breaking development in Chapter 8.

destruction of fossil fuel incumbencies.[7] Insofar as the green energy shift represents a major techno-economic paradigm shift, it is less a challenge of environmental policy, or even energy policy, than a challenge of techno-industrial policy: of *new industry building* and *legacy industry adjustment and dismantling.*

The second reality we observe relates to the central role of the state in expediting the green energy shift. Insofar as this shift is understood as essential to addressing the existential threat of climate change, it is widely accepted in scholarly, policy, and popular debate that national governments should do all within their powers to expedite it. This is arguably what distinguishes the green energy transition (GET) from previous techno-economic shifts. However, the question for policymakers is: what does 'all within their powers' actually entail? Insofar as the green energy shift represents a techno-economic shift embodying the process of 'creative-destruction' (CD), it seems obvious that state actors wishing to expedite it must simultaneously and successfully navigate two distinct but interrelated dynamics: the *creation* and *mass commodification* of new green energy technologies on the one hand, and the *destruction* of powerful, fossil fuel incumbencies on the other. We describe these dynamics as interrelated insofar as it is extremely difficult for governments to go about destroying FF incumbencies without first creating green energy alternatives and making them widely available at an affordable price. Similarly, it is very difficult (or at least very expensive) for governments to make green energy alternatives widely available at an affordable price without first destroying FF incumbencies, or else convincing incumbents to abandon fossil fuels and embrace green energies instead. In sum, if policymakers wish to expedite the green energy transition, they must be willing and able to expedite both the 'creative' and 'destructive' aspects of the Schumpeterian dynamic central to all major techno-economic shifts, not least the greening of energy systems.

The third reality we observe is that the 'creative' and 'destructive' aspects of the green energy shift often involve very different political constituencies and require different kinds of state capabilities. As a result, some state actors may be more willing and able to expedite 'creation' than 'destruction', thereby slowing a country's overall progress towards the green transition. Understanding the conditions—political, economic, and social—that might drive greater alignment between the state's 'creative' and 'destructive' ambitions and capabilities is thus critical to explaining long-term patterns of progress towards the green energy shift in particular national settings, and whether progress is likely to be sped up—or remain stalled—in the future.

This brings us to the aim of our book. In the chapters that follow, our primary objective is to *explain* Northeast Asia's distinctive pattern of performance in the green energy shift from the mid-2000s to the present and, on the basis of

---

[7] For ground-breaking Schumpeterian analyses of the green energy shift in NEA and more broadly see Mathews (2013, 2017b, 2020).

this understanding, to *anticipate* the most likely trajectory of that shift into the future. To this end, we seek to answer four interrelated questions. These questions are informed by our understanding of the green energy transition as a techno-economic shift embodying the Schumpeterian dynamic of 'creative-destruction'. We ask: (1) What has motivated NEA states to seek to expedite the green energy shift since the mid-2000s by embracing ambitious national greening strategies? (2) Why have these states appeared more willing and able to expedite the *creative* aspect of the shift in question (i.e., rapidly building green energy industries), rather than its *destructive* dimension (i.e., dismantling fossil fuel incumbencies and progressing rapid fossil fuel phase-out)? (3) What, if any, factors are now driving greater alignment between these states' 'creative' and 'destructive' ambitions and capabilities? And finally, (4) What obstacles remain to more rapid progress on the 'creative' and 'destructive' fronts, and are they likely to be overcome?

We seek to answer these questions through a detailed empirical analysis of the national greening efforts of two Northeast Asian countries: China and South Korea (hereafter Korea). We have chosen these countries for two main reasons. First, these states have both declared and demonstrated a high degree of ambition and capability on the green energy transition front—at least in terms of the 'creative' aspects of that transition—which has remained front and centre of the national policy agenda for more than a decade. In recent years, these countries' green energy ambitions have been the subject of sustained scholarly analysis, to which we have contributed individually and collectively.[8] A focus on these countries thus allows us to significantly deepen and extend existing understandings of the central role of the state in NEA's green energy shift.[9]

Second, Korea and China represent two very different regime types: an authoritarian dictatorship (China) and a developed democracy (Korea). A focus on these countries thus allows us to critically engage with the most influential existing explanation of the role of the state in Northeast Asia's green energy shift—that of 'authoritarian environmentalism' (Beeson 2010, 2018). Put simply here, and elaborated in Chapter 3, the authoritarian environmentalism perspective holds that authoritarian regimes are more capable than democracies of driving efforts to mitigate environmental degradation (Heilbroner 1974: 38). This is because authoritarian regimes such as China are more capable of mobilizing rapid, encompassing, and extensive greening programs—a view to which many now subscribe (Beeson 2010, 2018; Chen and Lees 2019; Gilley 2012; Moore 2014). At the same time, the process of democratization is said to weaken states' capacities to effect a rapid green energy shift, thanks in no small part to the state's diminishing

---

[8] Mathews (2013, 2015, 2017a&b), Tan (2018), Tan et al. (2021), Mathews and Tan (2013, 2014, 2015), Kim (2021), Kim and Thurbon (2015), Thurbon et al. (2021), Mathews et al. (2022)

[9] While we touch briefly on their experiences in Chapters 8 and 9, the analytical approach we develop in this book could also usefully be applied to the greening experiences of East Asia's other erstwhile developmental states of Japan and Taiwan.

abilities to exert 'power over' fossil fuel energy incumbents—an argument most recently applied to Korea (Kalinowski 2020). The authoritarian environmentalism approach is thus typically accompanied by explicit statements of pessimism on the part of Western analysts who claim that regretfully, we may just have to accept the fact that authoritarian regimes are more capable than democracies of meeting the challenge of climate change (Beeson 2010, 2018; Drahos 2021).[10]

We take serious issue with this view, rejecting both its foundational assumptions and its pessimism about the future.[11] A comparative analysis of China and Korea allows us to challenge the prevailing idea that authoritarian environmentalism can explain the effectiveness of Northeast Asia's greening strategies, and the related claim that democratization must compromise a state's capacity for strategic industrial governance. It also allows us to develop an alternative explanation for these states' progress towards the green energy transition.

A core argument of our book is that, when it comes to explaining China's and Korea's embrace of, and successes in, the green energy shift, the differences between these states are far less important than their similarities. The most significant similarity relates to the long-established developmental orientation and ambitions of their policymaking elite, and the recent evolution of traditional developmental ways of thinking into a new variety of the developmental mindset, which we call *developmental environmentalism* (Kim and Thurbon 2015). We argue that in both China and Korea, policymakers have embraced the green energy shift as an expression of their newfound 'developmental environmentalist' (DE) outlook. We further argue that to execute their greening strategies, the Chinese and Korean states have behaved less like 'top-down commanders' (as authoritarian environmentalism would have it) and more like the collaborative 'catalysts' characteristic of traditional developmental states (DS)—albeit with some important adaptations needed to deal with green concerns.[12] To advance this argument, we examine the emergence of a new mode of close, collaborative government business relations in China and Korea centred on hybridized industrial ecosystems (HIEs) that feature in some of these sectors (Kim 2019). This new mode of government–business collaboration, we argue, is crucial to these states' capacities to advance their green energy ambitions.

[10] On the other hand, a recent study makes the opposite argument: that democracies are better placed to expedite technology-intensive transitions like the green shift because democratic systems are more conducive to innovation (Aghion et al. 2021). We take issue with this view in Chapter 3, highlighting the limitations of 'regime-type' arguments more broadly when it comes to the effectiveness of techno-industrial governance.

[11] To be clear, while we reject the idea that China's greening successes should be attributed to its authoritarian model of governance, we agree with scholars such as Fengshi Wu and Ellie Martus (2020) who argue that the Chinese government's growing responsiveness to environmental concerns may serve to reinforce the regime's political legitimacy and stall democratic transition.

[12] Nevertheless, we acknowledge that there is an increasing concentration of political power in China, which may impact on approaches of the country's policy formulation and implementation in the future.

The value-added of developmental environmentalism

Our concept of developmental environmentalism (DE) provides a powerful framework for making sense of the green energy shift in Northeast Asia. It does so by both highlighting and paying serious analytical attention to the significant continuities *and* changes at the levels of elite ideation, strategic ambition, and policy action that are both driving and shaping the direction of the region's green energy shift. In terms of continuities, DE draws attention to the enduring influence in China and Korea of traditional developmental ideas about the state's primary goals and the appropriate role of the state in achieving them. In the developmental mindset, policymakers view local manufacturing capacity, technological autonomy, and export competitiveness as the essential foundations of domestic political legitimacy, national security, and international status and prestige, and embrace a central role for the state in advancing these goals through strategic interventions in the market.[13] As we will see throughout this book, these traditional developmental ideas continue to inform NEA governments' approach to the green energy shift—especially the overwhelming emphasis they place on nurturing local manufacturing capacity, technological autonomy, and export competitiveness as a necessary part of that shift.

Crucially however, we also observe something fundamentally transformative underway in Northeast Asia at the level of elite ideation, strategic ambition, and policy action; the green energy shift represents much more than continuity in NEA's erstwhile developmental states. Specifically, the enthusiastic embrace of the shift in question has been catalysed by policymakers' growing realization that their traditional 'fossil-fuelled' model of development is unsustainable economically, environmentally, and politically—in both the domestic and international (read: geopolitical) sense. This realization has led state agents to not just incorporate but increasingly to *centre* greening goals in their techno-industrial transformation strategies, not least by making a rapid shift towards renewables the central pillar of those strategies. To use the language of economists, it's about 'internalizing' greening objectives into their economic development strategies. In this sense— and as the term 'developmental environmentalism' implies—we take seriously not only the traditional *developmental* drivers of the green energy shift in NEA, but its *environmental* drivers (and indeed implications) as well.

It is here that our analysis departs fundamentally from many existing analyses of Northeast Asia's green energy shift. On the one hand, existing analyses tend to either dismiss or else understate the significant environmental considerations driving the shift in question, depicting it as 'developmental business as usual'.[14]

---

[13] On the origins, contours, and evolution of the traditional developmental mindset in Northeast Asia generally and South Korea in particular see Thurbon (2014, 2016).

[14] There are some important exceptions; Finamore's insightful intervention *Will China Save the Planet?* (2018) highlights the intense environmental concerns driving China's green shift from the early

On the other hand, many studies on environmental politics in NEA have not sufficiently taken the developmental drivers of the environmental initiatives into account. As our detailed case studies reveal, environmental concerns and their related political legitimacy challenges have featured alongside traditional developmental concerns as a key driver of techno-industrial policy ambition and activism in both China and Korea since the early 2000s. However, because in both contexts the state's domestic political legitimacy and international security has also hinged on its ability to deliver strong economic outcomes, the balance between the state's green energy industry creation and fossil fuel sector destruction efforts has not always been even. As we show in our case studies, the story of NEA's green energy shift is in many ways the story of these governments' efforts to reconcile their sometimes (but not always) conflicting developmental and environmental ambitions—to rapidly green their economies without compromising on the foundational developmental goals of local manufacturing capacity, technological autonomy, and export competitiveness.

Indeed, as we elaborate in Chapter 3, these states' enduring commitment to traditional developmental goals—alongside new greening goals—has had profound implications for both the policy sequencing and related pattern of performance of NEA's green energy shift observed thus far. Policymakers' enduring emphasis on local manufacturing capacity and technological autonomy has rendered them reluctant to simply substitute fossil fuel imports with imports of green energy and related technologies and equipment. Rather, their goal has been to substitute fossil fuel imports with *locally manufactured green energy and related technologies and products wherever possible*, with a view to solving the state's pressing energy/economic security and environmental challenges in one hit. While this has meant a strong early emphasis on the 'creative' side of the green energy shift, as domestic green energy capabilities have increased, so the balance between the state's 'creative' and 'destructive' ambitions and actions appears to be recalibrating, as we demonstrate in the case studies presented in Chapters 4 to 7.

Insofar as the concept of developmental environmentalism is intended to capture the actually-existing (i.e., empirically discernible) drivers and dynamics of NEA's green energy shift, it represents an exercise in inductive theorizing.[15] Like the concept of the developmental mindset (and the 'developmental state' before it), DE is principally intended to both *describe* and *explain* what is actually going on

---

to mid-2010s—not least China's coal-induced 'airpocalypse' (2018: 23). These environmental concerns have been a key factor driving investments in new and renewable energy industries, including EVs. For Finamore, the growing convergence of environmental and economic interests since that time indicates that there is something fundamentally transformative underway in China—a conclusion with which we agree.

[15] In the tradition of the foundational literature on East Asia's developmental states. For an insightful discussion of the inductive method in developmental state analysis with a focus on the work of Alice Amsden see Chu (2017).

in NEA—rather than what might or should be. More specifically, as we have indicated above and detail in Chapter 3, we use the term DE to capture an empirically discernible elite mindset, an associated legitimation strategy, and a distinctive policy approach (by which we mean an approach to 'creative' and 'destructive' policy *sequencing*, rather than specific policy *content*).

In this sense, 'developmental environmentalism' differs fundamentally from concepts such as Robyn Eckersley's 'green state', which are principally exercises in critically-informed normative theorizing (Eckersley 2004, 2018). Such efforts twin rigorous critique of the prevailing economic, social, and political structures that produce and/or perpetuate environmental harms with the articulation of alternative visions of what might (or should) be. Critically-informed normative theorizing plays a crucial role in debates about climate change generally and the green energy shift in particular. Yet as Eckersley (2018: 50) points out, to the extent that a good deal of this theorizing presents the challenge facing national governments as one of shifting from 'growth' to 'de-growth' (or from capitalism to a post-capitalist society), it can be inherently self-limiting and risk marginalizing the crucial voices of critical theorists in the politics of transition.

Specifically, by starkly framing the challenge as one of growth versus de-growth, critical theorists foreclose arguably more politically (and arguably environmentally) productive debates about the possibility of simultaneously advancing 'growth' and 'de-growth', that is, of growing the environmentally sustainable aspects of the economy (e.g., renewable energy industries) while 'de-growing' the harmful aspects (e.g., the fossil fuel sector) at the same time.[16] Such an approach would allow national governments to address environmental harms whilst avoiding the fiscal/financial (and related political legitimacy) challenges associated with an overall de-growth strategy. Eckersley thus calls for a new approach to critically-informed normative analyses of the global green shift, one that does not abandon the pursuit of transformative change but that takes certain problematic social structures as *provisionally given* 'in order to focus on political debates and policy prescriptions that are likely to carry high transformative potential' (2018: 50).[17] In the NEA context, we insist that state agents are focused on developmental goals as much as environmental (or climate-related) goals—and that it is the conjunction of two frames of reference that underpins the transformative potential of the NEA approach to the green energy transition.

---

[16] Of course, this leaves to one side the question of whether the empirical evidence supports the idea that 'green growth' can—under any circumstances—limit global warming to less than two degrees by 2050; for a comprehensive overview of available evidence on this question see Hickel and Kallis (2020).

[17] To give an example, we see the important work of scholars such as Susan Park and Tamara Kramarz as illustrative of such an approach. While acknowledging the imperative of a rapid green energy shift to mitigate climate change, Kramarz, Park and Johnson (2021) draw our attention to the disastrous social and environmental consequences associated with mining of renewables-related minerals and metals and offer a new way of conceptualizing those costs with a view to informing debates about developing more effective governance mechanisms.

Do we espouse 'developmental environmentalism' as an alternative vision for the future? As we argue in Chapter 9, there are both limits to the generalizability of this approach—given its distinctive domestic and geostrategic drivers—and some potential risks in its execution. However, we do see DE as an elite mindset, a legitimation strategy, and a policy approach with high transformative potential—insofar as it is currently transcending Northeast Asia's fossil-fuelled growth model and setting it on a more sustainable footing, while re-shaping the broader economic dynamics and geostrategic calculus of the global green shift. As such, while our book may not be categorized as an exercise in critically-informed normative theorizing, we do see it as consistent with Eckersley's call for scholars traversing the fields of International Political Economy (IPE) and Global Environmental Politics (GEP) to pay closer attention to the political conditions and contests that are currently producing and shaping genuine efforts to 'green' and 'grow' national economies. Our study of NEA's green energy shift differs from many existing analyses because we argue that what is going on in China and Korea is far from 'greenwashing' or 'business as usual', and that the economic *and* environmental consequences of the region's transformation are potentially profound for NEA—and for the globe.

In sum, we see the significance of this book in its taking seriously both the developmental *and* environmental considerations that are driving NEA's green energy shift, and in its providing fresh insights into policymakers' efforts to reconcile developmental and environmental goals. This enables us to provide a theoretically-informed and empirically-based assessment of the likelihood of future success. However, while state ambition is central to the story of NEA's green energy shift, we argue that a comprehensive explanation of the shift's drivers, dynamics, and most likely future trajectory must go further and explore the relationship between state ambition and *broader capitalist market dynamics*—especially the dynamic of 'creative-destruction'.

Bringing capitalist materialities back in

We argue that elite orientation and ambition is key to explaining Northeast Asia's pattern of performance in the green energy shift. However, we view capitalist market dynamics as an equally important explanatory factor, especially the transformative dynamic of 'creative-destruction' and the associated dynamics of technological learning and cost reduction. Here, we build on and go beyond existing analyses emerging from the field of IPE. As scholars such as Mat Paterson have pointed out, the issue of climate change has long been marginal to, if not a 'blind spot' in, the IPE literature.[18] Moreover, those IPE studies that do tackle this

---

[18] In 2020, the two leading IPE journals *New Political Economy* and *Review of International Political Economy* joined forces to publish two excellent special issues on 'blind spots' in IPE scholarship, nominating climate change as one of the most significant. See LeBaron et al. (2020) and Best et al. (2020). For

issue tend to either marginalize or neglect 'capitalism's materialities' (read: capitalism's essential characteristics, including its technological dynamics) and how they might be implicated in transformative action on climate change (Paterson 2020a: 401).[19] To the extent that the IPE literature (and we might add the GEP literature) does engage with questions of the relationship between capitalism and climate change, there is a tendency to assume an inherently negative relationship between the two, and that we must transcend the former to overcome the latter.

Our approach is different. We take as our starting point the idea that capitalism comes in different varieties, and that it is the fossil-fuelled, linear throughput variety of industrial capitalism that is problematic from a climate change perspective. So, if humankind is to avoid catastrophic climate change, the challenge facing the globe is not necessarily to transcend industrial capitalism but to comprehensively transform it—and perhaps most importantly to transform the energy system underpinning it. Moreover, we see capitalism as embodying its own transformative dynamic of 'creative-destruction'. Our distinctive contribution to the IPE literature is to centre this material feature of capitalism in our analysis and to explore the circumstances under, and ways in which, state actors might be compelled to harness the dynamic of 'creative-destruction' in pursuit of transformative change.[20]

Our argument

This brings us to the core of our argument about Northeast Asia's distinctive pattern of performance in the green energy shift since the turn of the twenty-first century. This decidedly mixed pattern, we argue, has resulted from varying degrees of (mis)alignment between these states' 'creative' and 'destructive' ambitions and actions. To elaborate, from the early 2000s to the mid-2010s, Korea and China were more committed to, and capable of rapidly expediting, the *creative* aspects of the green energy shift, thanks largely to these states' long-standing developmental ambitions. From the mid-2000s onwards, in light of twinned energy/economic

a masterful overview of the ways in which climate change is treated in the political economy literature more broadly (canvassing both orthodox and heterodox political economy scholarship) see Paterson and P-Laberge (2018).

[19] Although there are some important exceptions in the IPE field, see Bell (2020); Kim (2021); Thurbon et al. (2021).

[20] One prominent recent study in the field of economics highlighted the transformative potential of the 'creative-destruction' dynamic and argued that states should seek to harness this dynamic to address climate change (Aghion et al. 2021). However, this important contribution paid little attention to the conditions that might compel and/or enable states to act in such a way, apart from positing that democracies are more likely than authoritarian regimes to be effective in this pursuit—an argument that seems less than convincing when we consider the case of China—a point we take up in detail in Chapter 3.

security and environmental concerns, those traditional ambitions became manifest in a newfound 'developmental environmentalism'. Yet despite their successes on the 'creative' front, prior to 2015 these states' willingness and ability to progress the crucial *destructive* dimension of the green energy shift proved wanting. As we elaborate in Chapters 4 to 7, the reasons for this 'creative-destructive' misalignment centre on the perceived need to balance sometimes (but not always) conflicting developmental and environmental ambitions, and the complex political legitimacy and national security challenges associated with these twinned ambitions.

Yet since 2015 (or thereabouts), in both Korea and China we have seen a growing (though still incomplete) alignment between these states' 'creative' and 'destructive' ambitions and actions. That is, policymakers have been deepening and extending their techno-industrial activism, while at the same time taking significant steps to dismantle fossil fuel incumbencies, promoting coal-exit on the one hand, and the green re-orientation of state-owned power utilities and private sector FF incumbents on the other. We further identify the factors that explain this recent invigoration of the state's 'creative' *and* 'destructive' ambitions and actions in each setting. While some of these factors are context specific—and elaborated in Chapters 4 to 7—we identify four shared factors of particular significance that are common to each of our case studies.

The first is the nature of political leadership, by which we mean the heightened developmental-environmental ambitions of China's President Xi Jinping (2013–present) and Korea's former president Moon Jae-In (2017–2022).[21] The literature on Korea's erstwhile developmental state has shown that—given the country's quasi-imperial presidential system—the character of the president can often be a swing factor when it comes to the degree of ambition of the country's industry-building initiatives (Thurbon 2016). The same now appears true of China. As our detailed cases show, as their presidencies progressed, China's Xi and Korea's Moon proved themselves uniquely willing and able to expedite both the 'creative' and 'destructive' aspects of the green energy shift, and to mobilize local government actors behind 'creative' and 'destructive' initiatives. Political choices matter in the green energy shift.

The second (and closely related) shared factor is the changing geostrategic landscape, especially the growing great power rivalry between China and the US. This rivalry involves China's newfound ambitions for global economic and military primacy, and South Korea's increasingly frantic efforts to both stay ahead of China and catch-up with Japan at the technological frontier—especially in the strategic industries of the future. This growing geostrategic rivalry has had a profound impact on the focus, pace, and intensity of these states' strategic activism, especially but not only in the green energy arena. In both China and Korea, this activism

---

[21] We discuss the implications of Korea's recent change in president in Chapter 8.

has now morphed into what is best described as a kind of 'domestically-oriented economic statecraft', by which is meant 'government initiatives designed to reach for or push the high-tech frontier in order to fend off, outflank, or move in step with clearly defined rival powers—whether such rivalry is primarily economic or military' (Thurbon and Weiss 2019; Weiss and Thurbon 2020: 474). To be sure, there are important differences in the logic motivating this statecraft in the Korean and Chinese contexts. As indicated above, in Korea, domestically-oriented economic statecraft is driven primarily by a *geoeconomic* logic, and thus trained on the commercial objective of fending off an increasingly technologically competitive China, and catching up and/or moving in step with a technologically superior Japan.[22] In China, statecraft is arguably of a different (read: higher) order, motivated by the desire to establish global leadership—and challenge the US—in *both* the economic and military domains.[23] These different logics aside, the concept of domestically-oriented economic statecraft highlights the broader geo-economic and geo-political factors that are both informing and shaping the techno-industrial strategies of Korea and China—not least their greening strategies.

The third shared factor relates to the growing environmental problems associated with these states' traditional fossil-fuelled development strategies, which are now posing a major political legitimacy problem for the regimes in question. As indicated above, the environmental problem of greatest concern is not climate change—although this issue is most certainly gaining increasing attention. Rather, the more pressing problem is that of particulate pollution which shrouds major Chinese and Korean cities in thick blankets of haze for days and weeks at a time and causes untold damage to the health of the populations in question. The worsening of domestic environmental problems has coincided with growing international concern about, and action on, climate change. By changing cost calculations, growing international action is helping to transform global energy markets, creating massive new opportunities for green energy industry expansion—and massive new incentives for states to embrace more ambitious creative and destructive measures, as they are doing (we argue) in Northeast Asia.

This brings us to the last but by no means least important shared factor: the increasingly symbiotic relationship between NEA states' strategic activism and the distinctive market dynamics of industrial capitalism—a 'state-market symbiosis' in

---

[22] On the emergence of domestically-oriented economic statecraft in Korea in response to the China challenge in particular, and for an explanation of how this statecraft differs from both 'marketcraft' (Vogel 2018) and more generic 'industrial policy', see Thurbon and Weiss (2019).

[23] See Weiss and Thurbon (2020) for an extended discussion of the different logics that can drive domestically-oriented economic statecraft (i.e., geo-economic; geo-political; and fused geo-economic *and* geo-politically logics), with specific reference to South Korea, the US, and China. For the landmark analysis of what is best described as geo-politically driven, domestically-oriented economic statecraft in the United States see Weiss (2014); and Weiss (2021) on the evolution of the same in that context.

Stephen Bell's terminology.[24] The dynamics of most significance are the dramatic pace of technological learning and price reduction unleashed by these states' massive early investments in green energies—a by-product of the intensity of their developmental-environmental ambitions. Technological learning and price reduction is an inherent feature of all manufacturing processes—a feature that gives renewable energy derived from manufactured products (such as solar photovoltaic (PV) cells, wind turbines, and electrolysers) an inevitable price advantage over energy derived from extracting and burning fossil fuels. This rapid technological learning has resulted in the dramatic reduction in the price of renewable energies not just in NEA but globally.

These twin developments are now helping to transform the interests of the two most powerful political constituencies that have long stalled the Korean and Chinese states' destructive ambitions and actions: domestic energy consumers (both business and households) and fossil fuel incumbents. As international markets for carbon-intensive products have begun to dry up, FF incumbents are proving more willing to collaborate with the government to pioneer and seize first-mover advantage in emerging green energy industries from green hydrogen to offshore wind power and beyond. Thus, thanks largely to China's and Korea's long-term, dedicated efforts on the 'creative' front, the dynamic of the green energy shift in NEA now seems to have reached a tipping point; no longer does the dial seem stuck on the 'creative' side of the 'creative-destruction' dynamic. These states are now increasingly willing to advance the destructive dimension as well by introducing more aggressive prices on carbon and RE targets and setting ambitious timelines for FF exit. This is another reason why we see the green energy transition in East Asia as driven by states as much as by companies and markets. In this sense, our analysis supports the tentative conclusion drawn by Stephen Bell (2020) who posits that the world is now entering an era of 'symbiosis and mutually reinforcing leads' between national governments and markets that will continue to drive up clean energy investment, drive down clean energy prices and drive policymakers to take ever more ambitious strides towards a clean energy shift. To be sure, unforeseen events like the 2022 global energy crisis sparked by Russia's invasion of Ukraine might interrupt some governments' ambitious RE timelines in the short term, as leaders scramble to cover short-term supply interruptions (and minimize their economic, social, and political fall-out) by any means possible. However, the relentless progress of technological learning and price reductions for renewables means that those interruptions are likely to be temporary, a point we return to in Chapter 8.

In sum, we argue that China's and Korea's distinctive pattern of performance in the green energy shift since the turn of the twenty-first century can be explained

---

[24] On the potential for a 'state-market symbiosis' to drive forward the clean energy shift at a global scale, see Bell (2020).

by varying degrees of alignment between these states' 'creative' and 'destructive' ambitions and capabilities. Allowing for some leeway in exact dates, we see the year 2015 as marking an important transition. Following a period of misalignment characterized by a 'creative' emphasis (early 2000s–2015), we have seen growing alignment between the states' 'creative' and 'destructive' endeavours (2015–present) which we attribute to a range of factors—some of which are shared (i.e., presidential orientation and ambition, changing geostrategic landscapes, growing environmental concerns, and capitalist market dynamics) and some of which are context specific. On the basis of this growing alignment, we see cause for optimism about the future direction of NEA's green energy transition.

The green energy shift: Northeast Asia vs. the West

While the primary aim of this book is to deliver the first comprehensive analysis of the state's distinctive role in Northeast Asia's green energy shift, we also seek to articulate the ways in which this role differs from that typically observed in the industrialized West.

The first difference we identify relates to *motivation, ambition, and emphasis*. In the West, to the extent that states have sought to expedite an energy shift since the early 2000s, their primary motivation has been *energy security*. Thus, their emphasis has been on a shift away from energy imports towards domestic energy production, whether that locally-produced energy is green or not. This has typically involved a growing policy emphasis on exploiting local shale gas and deep-sea oil reserves, some of which are misleadingly branded 'clean' energies. We see the US as the stand-out example of this approach, which has effectively stunted its embrace of renewables (see Chapter 2 for comparative data) and informed its minimal engagement with international efforts to effect a global green shift. In a small number of Western countries, energy security motivations have been complemented by serious *moral-environmental* commitments and ambitions, leading to a greater emphasis on a truly 'green' energy shift. We see Germany and Northern European countries such as Denmark as the exemplars of this approach (see for example Weidmer 2008). Typically, these countries have been motivated to embrace green energies by growing community concerns about the existential challenge of climate change, and the threat it poses to human lives and livelihoods—and indeed the lives of all living things on Earth. These serious environmental ambitions have informed these countries' more vigorous engagement with international efforts to reduce carbon emissions. However, it is also fair to say that these countries recognize the economic *opportunities* inherent in a green shift, and some (especially Denmark and Germany) have become major exporters of renewable energy equipment and technologies, especially those related to wind power.

In NEA, we see a quite different set of motivations and ambitions at play. Here, environmental motivations have not been absent—despite frequent claims to the contrary. As indicated above and as we show in our case studies, in both China and Korea, environmental concerns have been an important driver of policy efforts related to both green energy industry creation and (more recently) fossil fuel industry destruction. Yet in stark contrast to the West, the environmental issue considered most pressing since the early 2000s has been that of particulate pollution rather than the more existential challenge of climate change, leading to these countries' relatively weak engagement with international carbon reduction initiatives—although this now appears to be changing, especially since COP26 at Glasgow in 2021. At the same time, while NEA governments have also been motivated to pursue an energy shift by energy security concerns, their severe natural resource constraints have informed a necessary emphasis on energies that can be locally *manufactured* (i.e., renewables) rather than those that depend on the extraction of fossil fuels, in which NEA countries are relatively poor.[25]

Moreover, alongside environmental and energy security concerns, an equally important driver of the energy shift in Northeast Asia has been the traditional developmental ambition of securing local manufacturing capacity, technological autonomy, and export competitiveness in the higher-wage, higher value-added industries of the future. This pursuit of business interests has further shaped these countries' strong emphasis on the development of manufactured (read: green) energies rather than on legacy fossil fuels. In sum, by promoting a rapid green energy shift, NEA governments are seeking not only to end their increasingly risky reliance on fossil fuel imports and to address pressing environmental concerns, but to shore up their economic (read: techno-industrial) security and export competitiveness. And as indicated above and explored in detail throughout this book, these traditional developmental motivations have only been amplified in recent years by intensifying geostrategic rivalries—leading to unprecedented efforts to expedite both the 'creative' and 'destructive' aspects of the green energy shift. These underlying developmental-environmental motivations and ambitions are what really distinguish NEA's green energy shift from those taking place elsewhere—especially in the US.

This brings us to the second key difference between Northeast Asia and the West, which relates to perceptions of the principal policy challenge facing national governments wishing to expedite greening goals. In NEA, thanks to their long-standing developmental orientations and ambitions, policymakers perceive the

---

[25] Of course, the production of renewables also depends to a significant degree on the extraction of critical materials such as copper, lithium, and rare earths. However, the natural resource constraints of renewables are considered to be of a fundamentally different nature than that of fossil fuels, insofar as these resource needs can be met—at least in part—through recycling efforts including urban mining and have the potential to be addressed through technological innovation. (For example, the emergent possibility of replacing lithium with salt in batteries).

principal challenge as one of *new green industry creation—and thus principally as a challenge of techno-industrial policy.* In the West, where the primary driver of the green shift is moral-environmental, the principal challenge is perceived as one of *reducing carbon emissions and (more recently) of phasing out fossil fuels altogether.* Thus, the greening challenge is perceived principally as a challenge of environmental and energy policy, rather than of techno-industrial policy more broadly.

These different perceptions have informed very different framings of the policy problem facing national governments in both political and scholarly debate—which is our third distinguishing feature. As Mat Paterson cogently reminds us, the framing of policy problems is important because it 'discloses possible responses, closing down certain policy options and opening up others' (2020a: 2). In NEA, governments have long framed the principal policy problem in positive terms: as one of new industry creation involving massive economic and environmental opportunities and benefits. In the West however, the policy problem is often framed in negative terms, i.e., in terms of what must be *stopped or destroyed* (rather than what must be *created,* as is the case in NEA). As Paterson (2020b) points out, this framing was originally reflected in the discursive emphasis on reducing or stopping carbon emissions both nationally and internationally. It is now reflected in the more recent rhetoric centred on 'the end of the fossil fuel era'.[26] To be sure, this newer framing has some important benefits, not least because—unlike the idea of 'carbon reduction'—it highlights the transformative systemic changes that are required if we are to avoid catastrophic climate change. Nevertheless, this framing has also had a number of unfortunate unintended consequences. In particular, it has tended to produce a very narrow emphasis in both political and scholarly debate on the challenge of dealing with extractive industries and their incumbents—and on the (often adversarial) politics of fossilfuel phase-out. In these stories, fossil-fuel incumbents are typically cast as the fierce opponents to—and indeed enemies of—the green shift.

However, as the NEA experience reminds us, the phasing out of fossil fuels is just one of the many challenges involved in effecting a global green energy shift. An equally important challenge involves helping those carbon-intensive sectors that will continue to play a central role in a low- and no-carbon society—such as transport and electricity generation and distribution—adapt to the new green order. Moreover, what is often overlooked in political and critical scholarly debate is that many incumbents in fossil-fuel extractive industries are also participants in, and

[26] Another kind of negative framing of the green energy shift typically in the West is the language of 'sacrifices and trade-offs'; the green shift is framed as a choice between 'jobs and growth' on the one hand and environmental protection on the other. This framing has had a number of unfortunate practical consequences. For example, in many contexts, it has allowed debate to be hijacked by fossil-fuel incumbents and their interests, who have been able to point to the economic costs of the green transition (for workers, consumers, and businesses) as a reason to take a more cautious and gradual approach.

emerging leaders of, renewable industries. Indeed, a key feature of the renewables shift in NEA has been close cooperation between FF incumbents (such as Korea's Hyundai and Korea Electric Power Corporation (KEPCO)) and the government in pursuit of a green shift.

These differences between Northeast Asian and Western approaches to, and framing of, the green shift now hold important lessons for other countries wishing to expedite the shift in question. While NEA is routinely held up as a model for developing countries, we argue that these lessons are relevant for developed and developing countries alike. We tease out these lessons in the ultimate chapter of this study—drawing on the detailed analysis of the cases we develop herein. Which brings us to the structure of this book.

Outline of the book

In Chapter 2, we begin by establishing empirically our claim that Northeast Asia's green energy shift has followed a distinctive pattern since the mid-2000s, with a primary focus on the macro-level data. We show how on the one hand NEA countries have led the globe in terms of their renewable energy investments, industrial expansion, and market share. Until recently however, these achievements on the industry creation front were not matched by efforts to phase-out fossil-fuels— although this pattern now appears to be changing. We also discuss the limitations of macro-level data analysis when it comes to illuminating not just the pattern, but also the drivers and dynamics of the clean energy shift. In doing so, we make the case for a fresh approach centred on the development of detailed longitudinal case studies, and the analysis of those case studies in ways that are sensitive to historical, political, and institutional factors—as well as to factors of capitalist market dynamics.

In Chapter 3 we introduce our novel analytical approach to both illuminating and explaining Northeast Asia's distinctive pattern of progress towards the green energy shift. As indicated above, our analytical approach synthesizes Schumpeterian understandings of 'creative-destruction' and techno-economic change with cutting-edge developmental state theorizing centred on 'developmental environmentalism'. Our key conceptual innovation is to reimagine DE as at once embodying an elite mindset, a political legitimation strategy, and a distinctive policy approach (by which we mean a distinctive approach to *sequencing* the clean energy shift). This reimagining, we argue, has significant analytical payoffs when it comes to understanding both the drivers and dynamics of the clean energy shift in East Asia.

In Chapters 4 through 7, we develop our detailed longitudinal case studies of green energy industry creation in China and Korea, canvassing developments from the 1980s up until the end of 2021.[27] In both countries, we focus on state efforts to support the rapid development and expansion of the electric vehicle and smart grid industries. We have chosen these industries because they are so central to the green energy shift not only in Northeast Asia but globally. They represent industries (automobiles and energy generation and distribution) that will straddle the fossil-fuel and green energy eras—and that have been very much under-analysed in the environmental politics and IPE literatures. In each case, we structure our analysis around these states' 'creative' and 'destructive' ambitions and capabilities—focusing on the factors that have fuelled 'creative' and 'destructive' ambitions at different points in time, that have enabled or constrained the execution of those ambitions, and that are now bringing those ambitions and capabilities into greater alignment. We also seek to identify the remaining obstacles to future progress on both the creative and destructive front, and how likely it is that these obstacles will be overcome.

In Chapter 8 we establish and analyse the similarities and differences between China's and Korea's developmental-environmental strategies and the factors that are driving and shaping them. Specifically, we reflect on the shared factors, identified above, that are now invigorating developmental-environmental ambition and driving greater alignment between these states' 'creative' and 'destructive' strategies (i.e., presidential orientation and ambition, changing geostrategic landscape, growing environmental concerns, and capitalist market dynamics). We also reflect on the distinctive workings of DE in each national context, considering the ways in which DE now manifests in China and Korea as a set of elite ambitions, as a political legitimation strategy, and as a particular approach to sequencing the clean energy shift.

In Chapter 9 we draw the threads of our argument together and offer a solution to our motivating puzzles. Namely, how was it possible that NEA countries started their green transition so late but then accelerated it to become world leaders in green industries within a decade? And how can we explain these countries' (taking China and Korea as prime examples) distinctive pattern of performance in the green energy transition—first enthusiastically embracing green energy industry creation, then fossil-fuel industry destruction? We then canvas the future trajectory of the global green shift in light of two key developments: escalating geostrategic competition between China and the US; and the ongoing challenge of economic development in a world beset by climate crisis. We close by teasing out the potential lessons of NEA's distinctive approach to greening for developing and developed countries alike.

---

[27] While our case studies end in 2021, we reflect on the implications of early 2022 developments, namely the global energy crisis and Korea's change in president, in Chapter 8.

2

Northeast Asia's Performance in the Green Energy Shift: What Does the Data Reveal?

For those familiar with the smog-clouded skies of cities home to heavy manufacturing such as Beijing and Tianjin in China or Ulsan in Korea, it may come as a surprise that the global renewable revolution is already well underway and is being led by Northeast Asia (NEA). In this chapter, we begin to evidence our central claims about NEA's green energy shift by homing in on the macro-level data. We pay particular attention to the question of what this data might reveal—and conversely what it might not reveal (or even obscure)—about the degree, dynamics, and ultimate direction of the shift in question.

The first claim we test against the data is that NEA has recently emerged as the centre of global renewable energy gravity. This claim is clearly affirmed by macro-level data depicting the dramatic increase in the region's renewable energy (RE) production, consumption, and investment, and the equally dramatic increase in the region's technological, manufacturing, and export capabilities in RE-related industries such as solar panels, wind turbines, batteries, electric vehicles, and smart grids.

The second claim we test is that Northeast Asia's impressive green energy shift has followed a distinctive pattern, characterized by two phases. Phase One—which began in the mid-2000s—involved a massive emphasis on the 'creative' (read: clean energy industry creation) side of the 'creative-destruction' equation, and the relative neglect of the 'destructive' (read: fossil fuel phase-out) side. The second phase (which began in the mid-2010s and continues today) involves the growing alignment between 'creative' and 'destructive' efforts, in which even more impressive green energy industry creation efforts are increasingly matched by bold efforts to reduce or eliminate fossil fuel production and consumption.

Regarding the 'creative' aspect of the shift, the data we provide below clearly shows that since around the mid-2000s, the NEA region (comprising China, Korea, Japan, and Taiwan) has not only rapidly increased its uptake of renewables in both the energy system overall and in the power sector specifically. The region has also made major advances—and indeed now leads the world—in the manufacture of equipment associated with renewable energy technology supply chains, such as solar, wind, EVs, and smart grids. Indeed, the data reveals that the uptake of renewables in the energy mix and the building of related industry have intertwined since the beginning of the green energy shift in NEA—indicating that

Developmental Environmentalism. Elizabeth Thurbon et al., Oxford University Press. © Elizabeth Thurbon, Sung-Young Kim, Hao Tan, and John Mathews (2023). DOI: 10.1093/oso/9780192897794.003.0002

the region intends to fuel its green energy shift with locally-manufactured rather than imported energy. The creation and growth of these new RE-related manufacturing industries stands out as a profound feature of the green energy shift in these NEA countries. Moreover, and in line with our claims about the two phases of the shift in question, since the mid-2010s the region's 'creative' activities have seemingly been turbocharged—affirming the idea of not just *continuity* but *acceleration* in 'creative' efforts across the first and second phases of the region's green energy transition.

When it comes to the 'destructive' aspect of the green energy shift however, the pattern that we claim exists is less apparent in the macro-level data. This data clearly supports the first part of our claim—that in phase one (the mid-2000s to mid-2010s), the region's ambitious 'creative' efforts were not matched by a similar level of 'destructive' action. But when it comes to our claim regarding a growing alignment between 'creative' and 'destructive' ambitions and actions in phase two, the macro level-data is less conclusive. For example, the data shows that the use of fossil fuels in NEA has continued to grow since the mid-2010s—albeit at a slower pace in recent years. At the same time, China has continued to build new coal-fired power capacity at a level dwarfing any other country in the world. And until recently, China, Japan, and Korea remained the top three public financiers of coal power projects in the world. In this context, the data also shows that coal consumption in the region has not declined markedly in recent years. Yet at the same time, energy intensity and carbon dioxide (CO_2) intensity in the region, measured by the ratios of energy consumption and carbon emissions to gross domestic product (GDP) respectively, have substantially declined (i.e., improved) since the mid-2010s.

Nevertheless, and as we elaborate in the concluding section of this chapter, we see important reasons to question precisely how much the macro-level data can reveal about the dynamics and direction of Northeast Asia's green energy shift and its most likely future trajectory. For this reason, when it comes to drawing conclusions on the basis of this data alone, we see serious limitations. We thus end the chapter with our call for a different—more qualitative and historically informed—approach to analysing NEA's green energy shift, which we elaborate in Chapter 3.

The creative dynamics of Northeast Asia's green energy shift: What does the data tell us?

The most arresting feature of the green energy shift in NEA is the rapidity of the transformation—from an industrial system largely dependent on fossil fuels at the turn of the century to one that is well on the way to a green transition in the current period. The growing appetite for renewable energies in NEA is evident in

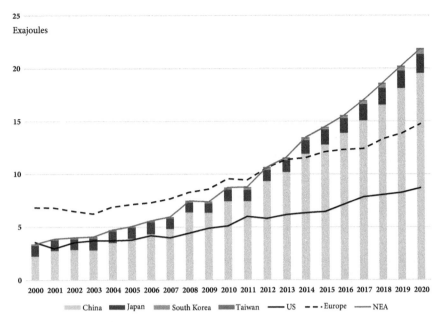

Figure 2.1 Renewables consumption, 2000–2020

Data: BP Statistical Review of World Energy

Figure 2.1. From 2000 to 2020, measured in energy units, the NEA region's consumption of renewables, including solar, wind, geothermal, biofuel, and hydro grew from 3.4 EJ (exajoules) in 2000 to 21.9 exajoules in 2020, an increase of 6.5 times over the 20 years. The rise of renewables in the NEA region has been particularly driven by the deployment of non-hydro RE technologies (solar and wind), which rose from 0.21 exajoules in 2000 to 9.73 exajoules in 2020. China and South Korea led the RE boom among NEA countries. Both countries recorded a compound annual growth rate (CAGR) of more than 30 per cent in their use of non-hydro renewables during the past two decades. Consumption of renewables in China exceeded the US in 2007 and Europe in 2014. Taken together, NEA countries substantially outperformed the rest of the world in the growth of their RE consumption. From 2000 to 2020, NEA's consumption of renewables and non-hydro renewables grew at a CAGR of 9.8 per cent and 21 per cent respectively, compared with a CAGR of 4.5 per cent and 13.2 per cent for the same indicators at world level.

Importantly, the use of renewables in the Northeast Asian countries has *outpaced* the growth of fossil fuels (FFs) and nuclear energy. Figure 2.2 demonstrates that the structure of energy consumption has indeed been shifting dramatically. From 2000 to 2020, the share of renewables in the total energy consumption in the region grew from four per cent to 12 per cent while the consumption of FFs

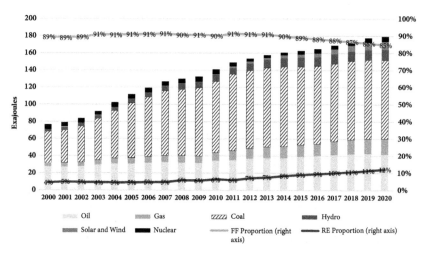

Figure 2.2 Energy consumption of Northeast Asian countries: Fossil fuels vs. renewable energies, 2000–2020
Data: BP Statistical Review of World Energy

declined somewhat from 89 per cent to 85 per cent. The pattern for nuclear energy also shows decreased levels (from six per cent to three per cent). The structural shift is even more sharply delineated if we focus just on power generation.

Figure 2.3 reveals that the share of renewables and hydropower in electric power generation in the region has increased steadily from 11.5 per cent in 2000 to 25.3 per cent in 2020—or a roughly 24 per cent shift in two decades. Renewables (including hydropower) took over from nuclear as an energy source in the national energy mix in 2006. During the same period, the share of fossil fuels in electricity generation has decreased from 71.4 per cent in 2000 to 67.1 per cent in 2020. We anticipate that the all-important crossover in power generation in Northeast Asia when power generated from renewables exceeds power generated from fossil fuels should occur by the end of the decade, in 2030.

How does NEA compare with the rest of the world? In Figure 2.4, it is evident that the region is not just shifting rapidly towards green energy sources, but it is doing so faster than any other part of the world. This means that NEA is playing an increasingly important, if not *the deciding factor*, in mitigating against climate change through steadily increasing the region's share in the world's renewable energy power generation. The region's global share was 12 per cent in 2000, well below that of European countries at 24 per cent and the US at 26 per cent, but by 2012, the region overpassed them in electricity generation from renewable sources, and the gap has continued to increase ever since. In 2020, NEA accounted for 33 per cent of global electricity generation from renewables.

The NEA region's leading global role becomes even clearer when we compare NEA's share of installed capacity into the two winning green energy generation

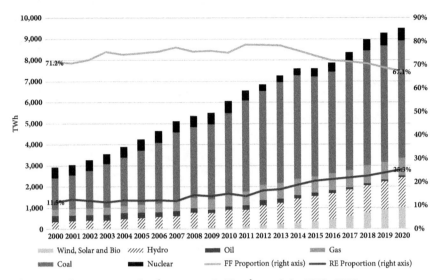

Figure 2.3 Power generation by sources in Northeast Asia, 2000–2020

Data: BP Statistical Review of World Energy

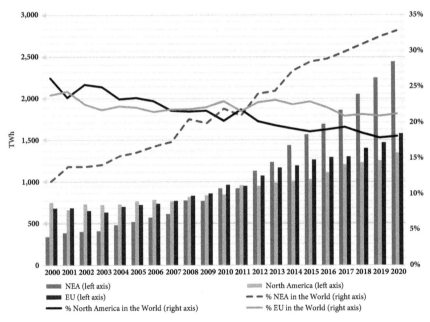

Figure 2.4 Global share of renewable energy power generation, 2000–2020

Data: *BP Statistical Review of World Energy*

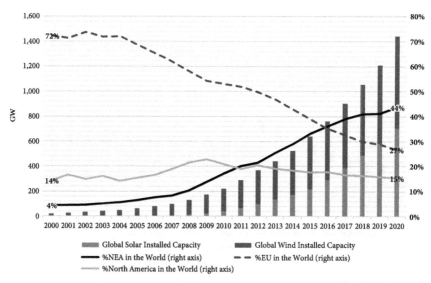

Figure 2.5 Share of installed renewable energy power capacity, 2000–2020

Data: BP Statistical Review of World Energy

technologies: wind and solar (Figure 2.5) (noting that wind and solar will also underpin the expansion of green hydrogen, which is emerging as one of the most critical technologies in global decarbonization efforts). In 2000, North American and European countries played dominant roles but, by 2020, NEA's share was 44 per cent of global installed capacity for wind and solar power—outpacing the European Union (EU) (27 per cent) and North America (15 per cent). The increase of the share is a result of the phenomenal growth of new installation of solar and wind power capacity in NEA, particularly in China and Korea, which expanded at a rate over 60 per cent and 40 per cent annually, respectively, on average since 2001.

The region's stellar performance is no accident. National authorities launched efforts to embark on the greening of their power systems backed up with enormous investments into installing green energy devices. Figure 2.6 provides a comparison of investment levels into renewable energy installed capacity from 2010 to 2019. During this decade, China, Japan, and Korea ranked amongst the top 20 markets for investments into RE capacity, totalling more than 1 trillion US dollars (USD) (USD 1,045 billion to be precise). This means that by around the end of the decade, Northeast Asia's investments into RE capacity were 1.8 times larger than those of the EU (USD 577 billion) and 2.3 times larger than those of North America (USD 451 billion).[1]

---

[1] Compared with those from China and Japan, the level of investment of Korea on renewable energies was relatively low. However, Korea's investment in RE seems to be accelerating. It rose by 31 per cent in 2019 compared with the level in 2018. The Green New Deal released by the Government of the Republic of Korea in 2020 aims to mobilize KRW 73.4 trillion (US$62 billion) by 2025, with a

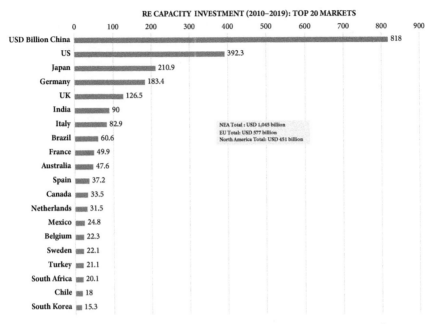

Figure 2.6 Renewable energy capacity investment, 2010–2019: Top 20 markets

Source: Based on data available from the FS UNEP Collaborating Centre

The significance of the figures above cannot be underestimated. As the 'factory of the world', the increasing installation, generation, and consumption of renewables in Northeast Asia's energy mix will have significant implications for reducing global carbon emissions—although not without a rapid phasing out of fossil fuels (more below).

Northeast Asia's efforts to green their power generation systems is also a story about the region's drive to build new domestic manufacturing industries in green energy technologies. Widely used green energy generating devices and systems such as solar photovoltaic (PV) technologies have been the subject of intense international competition (Figure 2.7). In 2019, China supplied 78 GW of PV modules, accounting for 63 per cent of global PV module shipments. Further, PV module shipments from Taiwan and Korea accounted for 5.6 per cent and four per cent, respectively, of the global total in 2019. Accompanying the greater scale of global PV module manufacturing, especially in Asia, is the rapid fall of costs. From 2010 to 2019, the price of PV modules decreased by over 70 per cent, from USD 1.5 per watt on average to USD 0.4 per watt.

focus of this investment in three areas, including green transition in cities, proliferation of low-carbon and decentralized energy, and development of innovative green industry ecosystems.

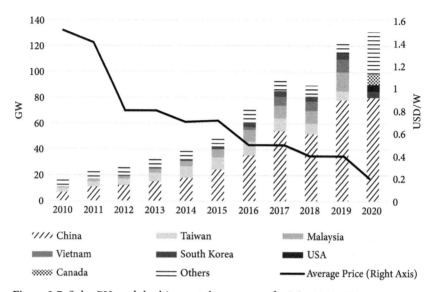

Figure 2.7 Solar PV module shipments by country of origin, 2010–2020

Data: IEA World Energy Investment (2020), available at https://www.iea.org/reports/world-energy-investment-2020; Bloomberg and REN21

The competitive advantages of NEA countries in the international solar PV market are more directly reflected in their export performance (Figure 2.8). In 2010, the European market share for solar PV exports was 59 per cent and NEA's was 27 per cent. By 2015, the tables were turned: the European countries' market share in the international solar PV market was reduced to 27 per cent and NEA's had risen to 47 per cent. The largest exporter of solar PV in NEA (and the world) is China, which averaged annual export values amounting to USD 25.5 billion from 2010 to 2020. This eclipses the figures for Japan (USD 4.6 billion) and Korea (USD 3.8 billion) during the same period.

In the key *enabling technologies* such as electric vehicles (EVs) and smart grids—the focus of this book—NEA countries have rapidly grown their market shares. In terms of battery electric vehicles (BEVs), an area once the domain of American and European countries, NEA manufacturers are now world leaders (Figure 2.9). In 2005, production of BEVs in the US and EU accounted for 58.6 per cent and 13.1 per cent of the global total while the NEA countries were completely shut out of this market segment. Yet, from the late 2000s onwards, the incumbents are now playing catch-up to new players from NEA. From 2008 to 2011, Japan overtook the EU and the US in a mere three-year period. Then, from 2014 to 2018, China and Korea joined the race and further enlarged the region's lead. By 2019, 58.8 per cent of BEVs in the world were produced in the NEA region.

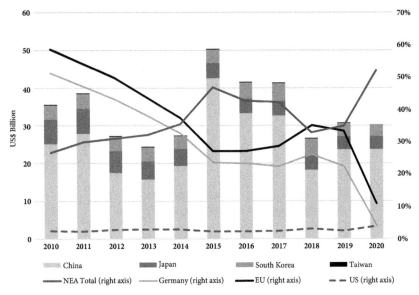

Figure 2.8 Solar PV exports by regions, 2010–2020

Sources of data: IEA, ISE, Statisita, and Nikkei

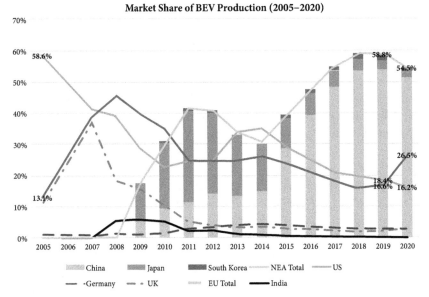

Figure 2.9 Production of BEVs as per cent in the world, 2005–2020

Data: KNOEMA

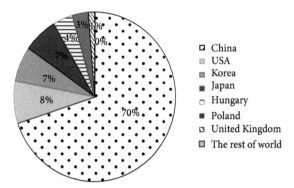

Figure 2.10 Global EV battery market share: Production lithium-ion battery by country in 2019 (MWh)

Source: Authors based on data available from Sun et al. (2021). Global competition in the lithium-ion battery supply chain: A novel perspective for criticality analysis. *Environmental Science and Technology*, 55, 12180–12190, Table S15

In Figure 2.10, we can see that Northeast Asian countries, in particular China, have dominated the global market for critical components in BEVs such as *batteries*. China accounted for 70 per cent of the global production of lithium-ion batteries (LIBs) in 2019, followed by the USA (eight per cent), Japan (seven per cent), Korea (seven per cent), Hungary (four per cent), Poland (three per cent), and the UK (less than one per cent). The rest of the world barely produced LIBs domestically.

While there are various types of emerging battery technologies, in terms of lithium-ion based products (a proven technology widely used by all of the major car manufacturers), the EU and Northeast Asia have been the two dominant exporters since 2012 (Figure 2.11). Chinese companies such as Contemporary Amperex Technology (CATL) and BYD, and South Korean companies including LG Chem and Samsung SDI are the stand-out performers. The region as a whole has been steadily expanding the value of its lithium-ion battery exports since 2012 (USD 8.8 billion) at a CAGR of 12.9 per cent to total USD 23.3 billion by 2020. However, Asian companies' LIB exports face increasingly intensive competition from companies in other regions. From 2012 to 2020, the share of exports of LIBs from EU countries in the international market increased from 21 per cent to 47 per cent, before this share plummeted to less than 30 per cent during the COVID-19 pandemic (Figure 2.11). In terms of Fuel Cell EVs (FCEVs) (an alternative type of EV technology to BEVs), according to data from Hyundai Motor Group,[2] Korea

---

[2] See: 'Popularising FCEVs: NEXO Sales over 10000 Units', *Hyundai Motor Group: Newsroom*, 20 November 2020, https://news.hyundaimotorgroup.com/Article/Popularizing-FCEVs-NEXO-Sales-over-10000-Units?sort=3&mainYn=Y

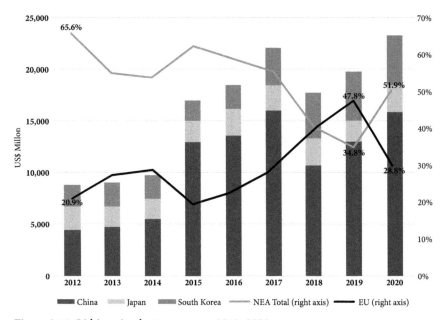

Figure 2.11 Lithium-ion battery export, 2012–2020

Data: UN International Trade Statistics database available at https://comtrade.un.org/Data/

is the global leader in this technology. In 2020, Hyundai achieved a year-over-year FCEV sales growth of 36 per cent, selling 6,600 units—which represented a 69 per cent share of the global market.

With regard to smart grid technologies, international competition remains fierce with no clear dominating region yet in sight. One of the main challenges in compiling data on smart grids is the fact that they are composed of a large array of technologies, devices, and systems—as opposed to EVs. As can be seen in Table 2.1 below, some of the main smart grid technologies include high-voltage grid transmission lines, transformers, energy storage systems (ESS), smart meters, uptake of EVs (as users and producers of renewable energy), demand response technologies, and microgrids. Table 2.1 also shows the different levels of progress in each of these aspects of smart grids in China, Korea, the US, and Germany.

There is little sense in making claims over a region's or country's progress in 'smart grids' as a whole. What *is* clear is that smart grid related technologies are projected to be of enormous value in the future. According to one broad estimate as shown in Figure 2.12, the 'Asia Pacific' area will become the biggest smart grid market by 2022 and is expected to capture approximately one-third of the global market by 2023. The global smart grid market is expected to grow at a CAGR of 20.6 per cent from USD 19.9 billion in 2017 to USD 61.3 billion in 2023 (Figure 2.12). In Korea alone, the cumulative installed capacity of energy storage

Table 2.1 Key data on smart grids in 2018

	China	South Korea	US	Germany
Length and Ratings of Lines	≥220 kilovolt (kV), 733,393 kilometres (km) UHVAC lines rated at 1,100 kV; UHVDC lines rated at 800 kV. By the end of 2020, total UHV line length reached 35,868 km.	Total 31,250 km long, including 835km of 765 kV lines, 8,653 km of 345 kV lines and of 21,530 km of 154 kV and below lines.	High-voltage transmission lines (miles) 642,000; Distribution lines (miles) 6,300,000.	1,845,385 km (up to 380 kV alternating current (AC), 500 kV direct current (DC) links planned) 220–380 kV: ~36,000 km 60–220 kV: ~96,000 km 6–60 kV: ~520,000 km 230/400 volts (V): ~1,120,000 km.
Capacity and ratings of transformers	≥220kV, 4,022,550 megavolt amperes (MVA)			
Number of Customers	6,844.9 terrawatt-hours (TWh)		145,000,000	50,468,192
Flexibility options in national grid	Hydro pump Storage	ESS		

Number of Smart Meters	471 billion	34 million smart meters by Nov. 2019. KEPCO is planning to distribute 100 per cent advanced metering infrastructures (AMIs) in private new buildings and more than 50 per cent in existing buildings by 2022, and achieve 100 per cent coverage in all sectors by 2025.	78,901,590	< 10,0000 (~ five Mio. binding)
Number of EVs	2.61 billion	60,000	1,116,483	53,861
Number and capacity of storage	29.7 GW	Grid-connected battery energy storage reached five GW in 2019; more than 1,250 battery ESS installed.	103 units/ 7,489 megawatts (MW)	Pumped storage: 27, 4.6 GW Battery storage: ~14,000, 78 MW
Number and example of demand response	28,000 demand response for peak load sheaving	More than 25 qualified demand response service providers; total capacity 4.3 GW.		Mainly industrial customers, e.g., chemical, steel, paper, automotive
Number of micro-grids	34	15/Investment 1.7 trillion Won (KRW)		
Number of Building Management System		116 KEPCO buildings by 2016		

Data: MI and Wuppertal Institut, and SGCC

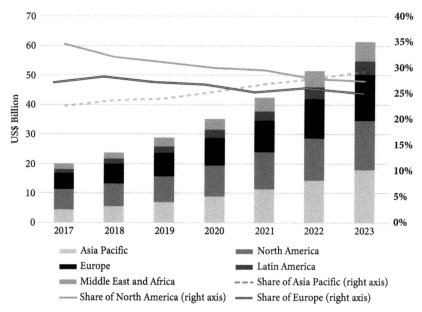

Figure 2.12 Global smart grid market size by region, 2017–2023 (est.)

Data: Authors based on data from Statista.com

systems is expected to grow from 0.5 GW (17.9 per cent of the world total of 2.8 GW) in 2016 to 6.9 GW in 2030—at a CAGR of 21 per cent.

A more meaningful way of measuring Northeast Asia's progress in the smart grid industry is by examining the region's performance in specific technologies. If we focus on just four core component systems—smart meters, super electrical capacitors, high-voltage direct current (HVDC) systems, and automatic regulators—it is possible to see that China and Korea are emerging as important manufacturers and exporters of smart grid components and equipment. As Figure 2.13 shows, from 2010 to 2020, the cumulative exports of the four categories from China and Korea were worth USD 234 billion and USD 28 billion, respectively. The sudden rise of China's share in 2015 was driven by the increases in its HVDC cable and automatic regulator exports (as discussed in the case study of China's ultra-high voltage innovations in Chapter 7). The export values grew by 91.7 per cent and 92.3 per cent respectively compared with 2014 levels. However, in 2018, US–China trade friction started dampening China's exports in this field.

As the world's major economies adjusted their tariffs and import regulations, Chinese exporting companies reduced their international business activities to minimize political, exchange, and collection risks. Overall, China achieved an average global share of 24 per cent with annual levels varying between 12 per

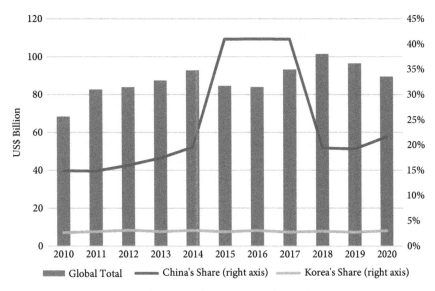

Figure 2.13 Export value of smart grid components (including smart meter, super electrical capacitor, HDVC and automatic regulator), 2010–2020

Data: UN International Trade Statistics Database

cent and 41 per cent, while Korea consistently retained a share of three per cent. The major customers for such componentry are utilities and, in Korea's and China's cases, state-owned utilities have played important roles in driving domestic demand for smart grid technologies. In Figure 2.13, the State Grid Corporation of China (SGCC, the world's largest utility) is shown to be a major purchaser of smart meters through its competitive-bidding system. From 2015 to 2020, SGCC bought 345.4 million smart meters (worth Chinese Yuan (CNY) 80.8 billion) from Chinese smart meter manufacturers.[3] In Korea, KEPCO has invested heavily into smart meters. During the period from 2010 to 2019, 8.48 million AMI meters were installed nationwide.[4] These developments show that Northeast Asian countries have demonstrated their ability to develop and commercialize smart grid related technologies, which has helped them achieve a growing presence in the global smart grid market.

---

[3] See: '2020年中国智能电表行业市场现状及发展前景分析 未来企业之间竞争将进一步加剧' [Analysis of the Market Status and Development Prospects of China's Smart Meter Industry in 2020], *Qianzhan Research Institute*, 6 August 2020, https://bg.qianzhan.com/report/detail/300/200806-03425b1a.html

[4] See 'Smart Meter, AMI development in Korea', *Vinatech*, 21 January 2020, https://www.vinatech.com/winko.php?code=blog_e&v=eng&body=view&page=1&number=38&category=&keyfield=&key=

The destructive dynamics in Northeast Asia's green energy shift: What does the data tell us?

For all their success in greening their power generation systems and growing green manufacturing industries, as we note in the introductory chapter, the Northeast Asian countries have been heavily criticized for their lack of progress in the phase-out of fossil fuels. China may be the region's and the world's largest investor and user of renewables (to generate electricity), but the share of water, wind, and solar (WWS) in the country's total energy consumption is only about 13.5 per cent as of 2020. Japan and Korea show even lower levels, at about 11 per cent and three per cent, respectively.

Unsurprisingly, the region's excessive reliance on imports of fossil fuels (since embarking on their industrial take-offs in the 1950s/60s) remains acute. While Japan, Korea, and Taiwan's oil imports have remained relatively stable through-out the following years, China's imports have expanded quickly since 2001. In 2020, China's annual oil imports reached 542 million tonnes, or about 80 per cent of its oil consumption in the year. Korea imported more oil than its domestic consumption, meaning the country relies almost entirely on crude oil imports to meet its domestic production and exports. Being net energy importers not only counteracts against efforts to green and grow the economy, but also exposes

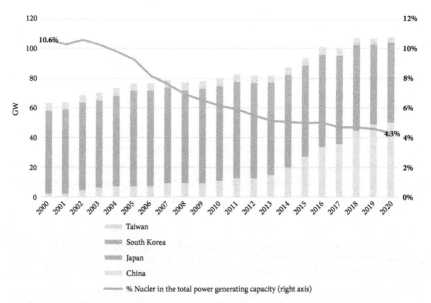

Figure 2.14 Nuclear power capacity in Northeast Asian countries, 2000–2020
Data: BoE TW, EPSIS KR, FEPC JP, NBoS CN

these countries to ongoing risks associated with highly volatile global oil prices. Calculated based on quarterly average West Texas Intermediate (WTI) oil prices, the annualized price volatility of oil prices was 31.6 per cent during the period from Q4 1999 to Q1 2020. In 2020, the volatility was as high as 84.5 per cent if calculated from average monthly crude oil spot price from December 2019 to November 2020. In Figure 2.14, we can see that the appetite for electricity generated from nuclear energy has also generally been declining in Japan and Korea since 2011 (the year of the Fukushima nuclear disaster). However, in China, the building of nuclear power capacity has continued to grow.

Coal phase-out

Much of the criticism of NEA countries' greening initiatives has been directed at the fact that coal continues to contribute a significant part of electricity generation. As Figure 2.15 shows, in the past two decades, NEA countries have added a total of 1,032 GW to their coal plant capacities and at the same time retired a total of 119GW. The net outcome was an expansion of 913 GW on their cumulative coal power capacities. The 1,032 GW was 40 times that of the US's new capacity of 25GW or 33 times that of the EU-28's new capacity of 31 GW during the same period. NEA's total retired 119 GW was higher than the EU-28's 98 GW but

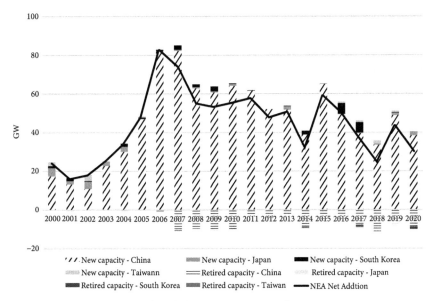

Figure 2.15 New and retired coal plant capacity in Northeast Asia, 2000–2020

Data: endcoal.org

lower than the US's 126 GW. Throughout the 20 years, the EU and the US reduced their cumulative coal capacities by 68 GW and 100 GW respectively. The annual net addition of NEA's coal plant capacity was built up quickly before 2006. Since countries in the region started retiring coal plants in 2007, the annual net addition gradually decreased from the peak of 82.7 GW in 2006 to 30.3 GW in 2020 with two reversals in 2015 (59 GW) and 2019 (43.6 GW). The annual growth rate of new coal capacity decreased by 47 per cent from 2015 (66 GW) to 2018 (34.9 GW). However, in 2019, this figure bounced back to 49.9 GW, thus reflecting little meaningful change from historical levels, especially in China. These NEA countries not only continue to build coal-fired power stations at home but also are the largest public financiers in the world for coal power projects abroad. As reported by the Global Energy Monitor, public financing by China, Japan, and Korea for coal capacity abroad—largely in developing countries—has significantly outweighed other countries such as India and Germany. From 2013 to July 2020, these three countries combined provided over 95 per cent of the public funding available to coal projects abroad.

However, Japan, and Korea pledged to stop funding overseas coal power projects in early 2021 and China made a similar announcement in September 2021. While international pressure for NEA countries to take more ambitious climate actions has contributed to their decisions, these moves were primarily driven by a rapidly changing market environment for coal projects abroad and the shifting policy orientation at home. Indeed, as our analysis elsewhere indicates in the case of China, its involvement in financing coal-fired power projects overseas had already decreased considerably during recent years, from 31 GW over the period 2015–2017 to 18 GW in 2018–2020 (see Tan et al. 2021).

The figures presented in this section indicate that the decarbonization of Northeast Asia's economies still has a long way to go. However, from a somewhat different perspective—measured by 'energy intensity', that is the amount of energy used to produce a given level of output or activity as generally measured by GDP, the energy intensity of NEA's economies (and the world as a whole) has been falling. As Figure 2.16 shows, although China and Korea exhibited higher levels of energy intensity than the world average, this began to drop from 2000 to 2019. In 2000, China consumed 0.226 kilogram of oil equivalent (koe) to produce one USD (2015 purchase power parities) worth of GDP, which was 0.122 koe higher than the level of Europe and 0.062 koe higher than the level of the US. By 2020, China had *reduced* its energy intensity to 0.145 koe/USD at an average annual reduction rate of 2.7 per cent, narrowing the gap with Europe and the US to a difference of 0.038 koe and 0.073 koe, respectively. During the same period, the energy intensity of Korea decreased from 0.186 koe/USD to 0.141 koe/USD. This is equal to an average annual reduction rate of 1.4 per cent.

In the context of climate change, a more concerning indicator is CO_2 emission intensity, as measured by the ratio between CO_2 emissions and GDP measured

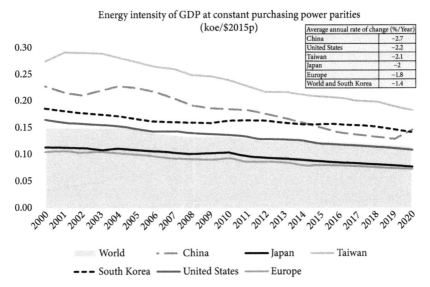

Figure 2.16 Energy intensity of GDP at constant purchasing power parities, 2000–2020

Data: EnerData

at purchasing power parity (PPP). The trend in CO_2 emission intensity is largely determined by the use of FFs as the major source of carbon emission and the level of economic growth. As shown in Figure 2.17, from 2000 to 2018 the carbon emission intensity of China, Japan, and Korea declined by 48 per cent, 40 per cent and 45 per cent respectively, compared with a fall of 45 per cent on average in emission intensity in the world. In other words, the major Northeast Asian economies do not seem to outperform the rest of the world in their reduction of fossil fuels in the contexts of their respective economic growth.

To further probe into recent trends of consumption of major fossil fuels in NEA countries, including coal, natural gas, and oil, we portray the growth rates of the use of these fuels in the NEA region as a whole (Figure 2.18) and in China which accounts for the lion's share of the FF consumption in the region (Figure 2.19). As suggested in Figure 2.18, the consumption of coal and oil in NEA countries grew fast in the mid-2000s and again in the early 2010s. However, since the mid-2010s, the growth of these FFs in the region has considerably slowed. In the case of coal, the consumption has either declined or barely grown since 2014. The growth rate of oil consumption has also continued to decrease from a level of 4.7 per cent in 2015, to one per cent in 2019 and −1.4 per cent in 2020. The exception is natural gas, which is seen by some as a cleaner energy source than coal and oil in the short- to mid-term transition towards sustainable energy systems. Consumption of natural gas continues to be at a high level of growth since 2015—although its reputation as an appealing 'transition fuel' is likely to take a significant hit following

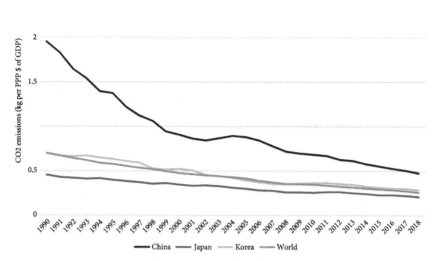

Figure 2.17 CO_2 emissions (kg per PPP $ of GDP): China, Japan, South Korea, and the world 1990–2018

Source of primary data: World Bank Database on World Development Indicators

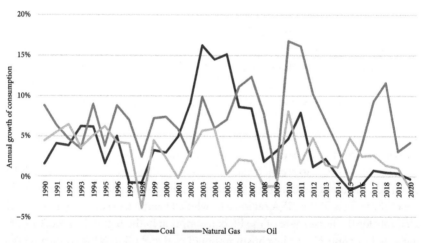

Figure 2.18 Growth of coal, natural gas, and oil consumption in the Northeast Asian region, 1990–2020

Source of primary data: BP World Energy Statistics

the Russia-induced energy crisis of 2022, which sent global gas prices soaring and turbocharged investments in renewable energies in Europe and beyond, as we discuss in Chapter 8. Similar and clearer patterns can be observed in the trends in consumption of major FFs in China in recent times (Figure 2.19).

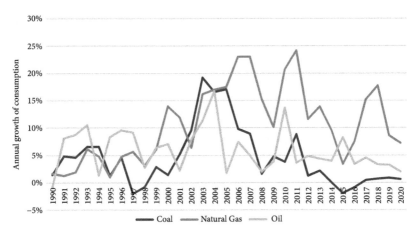

Figure 2.19 Growth of coal, natural gas, and oil consumption in China, 1990–2020

Source of primary data: BP World Energy Statistics

Making sense of the data and moving beyond the macro

The data we have presented in this chapter—most of which are at the macro level—sheds some important light on Northeast Asia's performance in the green energy shift. The data clearly reveals that the economies of China, Korea, Japan, and Taiwan have been ploughing resources into rapidly building globally competitive green energy industries and—especially in China's case—in rapidly expanding their use of renewables in local power markets—and that they have had significant successes in this arena. The data also tells us that these countries have so far failed to significantly reduce their use of fossil fuels or their greenhouse gas (GHG) emissions in ways that are reflected in macro-level national data.

The question thus arises: what broader conclusions are reasonable to draw from this data about the dynamics and direction of the changes underway in NEA? Based on the kinds of data we've presented in this chapter, some observers have drawn the conclusion that we should be sceptical of and pessimistic about NEA's green energy shift (see Chapter 1). Drawing on such data, they conclude that the idea of 'green growth' (GG) in NEA is a sham—that China's and Korea's clean energy building activities are just a continuation of 'old-style' developmentalism—and that these countries are far more interested in sustaining their national economic competitiveness than in seriously transforming their energy systems by moving away from FFs. In sum, based on the kinds of data we present in this chapter, some observers conclude that we were not really witnessing a transformative change in the region—we were simply observing 'business as usual'.[5]

---

[5] See for example Ha and Byrne (2019) on Korea and Erickson and Gabriel (2021) on China.

We take a different view and offer four main reasons as to why it is important for one to be cautious about drawing such conclusions from the macro-level data alone. First, the data itself tells us nothing about the domestic and international factors that are both *driving* the changes underway and powerfully *shaping* the direction they take. Specifically, the data tells us nothing about the very real domestic legitimacy and geostrategic challenges that originally compelled—and continue to compel—these countries to embrace a comprehensive green energy shift, and that point to fossil fuel phase-out as the logical end point (and ultimate goal) of this transformative process.

Second, the data reveals nothing about the powerful geostrategic logic that has informed these countries' *sequencing* of the green energy shift. We describe this as the logic of 'manufacturing energy security' (Mathews and Tan 2014). In this logic, *local clean energy industry creation is viewed as the strategic pre-requisite of fossil fuel phase-out—insofar as there is little desire in China and Korea to substitute FF import reliance with a reliance on the import of green energy equipment and infrastructure.* The logic of 'manufacturing energy security' explains why we might expect an early 'creative' emphasis to precede ambitious efforts to phase-out FFs—an effort that we argue is now in train, but not yet reflected in macro data.

Third, the macro data reveals nothing of the complexity of engineering a rapid green energy shift—especially one centred on the goal of localization. As we show in our case study chapters, this is not simply a matter of deploying solar panels and wind turbines and electric vehicles —but about the far more complex task of increasing the overall rate of electrification of the economy, and of rolling out the strong and smart grid infrastructures that can accommodate higher levels of renewables—along with charging infrastructures. This is a massive infrastructure challenge in and of itself but is made all the more challenging should a country wish for strategic reasons (as these countries do) to prioritize the development and deployment of *local grid and charging technologies* in order to enhance long-term energy security and economic competitiveness. In other words, the transition process is likely to be messy and certain patterns may not be yet reflected in macro data. For this reason, it is not surprising that the macro data on fossil fuel phase-out looks like it does—but we should not assume it will continue to look this way.

This brings us to our fourth and final—and perhaps most important—reason to be wary of an over-reliance on macro data for illuminating (not to mention explaining) Northeast Asia's performance in the green energy shift. That is, the macro data can deflect our attention from the fact that the overall (macro) green energy transition is made up of many micro-level transitions—that is, transitions *within* particular industries like EVs and smart grids—and in industries within those industries (e.g., for EVs, transitions within fuel cell and charging infrastructure industries). The macro data can also obscure how these industries are both geographically dispersed within countries and subject to multiple layers of governance (national and local). This means that we typically see rapid progress in some industry segments and slower progress in others, complicating the overall green-ing picture. Moreover, the effects of fossil fuel use, such as particulate pollution from coal-fired power stations or diesel cars, can also be geographically dispersed, and action to address these issues may be locally rather than nationally driven. The macro data can conceal the fact that significant destructive steps may be in train in particular industries in particular jurisdictions and while these changes are not yet reflected in macro data, they are contributing to the overall momentum of the shift taking place. This is especially the case when we factor in the momen-tum involved in the capitalist dynamics of learning and price reduction which can quickly bring on 'destruction'. There is also a high level of heterogeneity in the pace and scale of the green energy shift at the local level. For example, recent studies report that certain regions, such as Guangdong in China and Chungnam in Korea, are more aggressive in their phase-out of coal power stations than other regions in the country. We thus find good reason to question the conventional wisdom, espoused by influential scholars such as Vaclav Smil (2010), that energy transi-tions are necessarily prolonged affairs that take many decades to achieve. Indeed, as some excellent recent studies have shown, when they start in earnest, energy transitions can occur very quickly indeed: think France's near complete transition to nuclear, Kuwait's transition to oil, and the Netherlands to natural gas—all of which occurred within a decade or so (Sovacool 2019).[6]

For these four reasons, we argue that we should be cautious about making assumptions about the nature and trajectory of Northeast Asia's clean energy shift on the basis of macro data alone. To fully illuminate and account for the pat-tern of the shift in question—and to predict its most likely future trajectory—it is imperative to engage in detailed longitudinal case study analysis that pays seri-ous attention to both *state ambitions* and *capitalist market dynamics*—and the symbiotic relationship between the two.

In the next chapter, we draw upon the Schumpeterian idea of 'creative-destruction' and the Johnsonian concept of a 'developmental state' (and by exten-sion 'developmental environmentalism') to establish an analytic framework. We further develop four detailed longitudinal case studies at the industry level to address the puzzle we have shown in this chapter.

---

[6] Sovacool (2019) provides an insightful analysis of ten case studies of energy transitions affecting in aggregate around 1 billion people that took between just one and 16 years to achieve. He also provides a nicely nuanced discussion of the complexities of measuring the time of energy transitions. See also Sovacool (2016) and Sovacool and Geels (2016) on this topic. Newell and Simms (2021) also offer an insightful discussion of the potential for rapid energy transitions, drawing on historical examples.

3

A Novel Analytical Framework

Unlike the sceptics and pessimists, we argue that a genuine transformation is underway in Northeast Asia (NEA)—a transformation from a fossil-fuelled, linear throughput model of capitalism to a more economically, environmentally, and politically sustainable model based on renewable energies and a circular economy. We further argue that this transformation is following a distinctive pattern—but one that is both difficult to discern and impossible to explain by observing macro-level data alone. To fully illuminate and account for the pattern of NEA's green energy shift—and to predict its most likely future trajectory—it is imperative to engage in detailed longitudinal case study analysis that pays serious attention to both *state ambitions* and *capitalist market dynamics*—and the symbiotic relationship between the two.

In this chapter we introduce a fresh analytical framework developed precisely for this task. Our framework synthesizes and extends cutting-edge Schumpeterian and developmental state (DS) theorizing to produce a comprehensive explanation of the drivers and dynamics of Northeast Asia's green energy transition (GET) and its most likely future trajectory.[1] Our analysis is inspired by Schumpeterian theorizing insofar as we view capitalism as a dynamic system characterized by the relentless process of *creative-destruction*. In Schumpeter's words, the concept of 'creative-destruction' refers to 'a process of industrial mutation ... that incessantly revolutionizes the economic structure from within, incessantly destroying the old one, incessantly creating a new one' (Schumpeter 1942: 83). Drawing on the newest generation of Schumpeterian scholarship, we take as our analytical starting point the idea that

> essentially, greening is a process of creative destruction – a destruction of the entire fossil-fuel industrial order and its supersession by an alternative energy and resources order based on renewable inputs. This is not the mere substitution of one or two products by different products ... (but) a whole system transition or shift from one system based on fossil fuels to another system powered ultimately by renewables.
>
> (Mathews 2018: 245)

---

[1] The following three paragraphs draw on Thurbon et al. (2021).

Developmental Environmentalism. Elizabeth Thurbon et al., Oxford University Press. © Elizabeth Thurbon, Sung-Young Kim, Hao Tan, and John Mathews (2023). DOI: 10.1093/oso/9780192897794.003.0003

The approach we develop in this book pushes Schumpeterian theorizing in important new directions by illuminating the role of the state in the 'creative-destruction' dynamic embodied in the global green shift.[2] Conventional Schumpeterian scholarship emphasizes the role of *private sector entrepreneurs* in driving 'creative-destruction'.[3] In the context of the GET however, a primary focus on private entrepreneurs is problematic; it is now widely accepted that states have a crucial role to play in hastening the global green shift, not least because of the environmental urgency of the transition and the market and political power of energy incumbents seeking to block it (see for example Rodrik 2014). Moreover, it is now clear that in Northeast Asia generally and China and Korea in particular, state actors rather than private entrepreneurs have played a lead role in green industry creation, and are now actively promoting fossil fuel phase-out under their net-zero emissions pledges.[4]

To be clear, we do not seek to downplay or deny the crucial role of private entrepreneurs in Korea's and China's green transition, or in the global green shift more broadly. However, for the reasons just stated, we argue that to explain these countries' distinctive pattern of performance in the green energy shift we must take seriously the state's role in the 'creative-destruction' dynamic that underpins it. To this end, we engage in some conceptual innovation by deploying Schumpeter's 'creative-destruction' terminology in our analysis of the state's strategic activism. Specifically, we frame our analysis around (what we call) the state's 'creative' and 'destructive' ambitions and capabilities. To explain Korea's and China's pattern of performance, we identify the domestic and international factors that have influenced the state's will and ability to promote not just green industry *creation,* but also more recently fossil fuel sector *destruction.*

To account for these states' 'creative' and 'destructive' ambitions and capabilities, we draw on key concepts and insights from the newest generation of developmental state theorizing. In Korea and China, efforts to rapidly build and scale green energy industries have emerged from—and reflect the evolution of—these countries' longstanding developmental orientations and ambitions, which in the mid-2000s became manifest in a newfound 'developmental environmentalism' (DE). At the most fundamental level, DE refers to an elite mindset—a way of thinking about the state's primary goals and the most appropriate role of the state in achieving them. This is how the term was originally defined by Kim and Thurbon (2015), how it has since been invoked in the wider literature on Northeast Asia's

---

[2] We join a small but influential body of Schumpeterian scholarship investigating the state's role in driving and shaping economic innovation and change at the sectoral and national levels, including Mathews (2018) and Lee (2019).

[3] While some recent studies have highlighted the potential role of the state in supporting the transformative process of creative-destruction (e.g., Aghion et al. 2021), they do so in a way that limits their explanatory power, as we elaborate below.

[4] On the state's catalytic role in Asia's green shift see for example Mathews and Tan (2014) Mathews (2015) Kim and Thurbon (2015), Dent (2014), Kim (2019), Tan et al. (2021) and Thurbon et al. (2021).

green shift, and how we deploy it in this book. However, as we elaborate below, we argue that in the NEA context, DE can also be understood in more expansive terms. Specifically, DE captures not only an influential *elite mindset* (although this remains the most fundamental aspect of DE),[5] but also a related *political legitimation strategy* and a *distinctive policy approach*—by which we mean a distinctive approach to *sequencing the green energy shift* (rather than a fixed set of policies).

The value of the developmental environmentalism concept as we deploy it herein lies in its ability to shed important new light on the central role of the state in both the 'creative' and 'destructive' aspects of Northeast Asia's green energy shift. By 'the state' we mean both political and bureaucratic actors and the institutions through which they operate. There currently exists a large and growing body of literature devoted to both rationalizing and advocating 'green industrial policy' generally, and to analysing the detail and effectiveness of these policies in different national settings.[6] While this literature is valuable, it is also limited insofar as it is largely focused on *describing* what states are currently doing, and/or *prescribing* what they *could* or *should do*, to promote a green shift. To date, there have been few systematic attempts to *explain why* some states appear more ambitious and able to expedite both the 'creative' and 'destructive' aspects of the green shift in question.

One recent exception is the study by Aghion et al. (2021) which examines the potential for states to harness the transformative power of 'creative-destruction' (CD) to address major global challenges, including climate change. In contemplating the circumstances under which states might be compelled to do so, the authors devote a chapter to discussing the conditions that have—in the past— driven national governments to expand their fiscal capacity, to invest in education, and to engage in innovation and industrial policy—all activities that can support 'creative-destruction' (2021, ch. 14). Military threats, they argue, have historically provided states with such an impetus, citing Meiji-era Japan and Cold War America as key examples. Absent military threats however, and in an era of globalization, economic competition could potentially galvanize states into action—a point with which we wholeheartedly agree. And should states feel so compelled, the authors cite the US' Defense Advanced Research Projects Agency (DARPA) model as an example of innovation-oriented 'industrial policy' that they might follow.

Aghion's book is important because it draws much needed attention to the strategic role of the state in harnessing market dynamics to address major global challenges. However, given their significant focus on the global greening challenge, we find it surprising that the authors offer the US as a model of strategic activism while making no mention of East Asian governments' ambitious greening strategies, or the lessons they might hold for other countries—developed and

---

[5] Which, as our case studies reveal, can be present amongst not just national but also local policy elites.

[6] See for example Hallegatte et al. (2013); Rodrik (2014); Mazzucato (2015), Matsuo and Schmidt (2019).

developing alike.[7] Where Korea is discussed, the lessons drawn are largely histor-ical; emphasis is placed on the merits of its state-led industrialization model of the 1960s–1990s and of the government's (apparent) decision of the late 1990s to abandon its traditional conglomerate-centred, fast-follower growth strategy for one focused on smaller firms reaching for the technological frontier. In this story of strategic transition, the authors cast Korea's massive private conglomer-ates (known as *chaebol*) as the less innovative incumbents destined to be flies in the ointment of the government's frontier technology strategy (which is discussed in general rather than green terms). Yet as our detailed case studies will reveal, this story is partial, and confounded by the *chaebol's* longstanding efforts to pio-neer the green technologies of the future and their central role in the government's ambitious greening strategies from the outset. Aghion et al. overlook the Korean state's technology-intensive greening strategy and the central role of conglomer-ate incumbents in it—even in their chapter on Green Innovation and Sustainable Growth.

The authors are similarly silent on China's state-led greening strategy, which is overlooked apart from a brief acknowledgement of the country's growing capabil-ities in solar and electric vehicles (EVs) (Aghion et al. 2021: 185). Moreover, the authors' argument implies that when it comes to pushing for the tech frontier in the critical industries of the future (including green industries), there will be lit-tle to learn from the Chinese experience because '[i]nnovation needs democracy' (2021: 292). The reason they offer for this claim is that 'in a more democratic polit-ical system, vested interests have less influence on public officials, and it is harder to corrupt political power. When there is less corruption, there is more innovation' (2021: 292)—and thus a greater likelihood of transformative economic change. In other words, if innovation and economic transformation is the goal, democracy is the key. Absent democracy, frontier innovation and transformative economic change are more likely to flounder than flourish.

The limitations of this argument become apparent when we widen our analyti-cal lens to Northeast Asia. Authoritarian China's ambitious, technology-intensive greening strategy offers a powerful counter-case-in-point to the claim that demo-cratic institutions determine a state's willingness and ability to embrace innovation and transformative economic change. Similarly, the experience of democratic Korea unsettles the claim that close relationships between a strong executive and powerful incumbents (even of the fossil fuel variety) are likely to stall eco-nomic transformation. The weaknesses of Aghion et al.'s arguments stem from their emphasis on *regime type* rather than *elite orientation and ambition* as the key variable in the process of frontier innovation and transformative economic change.

---

[7] Their US-focus is even more surprising given America's evident lack of interest (until very recently) in supporting an ambitious greening shift, and the limited transferability of its DARPA-centred model of strategic activism. On the limited relevance of DARPA to 'industrial policy' debates and its limited transferability in practice, see Weiss (2014), and Weiss and Thurbon (2020).

As the history of post-World War II (WWII) Northeast Asia reveals, the developmental orientation of policymaking elites has long played a decisive factor in determining the pace and scope of these governments' successful techno-industrial transformation strategies, be it in democratic Japan, hard-authoritarian Korea, or soft-authoritarian Taiwan. And as our case studies reveal, it is the developmental-environmental orientation of policy elites in democratic Korea and authoritarian China that is now driving and shaping their greening strategies, which are firmly focused on the technological frontier. Moreover, in both Korea and China, DE-minded presidents have been using their extensive executive powers to expedite their countries' frontier technology innovation strategies—often in close collaboration with powerful, innovation-oriented incumbents.

In sum, our analytical approach adds value because it pays serious attention to elite orientation rather than regime type as a crucial factor both driving and shaping ambitious national greening strategies, especially those centred on the technological frontier. Importantly however, we see elite orientation as a necessary but insufficient explanation for the pace and scope of NEA ambitious greening strategies. To fully account for these strategies, and especially the growing alignment between these states' 'creative' and 'destructive' ambitions and actions, we must look beyond elite orientation to consider the material characteristics of capitalism itself, not least the dynamics of 'creative-destruction' and the related dynamics of technological learning and cost reduction. Thanks to these dynamics, we now see positive feedback loops emerging between NEA states' ambitions and actions and wider market forces, which finally appear to be pushing in the same direction. This increasingly symbiotic relationship leads us to draw more positive conclusions about the future trajectory of NEA's green energy shift.

A note on the importance of nomenclature

We appreciate the political sensitivities of using the term 'destructive' to describe a state's ambitions and actions; few policymakers would wish their policies—especially in the economic arena—to be described as 'destructive'.[8] Nevertheless, politics aside, we see two important analytical reasons for using Schumpeter's terminology in our analysis. First, following Schumpeter, we maintain that 'creative-destruction' is principally a *capitalist market dynamic*. It is probable that, absent state intervention, private entrepreneurs might seek to disrupt the existing fossil fuel order and pioneer green energy industries in order to capture first-mover profits.

We insist on Schumpeter's terminology to highlight the fact that in seeking to expedite 'creative-destruction', Korean and Chinese policymakers aim to

---

[8] This section draws directly on Thurbon et al. (2021), with permission.

kickstart and *harness the power of* market dynamics by employing the kind of 'market-conforming modes of intervention' (see Johnson 1982: 28) that have long distinguished Northeast Asia's developmental states. As Chalmers Johnson first observed in the context of post-WWII Japan, policymakers believed that national economic competitiveness (and national security) ultimately depended on private firms investing in new industries, rather than established industries destined for gradual decline. Yet they also believed that firms in established industries were more likely to try to protect their incumbent position rather than embrace radical change. Policymakers thus anticipated to find few, if any, powerful domestic interests favouring economic change.

Japan's post-WWII policymakers were thus faced with a problem very similar to that facing many policymakers worldwide today: while they knew that radical economic change was crucial to the nation's long-term prosperity and security, they faced powerful private resistance to it. Japan's policymakers thus saw for themselves a key role in aggressively supporting *new industry creation,* as well as *market competition* within new industries to ensure that local firms would be able to survive and thrive in global markets. This distinctive 'market conforming' approach to industrial policy—which involved trying to hasten and harness the market dynamic of 'creative-destruction' being resisted by powerful incumbents—was subsequently emulated by Korea and Taiwan.[9]

Second, while the term 'destruction' may appear contentious when viewed through the lens of electoral politics, we seek to foster a more nuanced understanding of the original meaning of 'destruction' in foundational Schumpeterian theorizing. For Schumpeter, the 'destruction' of established economic orders serves a transformative and ultimately productive economic and social purpose; it frees-up resources from 'old' industries (which in the case of energy are environmentally and socially damaging) to deploy more dynamic (and sustainable) 'new' industries. Moreover, while the 'destruction' of the established order *potentially* involves some economic pain for particular groups of firms and their employees, the nature and extent of that pain is by no means guaranteed *and can be mitigated by the state's activism.* That is, the destruction of the fossil fuel order need not involve the destruction of incumbent firms (and related jobs). Rather, it may involve incumbent firms—with government assistance—adapting to the new order by redirecting their investments towards emerging industries (and new job creation).

---

[9] In this context, it is significant Japan's post-WWII policymakers (and scholars) were not just familiar with, but impressed and strongly influenced by Schumpeter's economic ideas – especially the idea that technological innovation is the central component of economic competitiveness. On the influence of Schumpeterian thought on Japanese economic policymaking throughout the post-WWII period see Samuels (1994) and Metzler (2013). On Schumpeter's own very positive impression of Japan, and his "enormously enthusiastic" reception by Japanese scholars upon his lecture tour there in 1931, see the biography by Richard Swedberg (1991).

As we shall see, this is precisely what is occurring in Korea and China and in NEA more widely, where the state is encouraging the destruction of the fossil fuel economic order not by seeking to harm incumbent firms but by heavily supporting them to switch their investments towards 'green' projects. Thus, in Korea we observe the state's targeted support for established automaker Hyundai in its efforts to pioneer local and global fuel cell electric vehicle (FCEV) markets, and for coal-invested KEPCO to lead the nation's charge into green hydrogen for baseload power and other purposes. In this sense, when we write of the state's 'destructive ambitions and capabilities', we are not arguing that the state is engaged in efforts to destroy particular firms—and especially not Korea's 'national champions' like Hyundai and KEPCO that are so important to the national economy (and the state's traditional developmental ambitions). Rather, we are focused on the state's ambition to expedite the 'destruction' of the *established fossil-fuelled economic order*. In many instances, this involves the state working productively with incumbent firms to ensure they adapt, survive, and thrive in the new green economy. We insist that it is this central role of the state that accounts for the rapid rise in clean and green energy sources in NEA, as documented in Chapter 2.

Operationalizing our analytical framework

How do we operationalize our new analytical approach in the context of specific country cases? The approach we have developed consists of *three distinct analytical steps*. Each step addresses a structured set of questions designed to tease out the drivers and dynamics of the green energy shift in the cases in question. Importantly however, while these analytical steps are distinct, they are also interrelated. So, while we present the steps sequentially here, each chapter places varying degrees of emphasis on each, and explores the dynamic interplay between them.

Step One examines the *origins* and *emergence* of the state's 'creative' and 'destructive' ambitions and capabilities. So, for Korea and China we ask: 1) When and why did national policymakers first prioritize a green energy shift and devise their related strategies? 2) Why did these policymakers originally place greater emphasis on green industry creation than on fossil fuel destruction? And 3) Upon what pre-existing state capabilities did policymakers seek to draw to translate their new ambitions into action?

As already indicated, our answers to these 'origin' questions centre on the pervasive influence of traditional developmental ways of thinking amongst the policy and political elite, and the evolution of those ideas in the early to mid-2000s into the new mindset of 'developmental environmentalism'. Step One is our most self-contained in terms of both its relatively narrow analytical target (the DE mindset of policymaking elite) and its temporal boundedness (i.e., the historical context in which this mindset emerged and first gained currency in each context). Given its temporally contained nature, and our ability to draw on existing research to execute it, we complete Step One at the end of this chapter. This chapter is also the most logical home for Step One insofar as it invites further discussion of DE as more than an elite mindset, but also as a related political legitimation strategy and as a particular policy approach involving an emphasis on green energy industry creation before fossil fuel sector destruction. While we discuss these aspects of DE briefly in this chapter, we demonstrate them empirically in Steps One and Two—which focus on the *evolution* of the state's 'creative' and 'destructive' ambitions and capabilities over time.

Step Two is focused on the *evolution* of the state's *creative* ambitions and capabilities from the mid-2000s to the present. For both country cases we ask: 1) What factors have served to strengthen (or weaken) policymakers' 'creative' ambitions since the mid-2000s, and to shape the direction and detail of their industry creation strategies? 2) How/By what means have policymakers sought to translate their 'creative' ambitions into action? And 3) What factors have enabled and/or constrained execution of the state's industry creation strategies over time? As Step Two deals directly with the mechanisms and dynamics of policy *execution*, it demands a granular, longitudinal analysis of the state's targeted industry creation strategies in each national context. We have chosen to focus on China's and Korea's electronic vehicle and smart grid strategies, for reasons already outlined. We develop our longitudinal case studies of these industries across four separate chapters. Chapters 4 and 5 focus on EV-industry creation efforts in Korea and China respectively, while Chapters 6 and 7 focus on efforts to build smart grid industries in each country. Step Two's focus on strategic *execution* also demands that we extend our analytical gaze beyond the ambitions and actions of the national policy elite (the primary focus of Step One) towards the ambitions and actions of a wider set of actors—especially industry actors (i.e., private and public firms) as well as industry associations, research institutes, and regional and local governments. For as we shall see, to the extent that the states' creative ambitions have been realized in each country, success has hinged largely on government efforts to forge close, collaborative relationships with the business sector, rather than on the state's authoritarian imposition of its will on local firms.

Step Three shifts our analytical gaze again, but this time from the 'creative' to the 'destructive' side of the Schumpeterian equation. This step examines the state's evolving *destructive* ambitions and capabilities and seeks to identify the factors bringing 'creative' and 'destructive' ambitions and capabilities into closer alignment. We ask for each country: 1) What factors have strengthened or weakened policymakers' 'destructive' (read: fossil fuel phase-out) ambitions from the mid-2000s to the present? 2) How/By what means have policymakers sought to translate their 'destructive' ambitions into action? And 3) What factors have enabled and/or constrained the execution of 'destructive' strategies over time?

As already noted, while the analytical steps we identify are discrete, they are also deeply interrelated, insofar as successes in the 'creative' arena may make it easier for policymakers to pursue a more aggressive 'destructive' agenda (for example, by helping to drive down the costs of renewables vis-à-vis fossil fuels (FFs)). Moreover, in some instances, while it is useful to distinguish between the state's 'creative' and 'destructive' ambitions and capabilities for analytical purposes, in reality the lines between the two can be blurred. For example, should we classify government efforts to phase-out FFs by encouraging fossil fuel incumbents to invest in renewables 'destructive' efforts, 'creative' efforts, or both? To grapple directly with these issues, and to draw out the dynamic relationship between the state's 'creative' and 'destructive' ambitions and capabilities, we weave our Step Three analysis through our case study chapters. In this way, Chapters 4 through 7 serve two important functions. Empirically, they serve as detailed longitudinal case studies of the state's role in building two new green energy industries: smart grids and electronic vehicles. Theoretically, they allow us to tease out and illuminate the dynamic interplay between the state's 'creative' and 'destructive' ambitions and capabilities more broadly.

Developmental environmentalism (1): Conceptual contours

In this section we flesh out the concept of developmental environmentalism as we deploy it in this book before empirically tracing the emergence of DE in Korea and China in the early to mid-2000s. As already noted, we invoke the term DE in a very particular way in this study—to describe not only an elite mindset but also a related political legitimation strategy and a distinctive approach to sequencing the green energy shift. DE captures the idea that there is something transformative underway in NEA when it comes to the shift in question. Ambitious efforts to build and scale globally competitive, export-oriented green energy industries represent much more than 'business as usual' for these erstwhile developmental states. DE clearly conveys the fact that environmental considerations have emerged as a key factor both driving and shaping these states' green energy transition strategies—albeit alongside more traditional developmental ambitions. So, where some scholars believe it is inappropriate to associate the term 'environmentalism' with NEA's energy transition strategies, which they dismiss as examples of greenwashing[10], we take a different view.

Developmental environmentalism captures the complex ways in which developmental and environmental considerations are now entwined in the region, and how these entwinements are producing a distinctive approach to the green energy shift—one fundamentally different from that of the West. As noted at the outset, DE highlights the genuine intention and effort on the part of some NEA states to

---

[10] See for example Lee (2015).

fundamentally transform their fossil-fuelled, linear throughput growth model to a more sustainable model centred on renewable energies and circular economy principles—not only for energy and economic security reasons but for environmental reasons as well. Crucially however, these environmental reasons have had less to do with 'climate change' than the effects of particulate pollution—although climate concerns are now becoming more important. In sum, we take issue with perspectives that downplay or deny the environmental drivers and implications of NEA's green energy shift. Environmental considerations play a central role in the story of NEA's green energy shift, and this shift is likely to have major environmental implications not only for NEA but the world. In the sections that follow, we explain what we mean by DE as a mindset, a legitimation strategy, and a distinctive policy approach. We also highlight the analytical value added through this distinctive conceptual framing.

Developmental environmentalism as an elite mindset

As already noted, we invoke the term developmental environmentalism to capture an elite mindset—one that is currently discernible and influential in Northeast Asia's erstwhile developmental states. By 'mindset' we mean a particular way of thinking on the part of the state's policy elite that shapes policy action. In centring the DE mindset in our analysis, we build on and extend the newest generation of DS scholarship that posits *elite orientation and ambition* as the most important distinguishing feature of these states, in line with classical DS theorizing (cf. Johnson 1982).[11] According to this scholarship, to which we ourselves have contributed, a developmental mindset involves a particular way of thinking about the primary purpose of economic activity, about the state's primary economic goals, and about the appropriate role of the state in advancing those goals (Thurbon 2014, 2016). In the traditional developmental mindset, a strong economy is viewed as the key to both domestic political legitimacy and international security, status, and prestige. For developmentally-minded policymakers, the primary purpose of economic activity is to build and strengthen the nation. The state's primary economic goals are to promote local manufacturing capacity, technological autonomy, and export competitiveness, understood as the essential foundations of national economic strength. And, given the importance of these goals, policymakers view a long-term strategic approach to techno-industrial governance as both necessary and desirable.

It was the existence of a *developmental mindset*, we argue—rather than a shared set of organizational arrangements or policy practices—that was the most important unifying and distinguishing feature of Northeast Asia's pioneering post-WWII developmental states (cf. Thurbon 2014, 2016). And it is the evolution

---

[11] The following four paragraphs draw on Thurbon (2016).

and emergence of a *developmental-environmental mindset* that now unifies the experiences of the region's erstwhile DS and helps to explain their embrace of an ambitious green energy shift—as we elaborate below.

To be absolutely clear, in making this claim, we are certainly not suggesting that institutions and/or policies are irrelevant to developmental states in theory or practice. The existence of a developmental mindset (or indeed a developmental-environmental mindset) on the part of the policy elite means nothing without the institutional capacity required to translate ambitions into sustained policy action. As such, a mindset-centred approach does certainly not neglect institutions or policies, or imply that they are somehow unimportant. Institutions and policies matter fundamentally to the effective execution of a developmental project. However, in line with classical theorizing, we see the orientations and ambitions of the policy elite as emerging prior to, and as the pre-requisite of— developmentally-oriented institutions and polices, and thus as the preeminent feature of a DS (cf. Johnson 1982).[12] For absent the developmental mindset, how can one explain the emergence of institutional arrangements and policy practices that are so geared towards developmental goals? A mindset-centred approach thus puts developmentally-minded agents and their ambitions at the centre of the analysis, and then investigates the ways in which these agents go about navigating and manipulating their wider institutional (and indeed political and structural) environments in pursuit of their goals. In this sense, our approach is firmly grounded in the tradition of agent-centred historical institutionalism.[13]

A mindset-centred approach adds value to debates about the future of developmental states because it opens a window into the possibility that, as they develop and integrate with the global economy, these states may *adapt and evolve* rather than dismantle and decline. It thus provides an important corrective to the influential 'declinist' school of thought that emerged and gained prominence in scholarly and policy debate in the decades following the 1997–98 crisis. According to declinists, in an era of economic globalization, Northeast Asia's developmental states were no longer viable and were destined to 'normalize' and converge on a Western, neoliberal model of governance. However, those claims were often founded on a flawed conceptualization of a developmental state (see Thurbon 2014, 2016). That is, declinists tended to define DS in terms of static institutional arrangements

---

[12] As the originator of the developmental state concept, Chalmers Johnson also specified a number of organizational arrangements that he saw as central to developmental states (DS) as they emerged in Northeast Asia, including a meritocratic bureaucracy, a pilot agency, and a bank-based financial system. However, as Thurbon (2016) has shown, the tendency of subsequent analyses to focus on these states' shared organizational arrangements has obscured the central importance of other, nationally distinctive organizational features to developmentally-oriented policymaking in particular national contexts, such as the crucial role of the presidential office in Korea's DS.

[13] For pioneering studies of this approach see Bell (2011) and Bell and Feng (2013). For an application of this approach to the East Asian context see Thurbon (2016, 2019).

and/or policy practices, ignoring entirely their shared ideational foundations.[14] As a result, changes to institutions or policies were automatically interpreted as evidence of DS demise. The possibility of DS evolution and adaptation were ruled out by definition. A mindset-centred approach does not exclude the possibility of DS dismantling or demise. Its value is that it is not deterministic or predictive; it points to the possibility of varied outcomes depending on the combination of agential orientations, institutional and political enablers and constraints, and wider structural dynamics (including capitalist market dynamics) involved. In particular, it points to the possibility that when faced with domestic or international pressures for change, developmentally-minded policymakers might *adapt* their organizations and policies to better suit the new challenges at hand, without relinquishing their traditional developmental ambitions.

It is the idea of developmental state adaptation and evolution that provides the starting point for our analysis of Northeast Asia's green energy shift, and the state's strategic role in it. We argue that the green energy shift represents not only the ongoing influence of traditional developmental ways of thinking amongst the policy elite, but the evolution of that mindset into a new variety of developmentalism: developmental environmentalism (*cf.* Kim and Thurbon 2015).[15] In the mindset of DE, the traditional developmental goals of manufacturing capacity, technological autonomy, and export competitiveness retain their centrality. However, the established means of achieving these goals—by promoting fossil fuel based manufacturing industries—is viewed as no longer viable thanks to the growing environmental, economic, and political costs associated with this approach. In light of these costs—and in the context of an enduring developmental commitment—policymakers believe that the state can and should step in to help secure the country's leadership in the technologically advanced, environmentally-friendly manufacturing industries of the future, from renewable energies to smart grids to EVs and beyond. The ultimate ambition is to create a new growth model capable of simultaneously advancing developmental *and* environmental goals.

As a mindset, developmental environmentalism is not unique to Korea and China. However, since the mid-2000s, key segments of these countries' policy elite have enthusiastically embraced DE. Of course, neither Korea nor China use the term 'developmental environmentalism' explicitly; this is our term, coined for analytical purposes. As we discuss in detail below, in Korea, what we describe as the DE mindset originally found its expression in the language of 'green growth'—a concept enthusiastically promoted at home and abroad by Korean policymakers (Kim and Thurbon 2015; Kim and Mathews 2016). In China, the DE mindset has found expression in the language of 'ecological civilization' (Hansen, Li

---

[14] For a review of the declinist literature and its limitations see Thurbon (2014). For a comprehensive articulation of a mindset-centred analysis of developmental states and an application of the approach to South Korea and Taiwan see Thurbon (2014, 2016, 2019).

[15] The remainder of this paragraph draws on Thurbon et al. (2021).

and Svarverud 2018). However, as we also show below, these different discursive framings should not detract us from the shared DE orientations and ambitions that underpin them. And as our case studies reveal, these orientations and ambitions are now leading these states to adapt organizational arrangements and policy practices to meet pressing new challenges.

Developmental environmentalism as a political legitimation strategy

This book extends existing studies of developmental environmentalism by widening the definition to encompass not only an elite mindset, but also a related political legitimation strategy (and a particular policy approach, which we discuss in the next section). The idea of developmental environmentalism as a political legitimation strategy is already implicit in existing articulations of the concept. But we see value in drawing out this aspect explicitly, insofar as it helps to illuminate the complex political tensions that are both driving and shaping Northeast Asian governments' approaches to the green energy shift.

In this context, it is helpful to remind ourselves of the distinctive relationship between economic growth strategies and political legitimacy (domestic and international) that originally characterized Northeast Asia's developmental states. Throughout the post-WWII period, the authoritarian or one-party democratic regimes of Japan, Korea, and Taiwan sought to legitimate themselves in the eyes of both domestic and international audiences by delivering unprecedently high levels of economic growth with relative equity. Rapid and sustained economic growth thus came to be viewed as the key to bolstering not just regime survival at home, but the very survival of these war-torn and weakened nations in a hostile international arena, and of (re)building their international status and prestige in the eyes of the developed West (and with each other).

We see the emergence of developmental environmentalism in Northeast Asia as a response to the growing political legitimacy challenges associated with these states' traditional rapid growth strategies, centred as they were on fossil fuels. As we demonstrate empirically below, from the late-1990s onwards, the economic and environmental costs of those fossil-fuelled strategies were becoming increasingly apparent. These costs led to significant soul searching within the policy elite about the future viability of those strategies and whether they were capable of delivering the requisite political payoffs. A key argument of this book is that by promoting a rapid green energy shift, NEA governments are now attempting to address these serious domestic political legitimacy challenges and to further bolster their international security, status, and prestige. In this sense, DE has now replaced traditional developmentalism as a key political legitimation strategy.

An explicit focus on developmental environmentalism as a legitimizing strategy has a number of analytical payoffs. First, it allows us to draw attention to the growing responsiveness of Northeast Asian governments to pressing environmental concerns such as particulate pollution, waste management (see Wu and Martus 2020; Harrell et al. 2020), and more recently climate change. Second, it also allows us to highlight the increasingly serious political implications for these governments of failing to effectively address environmental issues—and the extent to which fears of those implications are helping to drive these governments' greening strategies. Such a focus also allows us to tease out the very complex political legitimacy challenges associated with policymakers' attempts to reconcile environmental and developmental ambitions and to translate those ambitions into policy action. These complex challenges can go a long way towards explaining the sequencing, pace, and scope of these government's green energy transition strategies.

We can see these complex political legitimacy challenges playing out across our case studies, particularly in the automobile industry which straddles the fossil fuel and green economies. Often, we see a tendency in the literature to assume that it is powerful FF incumbents who are resisting calls for faster change towards the green shift. But in the case of EVs in Korea we see both powerful incumbents and segments of the government wishing to push fast, but serious objections from labour (even labour strikes) about the idea of ramping up EVs more quickly due to labour loss concerns. The same complex dynamics can be witnessed in the electricity generation sector, where the arguments for continuing FF subsidies are coming not only from some powerful incumbents but from labour and wider social groups because of growing levels of inequality and cost of living. These are now massive electoral issues in Korea (and indeed elsewhere in East Asia and the West), where cheap access to energy is seen as a welfare matter.

It is here, we argue, that it is helpful to factor in the role of capitalist market dynamics in lending momentum to the greening shift and helping governments to reconcile the political tensions inherent in the initial phase of any greening strategy. In Northeast Asia, we are now seeing the transformative political impact of these governments' ambitious early emphasis on green energy industry creation, as capitalist dynamics help to drive green energy costs down and green job opportunities up. For these reasons, we posit that in the developmental-environmental mindset, green industry creation strategies (rather than fossil fuel destruction strategies) are viewed as the most effective means of addressing environmental problems—especially in the early phases of the transition. This is because green industry creation strategies help to sustain legitimacy and security enhancing growth while also addressing what are perceived to be the most pressing environmental concerns from a political perspective, especially particulate pollution.

Beyond the domestic arena, as our case studies reveal, there is also an international aspect to the complex political legitimacy challenges facing Northeast Asian states as they seek to balance their sometimes (but certainly not always) competing greening and growing goals. Both China and Korea have sought to leverage their developmental-environmental-inspired models of 'ecological civilization' and 'green growth' in ways that might bolster their international status and prestige. In this sense, these countries' greening strategies are also political strategies intended to demonstrate their willingness to take the lead on pressing global issues, as evidenced by Korea's lead role in the establishment and hosting of the Global Green Growth Institute and the Green Climate Fund. And for China in particular, the idea of ecological civilization is also increasingly tied to its attempt to establish its authoritarian model of governance as legitimate and desirable in the eyes of the international community. However, in seeking to politically leverage their new DE-inspired growth strategies in the international arena, these countries have also opened those strategies to close scrutiny. So, where they fall short on stated greening goals, these countries now risk doing serious damage to their international status and prestige. In this way, international political legitimacy concerns are also adding impetus to NEA's greening strategies.

Developmental environmentalism as a distinctive policy approach

The third and final way in which we discuss developmental environmentalism is as a *distinctive policy approach*, by which we mean a particular approach to sequencing the 'creative' and 'destructive' aspects of the green energy shift. As indicated above, this sequencing is shaped in part by the complex political legitimacy challenges associated with the shift in question. However, it is also shaped by the enduring influence of the traditional developmental goals of promoting local manufacturing capability, technological autonomy, and export competitiveness as the foundation of national economic security. As indicated in the previous chapter, these priorities mean that *local* green energy industry creation is viewed as the *strategic prerequisite* of fossil fuel phase-out—insofar as there is little desire in China and Korea to substitute fossil fuel import reliance with a reliance on the import of green energy equipment and infrastructure. The enduring influence of traditional developmental goals explains why we might expect an early 'creative' emphasis to precede ambitious efforts to phase-out FFs in Northeast Asia. It also explains these states' strong preference for solving environmental problems with new green industry creation strategies wherever possible.

In sum, we use the term developmental environmentalism to simultaneously capture the elite mindset, the political legitimation strategy, and the distinctive policy approach that has informed East Asia's approach to greening since the mid 2000s. To be clear, it is worth reiterating the point that DE is a term that we ourselves have coined for both descriptive and analytical purposes; it is not one that is actually used by political leaders or policy practitioners in Korea or China (or elsewhere in the region). What Korean and Chinese policymakers employ to describe their greening strategies are local terms, like 'Green Growth' (GG) (Korea) and 'Ecological Civilization' (China)—as we discuss in the section that follows. However, while these local terms do convey certain aspects of DE as we define it, they should not be thought of as synonyms for the same, as DE captures a much more expansive set of ideas that speak directly to the strategic role of the state in the greening process. To illustrate this point by way of example: the term 'Green Growth' first popularized by Korea and since promoted by international organizations like the OECD clearly conveys the idea that it is both possible and desirable to 'green' and 'grow' the economy at the same time.[16] Insofar as GG shares this key characteristic with DE, they stand in unified opposition to the ideas of 'zero growth' and 'de-growth', and the more nebulous idea of 'sustainable development', commonly advocated for in the West (see Mathews 2019). However, DE is also a far more expansive idea than GG—insofar as DE *insists upon a strategic role for the state in promoting and supporting green growth—while also capturing a political legitimation strategy and a distinctive policy approach.* The same can be said of the similarities and differences between DE and the idea of 'Ecological Civilization' popularized in China—as we discuss in more detail below. The point we wish to make here is that despite the distinctive local discourses devised by the Korean and Chinese governments, their actual approaches to greening their economies—and the ideas informing those approaches—are very similar, and the most important similarities are best captured by our term: 'developmental environmentalism'.

Developmental environmentalism (2): Empirical realities

In this section we empirically trace the emergence of developmental-environmental ways of thinking in the Korean and Chinese contexts. We pay particular attention to the domestic and international conditions that led policymakers to reimagine the relationship between economic and environmental goals in the early to mid-2000s, culminating in the emergence of DE as a mindset, a legitimizing strategy, and a distinctive policy approach.

The emergence of developmental environmentalism in South Korea

The focus of Korean policymakers over the post-war era (1960s to 1990s) was on economic 'catch-up'. In the broadest sense, this term meant closing the gap

---

[16] It is worth noting that since the mid-2010s, the idea of 'Green Growth' has also been re-defined by some to necessarily include democratic decision-making processes and distributive policy priorities, somewhat stretching the concept and complicating definitional discussions, which should not preoccupy us here.

in incomes, productivity, world market share, and technology between industrializing countries and the advanced industrial states (Lee 2013: 6–7). For the Koreans, catch-up had political significance. It was first and foremost about pulling ahead of North Korea (which posed an existential threat) and reaching parity (and surpassing) its former colonizer, Japan, closely followed by the bid to surpass European and North American countries. The Korean state sought to do so through nurturing large conglomerates (*chaebol*) responsible for spearheading local manufacturing capacity, technological autonomy, and export competitiveness. Promotion efforts were targeted towards sectors deemed to have strategic value. The first phase of industrial promotion centred on heavy industries such as automobiles and steel (Amsden 1989; Woo 1991). However from the 1990s, focus shifted to the creation of higher-tech fields such as semiconductors and telecommunications (Mathews and Cho 2000; Oh and Larson 2020).

Upon seizing power in the early 1960s, Korea's first developmentally-minded policymakers led by President Park Chung Hee fostered an institutional structure that enabled the dedicated pursuit of the country's rapid industrialization. At the top of this structure sat the presidential office endowed with vast executive powers and the ability to directly intervene in economic policymaking. As a result, in the Korean context, presidential orientation and ambition has long been a swing factor shaping the direction and dynamics of techno-industrial strategy (see Thurbon 2016). However, in an effort to ensure the routine development and execution of coherent, long-term strategies and to mitigate against the politicization of the same, in the early 1960s Korea's foundational developmental elite also established the Economic Planning Board (EPB). As the powerful 'super agency' formally responsible for coordinating national industrial development plans, the EPB was chaired by the Korean president and also had responsibilities over the budget and overall economic management (Evans 1995: 52–53). This agency was supported through the creation of a vast intelligence-gathering and analysing infrastructure in the form of governmental agencies and think tanks (Weiss 1998: 52–54). However, since the dismantling of the EPB in 1994 and the increasing technological sophistication of Korean firms, a shift towards more decentralized governance structures has been observed. Ministries with jurisdictions over specific technological sectors such as the former Ministry of Information and Communications (MIC) have assumed such roles as de facto or 'quasi-pilot agencies' over a specific technological field (Kim 2012). The state institutionalized channels of communication between state agencies and the conglomerates and privileged encompassing private-sector associations (such as manufacturing industry associations) to represent the interests of businesses and provide input into public policies (Weiss 1995: 55–64).

Importantly, for our purposes here, these ideational and institutional features of the Korean developmental state helped facilitate 'brown growth' industrialization, that is, energy-intensive and heavily dependent upon fossil fuel inputs.[17] The goal of rapid, fossil-fulled industrialization and expansion was prioritized above all else—not least environmental protection. Compromizing economic growth for environmental goals—or even seeking to balance the two as the universal language of 'sustainable development' recommended—was an unthinkable idea. This much was acknowledged by Korea's Presidential Committee on Green Growth (PCGG), the peak coordinating body established in 2009 to promote GG (which we discuss in more detail below). While such balancing might hold popular appeal in *some* countries (i.e., in advanced industrial economies with strong environmental movements), it was an entirely unrealistic principle in Korea (PCGG 2009b). According to the first Chairman of the PCGG, Hyung-Kook Kim, any concern for climate change amongst Koreans was overshadowed by the imperatives of late development (Kim 2010). Koreans would simply not accept an effort to protect the environment that came at the expense of continued economic development.

However, in 2008 two key developments led policymakers to rethink the relationship between economic and environmental goals and set the scene for the emergence of what we call developmental environmentalism. The *first* was the realization by key policymakers that Korea's brown growth economic trajectory was no longer able to deliver on traditional developmental concerns. These were Korea's extreme dependence on fossil fuel imports and the interruption to the supply of cheap fossil fuels from the early 2000s onwards. Korea has long depended upon imports to meet its energy needs. When President Lee Myung-bak came to power in 2008, 97 per cent of Korea's total energy requirements were being met by imports (PCGG 2009b: 13), and Korea the world's second and fifth largest importer of coal and oil respectively (UNEP 2010: 10). The country's fossil fuel import costs exceeded the combined income of its three largest export industries: automobiles, semiconductors, and ships (PCGG 2011: 13). While a high dependence on imports had long exposed Korea to international energy price fluctuations, from the early 2000s, two new factors heightened perceptions of *energy insecurity*. The first was increasing competition for energy resources from emerging economies (particularly China), which dramatically drove up energy prices between 2003 and 2007[18]. The second was the onset of the 2007/2008 Global Financial Crisis (GFC).[19] Taken together these developments undermined policymakers' faith in the ongoing ability of Korea's fossil-fuelled industrialization model to meet deeper developmental concerns.

---

[17] The following two paragraphs summarize Kim and Thurbon (2015: 218–219).

[18] The global price of oil increased from around USD 30 to over USD 100 per barrel and to USD 150 in 2008 (Kahn 2009: 7).

[19] Due to the GFC, between August and November 2008, the Korean Won fell 28 per cent against the USD, putting further pressure on import prices.

A *second* development was the articulation of environmental protection as a goal compatible with developmentalism through *internalizing greening as an economic opportunity*, not only as an economic cost. Protecting and improving the environment was not simply, or even mainly, about placing costs on polluters. Rather, policymakers came to view the development, commercialization, production, and export of green technologies, products, and processes as an economic development opportunity. And the principal opportunity as seen from the perspective of Korea would have been the rise of China as a competitive threat, which would call for innovative responses from Korea—as we detail in Chapter 4 on electric vehicles, where we outline the argument that Korea probably developed the FCEV initially as a means of differentiating its response to electrification from that of China.

These two developments gave rise to what Korean bureaucrats referred to as 'green growth'. This term refers to the belief that the pursuit of environmental protection through green industry creation could create a new green economic trajectory while phasing out the old brown growth trajectory. The developmental-environmental mindset of policymakers involved with the country's green growth project was made clearly evident by key individuals in the Lee administration. During a 2008 Address to the Nation, President Lee himself articulated the newly found symbiotic relationship between environmental and economic goals thus:

> Green Growth refers to sustainable growth which helps reduce greenhouse gas emission and environmental pollution. It is also a new national development paradigm that creates new growth engines and jobs with green technology and clean energy.[20]

President Lee's Secretary for Green Growth and the Environment, Kim Sang-Hyup, elaborated on why green growth marked a departure from the country's focus on brown growth:

> ... green growth seeks to advance the transition from quantitative growth to qualitative growth and the shift from the traditional, fossil fuel-dependent socioeconomic structure into a low carbon one ... Green growth identifies the measures that will allow us to mitigate climate change and its dependency on fossil fuel. In turn, these measures will also bring about new growth and create jobs.
>
> (PCGG 2011: 15)

---

[20] Lee Myung-bak, 'A Great People with New Dreams', Address on the Sixty-Third Anniversary of National Liberation and the Sixtieth Anniversary of the Founding of the Republic of Korea, 15 August 2008, accessed 16 August 2013, http://www.korea.net/Government/Briefing-Room/Presidential-Speeches/view?articleId=91000.

The recognition of green growth (GG) as a new economic growth engine for the national economy was articulated by high-level bureaucrats such as Soogil Young, former chairman of the PCGG:

> ... [GG] would work as a new development paradigm by harnessing green technologies and clean energies to create new growth engines and jobs ... The Korean view is that the old paradigm of brown growth would no longer work, not just for Korea or more industrialized countries, but also for the developing and emerging countries ... [21]

These ambitions were operationalized in the first Five-Year Plan for Green Growth (FYPGG) (2009–2013), which targeted 27 core technologies for promotion including electric cars and smart grids (UNEP 2010: 36–38). As we shall see in the chapters to follow, Korea's GG ambitions did not end in 2013 (after changes in political leadership) but has continued via the formulation of the second FYPGG (2014–2018) and third FYPGG (2019–2023).

In 2008, the institutional underpinnings of developmental environmentalism were made evident through the creation of a robust institutional structure of which the most important was the creation of the Presidential Committee on Green Growth.[22] This was an authoritative body designed to deliberate, consult, and review policies over green growth (PCGG 2011: 32–34). It was considered by policymakers such as Secretary Kim as one of the most important organizational embodiments of the GG initiative. With striking parallels to the ways in which former Korean presidents chaired the country's former centralized pilot agency (the EPB), President Lee personally chaired all PCGG meetings during his tenure (PCGG 2009: 10).[23] The authority of the PCGG was mandated in legislation. It was granted formal responsibility for formulating a long-term focused *National Strategy for Green Growth 2009–2050* and the more short-term goals involved in the Five-Year Plans for GG. However, the real power of the PCGG came from its ability to review and *reject* policy drafts over greening initiatives submitted by individual ministries.[24]

In 2009, in a significant boost to the PCGG's authority and capacity, the policy functions of all existing high-level governmental bodies established to promote

---

[21] Soogil Young, Keynote Speech for East Asia Low-Carbon, Green Growth Roadmap Forum. Jointly organized by UNESCAP and KOICA, 25–26 April, 2012, Seoul, Republic of Korea, accessed 1 July 2014, http://17greengrowth.pa.go.kr/?p=51182

[22] The following three paragraphs summarize arguments made in Kim and Thurbon (2015: 227–228).

[23] Former president Park Chung-hee (1961–1979) played a similar role in Korea's former pilot agency. See Choi (1988).

[24] The PCGG's mandate, composition, and responsibilities are provided in the Framework Act on Low-Carbon, Green Growth and the Enforcement Decree of the Framework Act on Low-Carbon, Green Growth. The Act came into force on 14 April 2010. The relevant legislation is available at http://www.moleg.go.kr/english/korLawEng?pstSeq=54751&brdSeq=33 (accessed 1 July 2014).

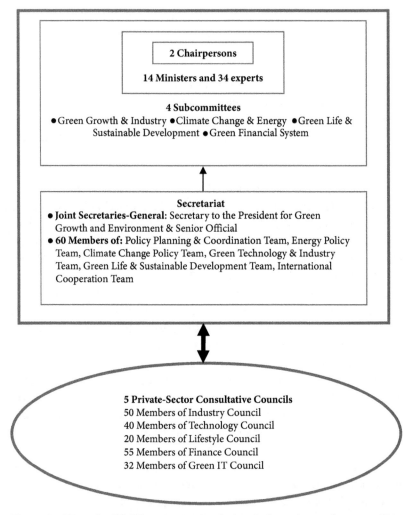

Figure 3.1 How the PCGG maintains insulation, information-gathering, and analysis functions

Source: Adapted from Kim and Thurbon (2015)

environmental protection and energy security were integrated into the body. These changes were underpinned by revisions to national legislation (PCGG 2011: 18). As can be seen in Figure 3.1, the PCGG sat at the apex of a vast bureaucratic network and possessed an independent capacity for information gathering and analysis (befitting a pilot agency). This provided the PCGG with the distance necessary to reach conclusions independently of special interests. The PCGG's Five Private-Sector Consultative Councils provided an avenue for industrial actors to have input into the design of policies over green growth (PCGG 2009: 10–12).

These organizational features of the PCGG and its relationship with business enabled 'insulation but not insularity' from private sector interests (and interests within individual ministries) which might otherwise derail the pursuit of long-term strategic objectives (Weiss 1995: 600–602).

In this sense, from 2009–2013, while not a full ministry, the Presidential Committee on Green Growth exhibited coordinative functions similar to the erstwhile Economic Planning Board. Unlike the EPB, the PCGG did not enjoy authority over the national budget, which in 2009 lay with the Budget Office within the Ministry of Strategy and Finance (MOSF).[25] For this reason, while the PCGG was highly effective in formulating sector-by-sector plans, it lacked some capacity in the sphere of implementation, especially when it came to countering ministerial resistance to its most radical proposals (as we shall see in our case study chapters). For example, the PCGG's proposal to phase-out the practice of electricity subsidization was thwarted by ministries responsible for traditional brown growth industries (see also Chapter 6).[26] Consequently, despite the government's substantial investments in green growth between 2009–2012 (discussed in full in the chapters on Korea's EV and smart grid industries), Korea's energy intensity *increased* over the same period. As we demonstrate in in our case study chapters, the limited reforms in this area do not detract from its significant achievements in promoting green technologies, which sit at the heart of developmental environmentalism. The point is that Korea's Green Growth strategy created the platforms from which Korean firms could launch their green industry creation initiatives—the full details and evolution of which we examine in the chapters that follow.

The emergence of developmental environmentalism in China

Developmentalism has been embraced by Chinese policymakers, sharing many similarities with other Northeast Asian countries, but with distinctive motivations and approaches.[27] For example, as a large country and an ideological rival of the West, China's developmental state approach reflected its concerns around developing a self-reliant economy with a reliable supply of energy and major resources. Similarly, the pathway from developmentalism towards developmental environmentalism in China in the past five decades shares similarities and differences with that of Korea.

The reform and opening up policy started by Chinese leader, Deng Xiaoping, in the late 1970s led to an unprecedented period of high economic growth. However,

---

[25] Author interview with Seung-Hoon Lee, Seoul, 27 November 2013.
[26] As explained by Seung-Hoon Lee, ibid.
[27] For an enlightening study tracing the neglected Chinese origins of East Asian developmentalism see Helleiner (2021).

two trends became increasingly profound during this period of economic take-off, which helped economic policymakers rethink the relationship between economic goals on the one hand and environmental goals on the other. *First*, environmental and resource constraints posed significant challenges to the country's aspirations for continuing economic prosperity. By 2000, the energy intensity of China, measured as joules of energy consumed per PPP GDP, was 50 per cent higher than the world average, 120 per cent higher than Germany, 93 per cent higher than Japan, and 40 per cent higher than the US.[28] Meanwhile, like Korea, China has a relatively poor resource base. According to the national sustainability report of China published in 2012, the amount of fresh water, arable land, and forest per capita in China was just 28 per cent, 40 per cent, and 25 per cent of the world averages respectively. Domestic supply of major energy and metal resources in China is also relatively poor—its oil, iron ore, and copper reserves per capita are at levels of 7.7 per cent, 17 per cent, and 17 per cent of the world averages, respectively. For Chinese policymakers, these realities made clear the ecological and energy limits to its explosive economic growth model. *Second*, and relatedly, although environmental protection has long been regarded as a major national policy, traditional efforts in this area were narrowly focused on 'end-of-pipe' treatments. Although environmental quality had improved in certain areas, this narrow approach was ineffective in addressing environmental crisis in China. As a result, the overall environment in China had been deteriorating despite tremendous investment in waste management (Huang, Zeng, and Jiang 2015). This in turn led to considerable dissatisfaction among Chinese people with the government, which directly threatened the legitimacy of the ruling party.

As a response to these two challenges, the term 'ecological civilization' was introduced as a core concept, along with the words 'scientific view of development', as the major narrative of the ruling party under the leadership of President Hu Jintao. The emergence of these concepts in China can be traced to the work of a researcher at the Chinese Academy of Sciences, Liu Zongchao, in the 1990s. Liu's work originally drew on an article published in Russia that described 'ecological civilization as a system that synthesizes concepts from social science (in the Marxist–Leninist tradition) with ecological studies' (Oswald 2017: 36). In the mid-1990s, the National Planning Office of Philosophy and Social Sciences (NPOPSS) in China approved a project on ecological civilization led by Liu in collaboration with researchers from other important institutions. Oswald (2017) suggests this event marked a formal endorsement of the concept by the Chinese authorities, given the strong connections of NPOPSS with the Party's Central Propaganda Department.

---

[28] Based on data available from the World Bank database.

In 2005, Yu Keping, a deputy director of the Compilation and Translation Bureau of the Central Committee of the Chinese Communist Party and a prominent political scholar in China, described the concept in another influential article (Yu 2005). According to Yu (2005), developing ecological civilization in China was by no means a call for people to 'passively live in a natural environment'. Rather, ecological civilization was a process built on a people-centred philosophy. The goal was to transform the ecological environment in ways that might improve the wellbeing of the people, while cultivating a harmonious relationship between humanity and nature (Yu 2005). Chinese leaders were receptive to such ideas. In 2007, the phrase first appeared in the party's political report delivered by President Hu in the party's Seventeenth Congress. In the report, the *internalization* of ecological costs became part of the overall goal of a 'moderately prosperous society' (the latter being the core goal of the Chinese government since the reform and opening-up period under Deng Xiaoping). The following objectives underpinned the goal for ecological civilization in the report, including:

> Development of an industrial structure, growth pattern and consumption model characterized with energy and resource saving and protection of the ecological environment; development of circular economy in a large scale and a significant rise of renewable energy; effective control of emissions of major pollutants and significant improvement of the quality of ecological environment; and establishment of the notion of ecological civilization in the society.

In the aftermath of the 2007 Congress, President Hu and senior officials continued to promote the idea of ecological civilization. Towards the end of his term in 2012, Hu made a remark to senior officials in China that 'the construction of an ecological civilization will be given a prominent place and included in all aspects and processes in economic, political, cultural and social development' (Meng 2012). In the party's Eighteenth Congress in 2013, in which a leadership transition from Hu Jintao to Xi Jinping took place, an entire chapter of the political report was devoted to ecological civilization.

The promotion of the notion of ecological civilization by the Chinese leadership and its resultant prevalence in the Chinese political discourse marked the emergence of what we call developmental environmentalism in China. It is now widely accepted by China scholars that by the early 2010s, environmental issues and their related political legitimacy challenges had 'climbed towards the top of the domestic agenda of China's leading officials' and that, despite the obvious implementation gap observable at that time, when it came to the issues of climate change mitigation, improving energy efficiency, and tackling problems of water and air pollution (among others), the 'expressions of intention and commitment from the highest leadership [were] remarkable' (Shapiro 2016, ch. 3).

However, as just indicated, when it has come to translating the slogan of 'ecological civilization' into action, the path has not been smooth—despite support at the highest levels of the Chinese state. As we detail in our longitudinal case studies, the challenges and obstacles have been numerous, from the relatively weak enforcement of environmental laws and regulations, to the misaligned political evaluation metrics at local governments, to vested interests within the different arms of the government and inter-agency rivalries.[29] As a result, prior to the mid-2010s, the government's development plans continued to heavily emphasize and deliver economic growth at the expense of environment protection (Geall and Ely 2018). While the concept of ecological civilisation has been used more and more frequently in governmental planning discussions and discourse since the early 2010s, it has only been in more recent years that we have witnessed a more serious operationalization of developmental environmentalism in China and the growing alignment between the state's creative and destructive ambitions and actions.

Four factors seem to have contributed to this development—factors that are broadly mirrored in the Korean case. While we explore these factors in detail in our case studies, it is worth prefacing them here.

The first factor has been the nature of political leadership, by which we mean presidential orientation and ambition. In the Chinese context, this means the developmental-environmental orientation and ambition of President Xi Jinping. Indeed, well before Xi's tenure as president, as a local official he coined the phrase 'Clear waters and green mountains are as valuable as mountains of gold and silver' (lüshui qingshan jiushi inshan yinshan, 绿水青山就是金山银山). By this, Xi sought to articulate the benefits of environmental efforts to economic development and in turn, the benefits for economic growth of pursuing environmental goals. Since Xi assumed office, the power and authority of the government over environmental issues has gradually been not just centralized, but also strengthened. As a result, since the mid-2010s, we have seen the strengthening of the institutional underpinnings of developmental environmentalism to support the implementation of ecological civilization. For example, the old Ministry of Environmental Protection was renamed as the Ministry of Ecology and Environment (MEE) in 2018, with a significant boost in the numbers of bureaucrats, and, partially as a result, growth in its authority. The ministry and its branches in provinces have launched a series of 'environmental protection storms' during which many energy- and pollution-intensive operations were forced to shut down (Tan 2018). Since 2015, and more formalized in 2019, a stringent environmental supervision program was established. Under the program, supervision teams led by senior party officials joined by high-level officials from the MEE, the Organisation Department

---

[29] The enormity of China's environmental challenges—and the complexities of addressing them—are catalogued in a number of excellent studies, see for example Economy (2010) and Yeophantong and Goh (2022).

of the Central Committee of the Chinese Communist Party (CCP), the Central Commission for Discipline Inspection and other party and government units were sent to local areas. These teams are powerful and their assessments could directly lead to disciplinary actions towards government officials.

The second factor influencing intensifying developmental-environmental ambitions and actions in China (and Korea) relates to the changing geostrategic landscape, especially the growing competition between China and the US for regional (and arguably global) hegemony. Insofar as clean energy is now viewed as a frontline in the competition between the superpowers, we have seen growing efforts on China's part to expedite the development of clean energy technologies and industries, and to secure local self-sufficiency in the same. This competition has had a knock-on effect for Korea, which now sees itself as locked in a battle to stay ahead of China in the race for techno-industrial competitiveness and local capability building.

The third factor relates to intensifying environmental issues and the political legitimacy challenges that they pose to the ruling party in China (and incumbent governments in Korea). As China's economic progress has grown rapidly, so have the levels of pollution in air, water, and land, causing great social and political unrest. Since the early 2000s, the growing popularity of the internet combined with the proliferation and marketization of more traditional mass media (including radio stations, newspapers, and TV channels) has made these socially significant problems more visible (Korolev 2015), and increased public pressure on governments at all levels for meaningful policy action, not least the problems of environmental pollution and degradation. The Chinese government has also faced mounting international pressures on climate action. Meanwhile, after 30 years of high economic growth, the Chinese economy has begun to slow down. In this context, the idea of ecological civilization has become both desirable and *necessary* to drive new sources of economic growth for the nation. The developmental potential of greening was made evident in a major government document published in 2015: *Opinions of the Central Committee of the Communist Party of China and the State Council on Further Promoting the Development of Ecological Civilisation.* According to Geall and Ely (2018), the document does not place emphasis on the reagriculturalization of the economy, nor redistribution of wealth, as some early advocates of ecological civilization had envisioned. Instead, the document sets out a range of policy priorities which reflect the spirit of developmental environmentalism. These include technological innovation, urbanization, improved economic structure through the development of strategic emerging industries and 'green' industries, the meantime reduction of energy- and pollution-intensive industries, efficient use of resources and energy, and improved institutions in this area. These priorities were subsequently integrated into the Thirteenth Five-Year Plan covering 2016–2020 and policies in specific areas. We see the same dynamics at play in China (and Korea) at the local levels. As we demonstrate in our analysis of the phase-out of coal power stations in the Guangdong province of China, more economically developed provinces and cities now have stronger motivations and capacities to engage with the narrative for local reasons (Tan et al. 2021).

The fourth and final factor is the dynamic interplay between state ambitions and capitalist market dynamics. Increasingly, this interplay has helped to drive down the prices of green energy technologies and products far more quickly than previously predicted. These price reductions have helped to neutralize at least some of the entrenched political resistance to the idea of fossil fuel phase-out—especially from erstwhile FF incumbents, many of which are emerging as key players in the green energy industries of the future. As a result, Northeast Asian governments and market forces now appear to be pushing in the same direction—towards ever greener energy systems—although obstacles to the transition clearly remain.

Concluding remark

This chapter has outlined our novel analytical framework for analysing Northeast Asia's green energy shift and the state's strategic role in it. By synthesizing cutting edge Schumpeterian and developmental state theorizing, our approach focuses attention on complex interactions between elite orientations and ambitions on the one hand and capitalist market dynamics on the other, and how these interactions are producing a distinctive approach to the shift in question. In the detailed longitudinal case study chapters that follow, we operationalize our analytical framework, paying particular attention to the domestic and international factors that have at various historical moments enlivened the states' 'creative' and 'destructive' ambitions and capabilities, and that are now bringing these ambitions and capabilities into greater alignment.

4

Creative-Destruction in Korea's Hydrogen Fuel Cell Electric Vehicle Industry

When the Republic first manufactured its own vehicles, the technology gap with the advanced countries amounted to at least 50 years .... However, the Republic grew into a technology powerhouse, which ranks ... fifth in automobiles. If we make up our minds before others and take action, we will be able to lead green growth and take the initiative in a new civilization .... I will make sure that the country comes up with new green growth engines for the next generation to use for 10 to 20 years ... great emphasis will be placed on nurturing eco-friendly and highly efficient green cars as one of the new growth engines .... I will help empower Korea to emerge as one of the top four nations producing green cars in the world.

(President Lee Myung-bak, 2008)

The hydrogen economy will become a new source of growth not just for every car manufacturer but for R&D personnel and relevant businesses. About 300 domestic parts makers are already involved in development and production, and numerous [SMEs] and leading mid-market companies are participating in the production, storage and transport of hydrogen ... Whereas carbon-based energy results in greenhouse gas and fine dust emissions, hydrogen is a clean energy source ... hydrogen-powered cars actually have the effect of purifying air by filtering fine dust while running. When hydrogen-powered cars are as widely distributed by 2030 as the Government plans, an estimated 30,000 tons of fine dust, or 10 per cent of the amount currently produced, will be removed ... As of now, [Hydrogen] is commonly extracted from fossil fuels, but it will become commonplace to produce it while utilising renewable solar, wind and bio energies ...

(President Moon Jae-In, 2017)

Developmental Environmentalism. Elizabeth Thurbon et al., Oxford University Press. © Elizabeth Thurbon, Sung-Young Kim, Hao Tan, and John Mathews (2023). DOI: 10.1093/oso/9780192897794.003.0004

The pattern

In 2008, as the full force of the Global Financial Crisis (GFC) bore down on Korea, newly elected president Lee Myung-bak declared an ambitious new vision for the country's hard-hit automobile industry: within the decade, Korea would seize global leadership in the 'green car' industries of the future. As part of this strategy, Korea would strive to conquer the battery-powered electric vehicle (BEV) market. A big BEV push would allow Korea's automakers, headed by Hyundai, to leverage the country's established capabilities in battery technology and production, fostered through decades-long government support of the chemicals and IT industries. To bring this ambition to life, the president's top economic advisors looked naturally to Korea's leading automaker, Hyundai Motor Company (HMC), who they believed should lead the charge. In a personal visit to HMC headquarters, Blue House officials made the president's expectations clear: Hyundai should waste no time in designing and building a fully electric battery-powered vehicle, and in doing so, turbocharge the nation's green car future.[1]

But there was a problem. At the time, Hyundai Motors president of research and development (R&D) was one Lee Hyun-Soon, a formidable engineer who in the 1980s had personally designed and built Korea's first internal combustion engine (ICE) to world-class standards and international acclaim. Dr Lee had no qualms with the new government's desire to build a world-leading, fully-integrated, technologically-autonomous green car industry, insofar as it largely aligned with Lee's—and Hyundai's—own ambitions. Indeed, since the early 1980s, Lee had personified Hyundai's distinctive corporate strategy of technological self-reliance—a strategy that had been encouraged by Korea's political leaders since the 1960s.[2] Since his appointment as head of Hyundai's R&D division in 1984, Lee had relentlessly pursued HMC's technological independence and vertical integration in ICE vehicles, and in doing so had helped thrust the company into the ranks of the global leaders. Moreover, since the 1990s, Lee had demonstrated a strong personal commitment to the idea of developing technological autonomy and market leadership in the eco-friendly cars of the future. In 1999, Lee himself had initiated the struggle to develop a Korean hybrid car and weathered an exhausting six-year battle against Japanese meddling and manoeuvring intended to stop Korea in its tracks.

---

[1] For a lively discussion of this period from the perspective of Hyundai's then president of R&D Dr Lee Hyun-Soon see Lee (2020).

[2] It is no secret that Hyundai's founder, revered industrialist Chung Ju-yung, shared a close personal bond with President Park Chung-hee (1961–79), the so-called 'father of developmentalism' in South Korea. Chung and Park had bonded over their fierce nationalism and desire for Korea's economic independence, and HMC arguably emerged as the greatest corporate embodiment and beneficiary of Park's relentless developmental drive. It was Chung who threw Hyundai behind Park's vision of creating a fully 'Korean Car' in the 1970s. For an excellent analysis of the role of the state in Korea's auto industry development from the 1960s onwards, with a focus on conventional internal combustion engine vehicles, see Doner et al. (2021).

However, while Hyundai's Lee shared the government's green car *ambitions*, he was sceptical of its desire to make BEVs a key part of its strategy.[3] In Lee's view, BEVs were unlikely to find a mass market due to concerns about range anxiety, not to mention high production and infrastructure costs—in terms of both charging infrastructure and electricity generation. In fact, Lee estimated that if Korea wanted to rapidly replace its fossil-fuelled internal combustion engine vehicles with BEVs, it would need to build five new nuclear reactors simply to meet the charging needs! A more logical bet for Korea would be to focus on hydrogen fuel cell electric vehicles (FCEVs). After all, Hyundai had been developing its FCEV technology with dedicated government support since the early 1990s under the state's 'G7 initiative', designed to thrust Korea into the ranks of global technological leaders. In Lee's view, FCEVs would not only trump BEVs on cost and range, but they could also be powered with hydrogen derived from Korea's expansive gas production systems. Unspoken at the time was the fact that gas-derived (read: fossil fuel) hydrogen is not truly 'green'. But at least FCEVs powered with gas-derived hydrogen would be an improvement on ICE vehicles which spewed CO_2 and particulate pollution from their exhaust pipes into Korea's cities and villages to devastating environmental effect. The only thing that FCEVs spilled from their exhaust pipes was clean water.

Significantly, these divergent views about the most desirable emphasis for Korea's green car strategy resulted in less conflict than compromise and cooperation between Hyundai and the government. Despite disagreeing with policymakers' desire to promote BEVs, Hyundai swiftly acted on the government's request, successfully designing and delivering a fully Korean BEV in record time and collaborating with the government on the development of BEV-charging infrastructure. And while certainly not relinquishing its BEV ambitions, the government also ramped up its longstanding support for FCEV development as part of its National Strategy for Green Growth. Yet for reasons canvassed below, despite significant technological breakthroughs, the government's efforts to scale up the local market for both BEVs and FCEVs faced significant obstacles over the 2008–2015 period. The government continually missed its aggressive EV sales and charging infrastructure targets and made no progress on phasing out ICE vehicles or finding a truly 'green' hydrogen source for FCEVs.

Flash-forward to 2021 and the landscape has changed significantly. After successfully creating the world's first FCEV for commercial production in 2013—one year ahead of Japan—Korea now leads the world in this cutting-edge automotive technology and has seized an overwhelmingly dominant global market share (see Figure 4.3 below). What's more, a solution to the 'green hydrogen' problem has now been found and, through collaborative efforts between government and business, Korea is leading the world in efforts to transition to 'green' hydrogen as an

[3] See Lee (2020) for a discussion of his BEV reservations and preference for a FCEV focus.

emissions-free energy source—not just for FCEVs but for its energy system more broadly.

At the same time, the government's early optimism about the mass-market viability of BEVs has proved prescient. With foreign BEV firms—namely Tesla—now threatening Hyundai's home turf, the government and national champion have swung into action, collaborating on a K-battery alliance to help Hyundai regain lost ground in the domestic and international market. Korea's local FCEV and BEV expansion plans both now rank amongst the world's most ambitious, and external observers anticipate the local market to expand exponentially, with EVs predicted to make up 60 per cent of new vehicle sales by 2040 thanks to massive government support (China is expected to reach just over 70 per cent) (BNEF 2021). Local market expansion is now also being supported by the decision of major local governments to ban diesel cars from city limits and set firm dates for the phase-out of diesel vehicles for public use. For its part, the national government has now pledged to ban ICE vehicles sales by 2035—having long lagged behind other countries in this important policy step. Finally, when it comes to the possibility of ICE vehicles phase-out in Korea, the question now seems less 'if' than 'when'.

The puzzle

In this case we detail and explain the Korean government's strategic activism in the FCEV arena, and its distinctive pattern of progress towards greening the auto industry more broadly. We ask: what has motivated the state to become so involved in green car industry creation, especially in the arena of FCEVs? How have Korean policymakers pursued their 'creative' ambitions? Why has the government appeared more ambitious and active in 'green car' industry creation than in ICE vehicles industry destruction? To what extent is this 'creative-destructive' misalignment now resolving? What factors are driving this realignment, and what obstacles to a fully green shift remain? To address these questions, we divide the case study into three parts, structured temporally. A linear temporal structure allows us to both demonstrate and explain the varying degrees of alignment between the state's 'creative' and 'destructive' ambitions and capabilities from the 1980s to the present.

In Part One (which covers the 1988–2008 period) we examine the logic behind the government's initial decision to promote FCEVs as a strategic industry, starting in the late 1980s. We argue that these early 'creative' initiatives had everything to do with the state's longstanding developmental ambitions of building technological autonomy, manufacturing capacity, and export competitiveness—but little to do with environmental concerns.

In Part Two we examine the *intensification* of the government's 'creative' initiatives and the *emergence* of more destructive ambitions in the automobile arena over the 2008–2015 period. We also show how these developments were linked to the emergence of 'developmental environmentalism' (DE) as a new political-economic philosophy amongst key segments of the policy and political elite. This new DE orientation meant that for the first time, policymakers sought to combine their EV industry creation initiatives with efforts to reign in dirty fossil-fuelled cars. Ultimately however, we show that this period was characterized by 'creative-destructive' misalignment, which cut along two dimensions. First, the government's 'creative' ambitions far outweighed its destructive ambitions during this period. Second, policymakers faced significant obstacles in both the 'creative' and 'destructive' arenas. So, while the government's FCEV industry-building efforts proceeded apace, its ambitious local market expansion targets were not met while its more modest dirty-car displacement efforts were ineffective.

In Part Three (2015–present) we trace the growing alignment between the state's 'creative' and 'destructive' ambitions and actions in the FCEV arena, and identify the factors driving this more positive trend. We also identify the remaining obstacles in the 'creative' and 'destructive' spheres and consider the conditions under which they might be overcome.

Part One: The developmental origins of Korea's FCEV focus (1988–2008)

We trace the Korean government's FCEV activism to the late 1980s.[4] This activism, we argue, was both motivated and shaped by the emergence of two major new external pressures: first oil-shock related energy insecurity, and then China's unexpectedly rapid rise. These pressures served to amplify the traditional developmental ambitions of Korea's policy elite and compelled them to re-think their fossil-fuelled, fast-follower developmental strategy. The determination to develop FCEVs (and a hydrogen industry more broadly) was the outcome of this strategic re-thinking, the result of which was a shift from 'fast-followership' to a focus on pioneering markets at the technological frontier. For these reasons, in this first phase of Korea's FCEV story, we argue that developmental motivations played the primary role, while environmental considerations were marginal at best.

Energy insecurity sparks soul searching about Korea's traditional developmental strategy

As we saw in Chapter 3, by the late 1980s a series of oil shocks had triggered some intense soul-searching amongst Korea's policy and political elite. Many

---

[4] Parts of this chapter build on and extend the case study published in Thurbon et al. (2021).

policymakers were deeply concerned about the implications of growing energy insecurity for the viability of Korea's traditional developmental strategy. That strategy centred on rapidly catching up with advanced economies by making massive investments in established fossil-fuelled industries—including automobiles—that could be quickly scaled for export. However, Korea's extreme dependence on oil imports for its energy needs had created a strong and often damaging connection between international oil prices and the competitiveness of Korea's most important export industries. When oil prices went up, so too did the price of Korea's main exports (including automobiles), throttling national income and shrinking the economy. So, in the late 1980s, desperate to break the connection between the price of oil and national competitiveness, Korean policymakers began searching for new energy alternatives with a view to improving Korea's energy security.

These energy security concerns lay behind the government's *Alternative Energy Technology Development, Use, and Deployment Promotion Act* of 1988. This Act marked the start of the state's commitment to exploring hydrogen as an alternative energy source, and hydrogen FCEVs as the means of securing the fortunes of Korea's auto industry, centred as it was on conventional ICE vehicles. Briefly, FCEVs work very differently from ICE vehicles. In an ICE vehicle, motion is produced via the controlled explosion of petroleum-derived fuel, which drives pistons up and down. In an FCEV, fuel cells convert chemical energy stored in the hydrogen-based fuel directly into electrical energy that drives the motor. The advantage of FCEVs over ICE vehicles is that there is less energy lost as waste, heat, light, and sound. The only by-product of the energy creation process is the water emitted from the vehicle exhaust pipe. Fossil fuel combustion on the other hand creates a host of nasty by-products, not least CO_2 and small particulates like particulate matter (PM) 2.5 that are so hazardous to human health.

Importantly for our purposes however, the potential environmental benefits of FCEVs did not factor into Korea's promotion efforts of the late 1980s. Indeed, the FCEVs being considered at that time were not completely 'green'. This is because, as noted earlier, they would be powered not by 'green hydrogen' derived from renewables like wind and solar, but by hydrogen derived from fossil fuels (mainly gas) using a process that created significant volumes of CO_2.[5] The reality is, in the 1980s (and the 1990s and early 2000s) Korean policymakers were simply not interested in renewable hydrogen, or a green transition more broadly.[6] They

---

[5] Hydrogen, while abundant in the atmosphere, has to be derived from a primary energy source, and historically it has been derived from fossil fuels rather than clean energy sources.

[6] In this sense, Korea stood in stark contrast to other countries, not least the UK, where there has long been a focus on the production of hydrogen from renewable sources combining with PV or wind. Even as recently as 2013, scholars have noted that 'there is literally no Korean R&D project ongoing for hydrogen generation from renewable sources' (Park 2013: 6560). The situation has radically changed since 2015, as we explain below.

were interested in solving Korea's energy insecurity and export competitiveness problems, and this is where their FCEV focus came in.

The 1988 Act ushered in a period of serious public and private investment in hydrogen and fuel cell R&D programs under the leadership of the Ministry of Science and Technology (MOST) (focused on blue-sky R&D) and the Ministry of Commerce, Industry and Energy (MOCIE) (focused on more commercial projects). Korea's lead auto firm Hyundai soon followed suit with its own FCEV development programs. FCEV initiatives were lent extra impetus in the late 1990s under the government's Group of Seven (G7) programs—intended to close the technology gap between Korea and G7 nations in critical areas, including hydrogen and related products. This included the 'G7 Next Generation Vehicle Technology Development Initiative', which saw the government and Hyundai collaborate closely on FCEV development.[7] Between 1988 and 2003, combined public–private investments in hydrogen and fuel cell technologies totalled USD 91.5 million (Haslam et al. 2012). These early investments were significant in that they secured Korea's place amongst the world's forerunners in FCEV-related R&D.

China's rise, a new developmental strategy, and the embrace of economic statecraft

In the early 2000s, a new set of competitiveness concerns added fresh momentum to Korea's FCEV and broader hydrogen development efforts, which were still to bear commercial fruit. These new concerns further diminished policymaker's faith in Korea's traditional fast-followership development strategy, and fuelled support for a new strategy centred on dominating the technological frontier via 'domestically-oriented economic statecraft' (cf. Thurbon and Weiss 2019), as we elaborate below.

The most significant concern was that China's unexpectedly rapid rise, lent fresh force in 2001 by the World Trade Organization (WTO) accession, increased access on the part of Chinese firms to foreign capital and markets. As Chapters 5 and 7 reveal, the Chinese government seized upon these new opportunities to drive forward its ambitious transformative agenda. At the same time, Japan's apparent economic revival further amplified Korea's competitiveness concerns. In the early 2000s, Japan's ambitious post-1997-crisis investments in advanced technology appeared to be paying off. By contrast, Korea's growth remained sluggish, hampered by weak corporate investment and the *chaebol*'s newfound enthusiasm for offshoring production to China. Taken together, these new challenges helped to crystalize the belief amongst Korean policymakers that the nation had only a

---

[7] On the G7 Initiatives and wider hydrogen-related initiatives during this period see Choi, Park, and Lee (2011).

narrow gap in which to cement its technological lead over China and to close the technological gap with Japan (see Thurbon 2016: 99–101). To achieve this goal, Korea would have to cast off its fast-follower approach and adopt a frontier technology strategy centred on pioneering the advanced-tech industries of the future.

Thus from 2003 onwards, we see Korea begin to engage in what is most appropriately described as 'domestically-oriented economic statecraft'—policy initiatives aimed squarely at defending a country's international position by bolstering its domestic economic strength.[8] Specifically, domestically-oriented economic statecraft involves 'government initiatives that reach for or seek to push the technology frontier to fend off, outflank, or move in step with rival economic powers', especially initiatives devoted to 'the making and growing of markets at the techno-industrial frontier' (Thurbon and Weiss 2019: 109). In 2003, to directly address the China challenge, and with the full support of newly elected president Roh Moo-Hyun, Korea's key scientific and economic ministries began devising plans to promote a range of new frontier technology growth engines under the banner of the Twenty-First Century Frontier Technology Program. This program lent fresh momentum to the nation's existing FCEV push, which featured strongly in a succession of national development plans.[9] Those plans laid the foundation for greater coordination between government and private sector investments in hydrogen-related industries.[10] By 2007, Korea's public and private investment in fuel cell technologies exceeded USD 110 million per annum (see Haslam et al. 2012), and Korea had narrowed the technology gap with industry leaders Japan and the US to between two and five years (Song and Chen n.d.:6).

Yet for all its focus on FCEVs, it is important to reiterate that prior to 2008, environmental concerns hardly rated a mention in FCEV debates, even as the early 2000s progressed (see Park 2013).[11] Rather, FCEV promotion efforts were motivated by the longstanding developmental desire to enhance domestic manufacturing capacity, technological autonomy, and export competitiveness, as part

---

[8] See Thurbon and Weiss (2019: 109), see also Weiss and Thurbon (2020).

[9] This included the 2003-2005 'Twenty-First Century R&D Technology Program' which had a particular focus on FCEVs.

[10] For example, in 2003, Korea launched its first major hydrogen-focused, public-private R&D Research Program, involving the Ministry of Knowledge Economy (MKE) the Ministry of Education, Science and Technology (MEST), the National Hydrogen Energy R&D Centre, and private firms. In this 10-year program, the government would invest USD 111 million and the private sector USD 16 million (see Haslam et al. 2012). At the same time, MOCIE announced its 'Hydrogen and Fuel Cell Automobile Research Program' with the aim of constructing the nation's first hydrogen station and building and testing the first FCEVs for commercial use. Then in 2005, MOCIE announced the *National Vision of the Hydrogen Economy and the Action Plan* with a view to developing core fuel cell parts and technologies, and to test-driving locally-produced FCEVs by 2010.

[11] On the limited resonance of environmental discourse amongst the policy and political elite prior to 2008, see Kim and Thurbon (2015: 217–219). Prior to 2008, environmental concerns were couched in the language of 'sustainable development' and expressed in policies designed to protect the environment by placing costs on polluters (read: Korea's most competitive exporters). Environmentalism and developmentalism were thus widely viewed as incompatible goals.

of a broader quest to enhance national economic security and international status and prestige. So, while the government was happy to invest in FCEVs as a frontier technology for geo-economic reasons, there was certainly no talk of a broader 'green car' revolution, and the idea of vigorously promoting a wider range of EVs, such as battery-powered EVs, was not seriously on the government's agenda. This is despite moves on the part of Japanese and European manufacturers to invest heavily in a range of EV technologies in the early 2000s, including BEVs.

Korea's early neglect of BEVs can also be explained by the belief of Korea's lead automobile firms (namely Hyundai and its subsidiary Kia) that the future of EVs lay with FCEVs and hybrids, not BEVs, which it deemed impractical from both a cost and range perspective (Lee 2020). We also speculate that by pushing FCEVs and hybrids rather than BEVs, Hyundai may have had one eye on fending off potential competition from Korea's large electronics and battery companies (namely, Samsung and LG). Their technological know-how would likely give these companies a real advantage in the BEV market, should they choose to pursue it aggressively in the future.[12] FCEVs were thus a safer bet for Korea's established automakers looking to mitigate energy insecurity concerns, secure their competitive advantage, and protect their market share both nationally and globally.

Part Two: From developmentalism to developmental environmentalism in Korea's FCEV strategy and creative-destructive misalignment (2008–2015)

The limited resonance of environmental concerns and the government's narrow focus on FCEVs changed dramatically in 2008 with the onset of the GFC. The GFC marked the enthusiastic embrace of developmental-environmental ideas amongst key segments of the Korean policy and political elite, and the start of the government's ambitious drive to promote 'green cars' more broadly (i.e., both FCEVs *and* BEVs) as cornerstones of the nation's future economic prosperity. How can we account for this shift?

Like previous crises, the GFC amplified concerns about Korea's energy security and its export competitiveness. However, unlike other crises, the GFC occurred against the backdrop of growing global concerns about climate change and of serious *action* to address it.[13] It also coincided with President Lee's Global Korea

---

[12] Samsung had attempted to diversify into the auto industry in 1994 via the creation of Samsung Motor Company but was hit hard by the 1997–8 financial crisis and eventually acquired by Renault in 2000, which bought 80 per cent of the company. Since that time, Renault has operated in Korea under the name Renault Samsung Motors.

[13] For a comprehensive discussion of the emergence and institutionalization of developmental-environmental ideas under the presidency of Lee Myung-bak see Kim and Thurbon (2015).

policy, and Korea's search for issue areas in which it might exert middle power leadership, with climate change being an obvious choice. And when it came to tackling climate change, for most advanced economies, the transport sector (land, sea, and air) was the logical place to start, as these make up such a significant proportion of national greenhouse gas emissions (GHG). In the mid-2000s, Korea was no exception. Since 2002, transport has outpaced manufacturing to become the country's second largest CO_2 emitter, just after electricity and heat production (Ritchie, Roser and Rosado 2020). In 2016, Korea's transport sector emitted 98.8 million tons of CO_2, 14.2 per cent of the national total (OECD 2020). Of this, road transport contributed 94.6 million tons, or 95.8 per cent (Greenhouse Gas Inventory and Research Centre of Korea 2019: 118–119, Tables 3–33). So as governments around the globe sought to ward off the worst effects of the GFC through significant stimulus packages, they placed major emphasis on *green* stimulus, including ambitious spending programs to promote the development and uptake of green cars.

In light of these shifting global conditions, a small segment of Korea's policy and political elite began to see the writing on the wall for Korea's automobile industry: the trajectory of the global economy was changing. Climate change concerns were here to stay and Korea was at risk of being left behind in this critical industry of the future if it did not urgently lift its game—especially in light of the early moves of Japan, Europe, and China in the EV space. In the words of one Ministry of Knowledge Economy (MKE) official in 2008:

> Electric vehicles are not a choice but a must for the local automobile industry because the governments of key industrialized nations, such as Japan, Germany and China, are taking aggressive steps to develop and promote electric vehicles. We need much more aggressive government measures to promote their development.[14]

At the outset, this small group of agents were concentrated in the presidential office and included President Lee's closest advisors, among the most important being Kim Sang-Hyup, Presidential Secretary for National and Future Vision, and key architect of Korea's green growth strategy. While Kim and his associates could see that the global economy was changing, they also believed that these changes held an enormous new opportunity for the nation. By focusing on the creation, commercialization, and export of environmentally-friendly technologies, Korea had the chance to solve its economic competitiveness and energy insecurity challenges in one hit: to 'manufacture energy security' (c.f. Mathews and Tan 2014). At the same time, by ambitiously promoting 'green growth', Korea had the chance to establish itself as an outstanding citizen in an area of major global concern,

---

[14] Cited in 'Full Speed Electric Car Unveiled', *Korea Herald,* 9 September 2010.

enhancing the nation's international prestige (a core developmental concern). Thus was born the philosophy of developmental environmentalism in Korea.

The story of how this small group of change agents were able to promote developmental environmentalism as a shared way of thinking amongst the wider elite, and to translate their ideas into meaningful policy action, has been elaborated elsewhere and cannot detain us here.[15] Rather, it is helpful here to identify what we see as the key differences in the focus and form of government strategic activism in the automotive arena that emerged during this period.

The government's strategic activism in the electric vehicle arena over the 2008–2015 period differed from the activism observed over the 1988-2008 period in four key ways. We have already alluded to the first key difference, which centres on the shift in *motivation* driving policy action, that is, the shift from developmentalism to developmental environmentalism. From 2008 onwards, key segments of Korea's policy elite were focused on the goal of growing *and* greening the economy at the same time. So, while traditional developmental concerns of manufacturing capacity, technological autonomy, and export competitiveness remained absolutely central to the government's industry creation efforts, for the first time environmental considerations also came seriously into play.

These environmental considerations informed the second and third key differences we observe in the government's strategic activism over the 2008–2015 period. The second difference was the expansion of the government's industry creation efforts to promote 'green cars' broadly, rather than just FCEVs. The third difference was the new focus on what we describe as 'destructive' policies in both electricity generation (discussed in Chapter 6) and in the auto industry. Over the 2008–2015 period, destructive policies in the auto industry were aimed at reducing the proportion of ICE vehicles on Korean roads and at changing the pattern of ICE vehicle production and consumption by discouraging the purchase of 'dirty' gasoline cars while encouraging the purchase of (what were assumed to be) more energy efficient/less environmentally damaging 'clean diesel' vehicles (although this policy turned out to be misguided from an environmental perspective, as we shall see).

The fourth and final difference in the government's strategic activism over the 2008–2015 period relates to the *form* of its industry creation efforts, specifically, the emergence of a new mode of industry promotion centred on what Kim (2019) refers to as 'hybridized industrial ecosystems' (elaborated in the section that follows). We now briefly discuss the state's key 'creative' and 'destructive' initiatives over the 2008–2015 period before turning to the question of 'creative' and 'destructive' obstacles and misalignments.

---

[15] See Kim and Thurbon (2015) for a foundational discussion of the emergence and institutionalization of developmental-environmental ideas in Korea. Thurbon (2016) provides an agent-centred analytical framework for investigating the emergence and evolution of developmental ideas and practices in different national contexts and applies it to the case of Korea over the 1901–2015 period.

From developmental-environmental ambition to action in the 2008–2015 period

Key creative actions: In 2008—as previously noted—there emerged strong support for developmental-environmental ideas amongst key segments of Korea's policy and political elite. And within that elite, 'green cars' (including BEVs and FCEVs) were viewed as a logical centrepiece for a developmental-environmental strategy. Support for promoting EVs came from the very top, with newly elected president Lee routinely emphasizing green cars as a central pillar of his 'green growth' vision, and a key means by which Korea might establish itself as a leader of industries of the future, as the epigraph at the start of this chapter indicates. The government's support for EVs was formalized in the Lee administration's National Strategy for Green Growth (2009–2050), and its related first Five-Year Plan for Green Growth (FYPGG) (2009–2013). That plan allocated no less than USD 1.8 billion to the development of low carbon vehicles. Indeed, so central were low carbon vehicles to the first FYPGG that one-third of the 27 technologies it identified for strategic promotion were related to their production (Kim and Thurbon 2015: 225).

The 2010 Green Car Roadmap articulated the government's EV industry creation goals and strategies in even greater detail. These ambitious EV industry creation plans were overseen by the Presidential Committee on Green Growth (PCGG), one of the most important institutional innovations of the Lee administration (see Chapter 3 for a more detailed overview). The PCGG performed the function of a 'control tower' coordinating and monitoring the activities of key ministries and their policy programs. The most significant EV-related ministries over the 2009–2013 periods were the MKE and the Ministry of the Environment (which jointly oversaw the Green Car Roadmap). As Kim and Thurbon (2015) have pointed out, Korea's EV promotion programs over the 2008–2015 period were distinguished by their developmental character—that is—their emphasis on promoting local manufacturing capacity, technological autonomy, and export competitiveness. As such, the overriding theme of these programs was *localization*. As much as possible, Korea's EV and related infrastructures were to be built using locally-developed and manufactured technologies, components, and materials. In other words, the aim was to create a *nationally-integrated industry* that could then form the basis of a new export platform (2015: 225).

The key mechanism for the operationalization of these industry creation initiatives was the establishment of *hybridized industrial ecosystems* (HIEs)—another significant institutional innovation with origins in the Lee administration. As S-Y Kim explains, HIEs represent 'a fusion of public and private features which bring together all major players in the production and innovation value chain' (2019: 3), from large firms to small- and medium-sized enterprises (SMEs) and high-tech start-ups, to state agencies and government research institutes. The purpose of

HIEs is 'to [develop] and [export] complete technology solutions or systems [think locally developed EVs or EV charging stations], not just individual components such as microprocessors or electronic devices as occurred in earlier periods of development' (2019: 14). Of course, HIEs are not exclusive to the EV arena—Kim's pioneering study of this phenomenon traced their emergence in the smart grid space (see Chapter 6 for further details of smart grid related HIEs). However, HIEs have also been (and continue to be) central to the state's EV promotion strategy. For example, Korea's quest to develop a fully-local, full-speed, full battery-EV, involving 44 local firms led by Hyundai in collaboration with public research institutes, stands out as one example from the first FYPGG era (see Kim and Thurbon 2015: 226). We might add to this the 'Smart Transport' projects initiated under Korea's smart grid pilot project on Jeju Island,[16] which involved the creation of three key consortia (each led by a different firm) aimed at developing and commercializing BEV charging infrastructures (the most successful of which has involved state-owned power company KEPCO).

Key destructive actions: The government's ambitions and actions on the destructive front were far more modest than in the 'creative arena', for reasons we canvas in the following section. During this period, as noted previously, the government set concrete targets for EV market expansion (i.e., to have EVs make up 21 per cent of new car sales by 2015). To the extent that this necessarily implied the displacement of internal combustion engine vehicles (i.e., reducing these vehicles from close to 100 per cent to 79 per cent of new sales), it may also be considered a 'destructive' goal. However, the government stopped short of taking more concrete action to advance this goal, such as specifying clear limits on the production or sale of combustion engine vehicles or nominating a target date for ICE vehicle phase-out (to be fair however, neither did any other country in the developed world at that time). Nor did the government appear to be proactively pursuing 'green hydrogen' alternatives for fuelling FCEVs during this period.

At the same time, the government sought to change consumption patterns in the ICE vehicle car market over the 2008–2015 period by encouraging consumers to switch from 'dirty' gasoline to so-called 'clean diesel'. It did so by introducing significant tax breaks for diesel (which effectively functioned as a tax on gasoline). While it is clear that in retrospect promoting 'clean diesel' over gasoline was hardly beneficial for the environment, some background to this policy action is important here, because Korea was by no means an outlier in considering 'clean diesel' an environmentally-friendly alternative in the mid-2000s. Indeed, in the early 2000s, 'clean diesel' was being vigorously promoted by Europe's big three car manufacturers—Mercedes, Bayerische Motoren Werke (BMW), and Volkswagen

---

[16] For analyses of this project as it relates to smart grids see Kim and Mathews (2016) and Kim (2019), the latter of which examines the emergence of hybridized industrial ecosystems in the smart grid space.

(VW)—as an environmentally-friendly alternative. Working in an alliance, these three had developed a technology to produce low-emissions 'clean diesel' by adding an ammonia derivative to fuel.[17] Before long however, VW decided to go it alone in what would become the 'clean diesel' race between the European majors.[18] So from the mid-2000s, the idea of 'clean diesel' was being vigorously promoted in Europe as an environmentally-friendly alternative to conventional combustion engine vehicles, and was starting to appeal too in the US.

The idea of 'clean diesel' piqued the interest of Korea's Roh Moo-hyun administration (2003–2007), which was grappling with a spike in global gasoline prices and looking for a solution to this significant economic problem. Prior to that time, diesel had (rightly) been considered a very dirty fuel in South Korea,[19] and automakers were not permitted to sell diesel passenger vehicles in Korea due to emissions concerns—even though Hyundai and Kia both produced diesel passenger cars for export.[20] Only commercial vehicles and trucks were permitted to use (very cheap) diesel, given the economic benefit—much to the ire of environmental campaigners. However, the 'discovery' and vigorous promotion of 'clean diesel' by European carmakers—and the simultaneous spike in international gasoline prices—changed the government's calculations. In 2005, President Roh revised Korea's diesel regulations, paving the way for the introduction of 'clean diesel' passenger vehicles in Korea. Soon after, in 2007, the government fixed the price of diesel at 15 per cent below the price of gasoline, in an attempt to further encourage the diesel switch. From that point, the sale of diesel passenger vehicles expanded rapidly in Korea—albeit less for environmental reasons than those to do with 'conspicuous consumption'; most diesel sales in Korea were of luxury European mid- or large-sized cars purchased by image-conscious young Koreans looking to stand out from the crowd (insofar as the local car market was overwhelmingly dominated by locally-made compact cars).[21]

---

[17] 'Exhausted by Scandal: "Dieselgate" Continues to Haunt Volkswagen', *Wharton School of the University of Pennsylvania*, 21 March 2019, https://knowledge.wharton.upenn.edu/article/volkswagen-diesel-scandal/

[18] As we now know, this race ended in a massive crash in 2015 in the form of the VW diesel emissions falsification scandal. This scandal revealed that many of the so-called 'clean diesel' cars being sold by European carmakers were not clean at all—and that their emissions data had been deliberately falsified (a point we return to below). In this sense, governments' working assumptions that 'clean diesel' vehicles were more environmentally-friendly than gasoline ones were false.

[19] Korean oil refineries very much lagged behind their European counterparts in their capacity to strip sulphuric content from diesel, and so the diesel they produced was extremely dirty. See 'Diesel-fuelled Passenger Cars Fuelling Debate', *Chosun Ilbo*, 10 February 2003, http://english.chosun.com/site/data/html_dir/2003/02/10/2003021061004.html

[20] 'Automakers Urge Go-ahead for Diesel-fuelled Cars', *Chosun Ilbo*, 9 December 2002, http://english.chosun.com/site/data/html_dir/2002/12/09/2002120961002.html

[21] 'Diesel-powered cars gain traction in South Korea', *NikkeiAsia*, 16 March 2015, https://asia.nikkei.com/Business/Diesel-powered-cars-gain-traction-in-South-Korea; Between 2005 and 2010, the share of diesel vehicles in the domestic passenger market skyrocketed from 0 per cent to 30 per cent. See 'Automakers look to benefit from VW's woes'. *Korea Joongang Daily*. 8 October 2015, https://koreajoongangdaily.joins.com/2015/10/08/industry/Automakers-look-to-benefit-from-VWs-woes/3010122.html

In 2008, 'clean diesel' became an important pillar of President Lee Myung-bak's 'Low-Carbon, Green Growth Strategy'. As part of that strategy, President Lee's clean diesel policy provided various incentives for consumers to choose (what were believed to be) 'low-emissions' diesel vehicles over gasoline powered ones— so long as the diesel vehicles met the strict Euro five emissions standard. The idea of clean diesel was appealing to Korea's newly minted political leadership, inso-far as it looked like a reasonably quick fix to some of Korea's spiralling carbon emissions—and certainly a logical stop-gap during the EV scale-up phase. Incen-tives introduced under President Lee's clean diesel policy—which were retained by President Park—included tax breaks and discounted registration, parking, and toll fees. Thanks to these incentives, between 2011 and 2018, the ratio of diesel cars on Korea's roads rose from 36.3 per cent to 42.5 per cent (so in 2018, 9.58 million of the nation's 22.53 million cars were diesel).[22]

Having now outlined the government's key 'creative' and 'destructive' ambitions and actions in the green car arena over the 2008–2015 period, what can we say about their success? Despite some important institutional innovations and sig-nificant policy efforts, progress under the Five-Year Plan for Green Growth and 2010 Green Car Roadmap was far from smooth sailing—on both the 'creative' and 'destructive' fronts. For while developmental-environmental ideas exerted a powerful influence amongst *some* Korean policymakers from 2008 onwards, these ideas were contested both inside and outside the state. As such, DE-minded poli-cymakers faced serious obstacles when attempting to translate their 'creative' and 'destructive' ambitions into action.

Creative-destructive misalignment in the 2008–2015 period

Conflicts within the state over industry creation initiatives: In the previous section, we saw that Korea's Science and Industry Ministries made serious invest-ments in EV-related RD&C programs under the Five-Year Plan for Green Growth, and serious headway in developing new products for export. However, lack of consensus within the state about the direction of Korea's EV industry creation strategy meant that the government would fall far short of the ambitious industry expansion targets established under the 2010–2015 Green Car Roadmap.

The most significant obstacle to the government's 'creative' efforts was the lack of consensus within the state about the desirability of making a swift transition from ICE vehicles to EVs. Despite strong presidential support for an aggressive EV push, the Ministry of Strategy and Finance (MOSF) was reluctant to come on board. The ministry's key concern was the potential for the domestic embrace of

[22] 'Korean Gov't to Do Away With Incentives for Diesel Cars', *BusinessKorea*, 9 November 2018, available at: http://www.businesskorea.co.kr/news/articleView.html?idxno=26428.

EVs to reduce gas consumption and thus gas tax revenue—a critical source of tax revenue in Korea. Compared with other countries, Korea has historically taken a large share of gasoline prices as an oil tax.[23] Thus the MOSF proved reluctant to place support behind Korea's early EV push and kept an unhelpfully tight hand on the purse strings. For example, in light of weaker than anticipated domestic demand for EVs, the Ministry of Strategy and Finance slashed the Ministry of Environment's EV budget by a massive 50 per cent in 2012.[24] It then refused to reinstate supports in response to the Ministry of Environment's appeals over the 2013–2014 period. Similarly, the MOSF proved unwilling to fund an aggressive national roll out of EV charging infrastructure, which would have supported domestic EV uptake.

Interestingly, key figures within Korea's leading industry ministry (whose name changed from the MKE to Ministry of Trade, Industry and Energy (MOTIE) in 2014) also proved reluctant to support the government's ambitious BEV promotion goals during this period, joining forces with the MOSF to reject calls for an increase in domestic BEV subsidies in 2013. Some commentators have attributed MOTIE's position to its concerns about reduced tax revenue (which could hit the ministry's budget). However, the ministry's position might also be explained by its close relationship with Korea's top auto firm Hyundai, which, as already noted, was sceptical of the government's BEV push and much preferred an emphasis on FCEVs.

Yet even where the government and Hyundai were closely aligned in their 'creative' ambitions (i.e., FCEVs), conflicts within the state continued to compromise aggressive market creation goals. As noted previously, with full government support, Hyundai had been investing in FCEV development since the early 1990s—though not for environmental reasons. However, by the mid-2000s, hydrogen's decarbonizing potential—and the potential benefits of FCEVs over BEVs—were becoming clearer. For example, while battery powered EVs (BEVs) can reduce passenger vehicle emissions, hydrogen FCEVs have more potential to decarbonize heavier vehicles—from buses, trucks, and trains, to even ships and planes—thanks to hydrogen's energy density. Density also means that hydrogen fuel cells can be deployed beyond transport in stationary settings including electricity generation. Eventually, green hydrogen power plants could replace fossil-fuelled ones—including coal and nuclear plants and oil refineries—and generate enough energy to power entire nations. Thus, it is now widely acknowledged

---

[23] In 2013 Korea took 52.24 per cent of the gas price as tax, compared to 11 per cent in the US. In 2013 alone (on MOSF figures) the government collected 19.4 trillion won (USD 17.5 billion) in oil taxes— which accounted for about 9.5 per cent of total tax revenue for the period, see: J. Park. 'Popularization of Electric Vehicles Taking Time in Korea', *BusinessKorea*, 2 December 2014, http://www.businesskorea. co.kr/news/articleView.html?idxno=7572

[24] J. Seo. '2020 road map for development of electric vehicles faces bumpy road', *The Korea Herald*, 17 December 2012, http://www.koreaherald.com/common/newsprint.php?ud=20121217000841

that hydrogen provides an incredibly powerful platform for decarbonizing not just particular sectors like transport, but the whole economy (IEA 2019).

In light of hydrogen's decarbonizing potential—and the government's long-standing support for FCEV technology development—it is not surprising that the government significantly increased its FCEV funding under its first Green Car Plan. In 2013, these dedicated investments in new industry creation finally bore fruit as Hyundai became the first company in the world to produce an FCEV for commercial sale—the Tucson ix FCEV. With a range of 400 km (249 miles) per charge, it provided a real alternative to BEVs, effectively eliminating the problem of 'range anxiety'. This development established Hyundai as a world leader in this frontier technology arena.

The problem was, thanks to the MOSF's general green car scepticism, the government had failed to roll out *any* public re-fuelling infrastructure for hydrogen cars—a hugely expensive endeavour. Indeed in 2013, there were no publicly available hydrogen re-fuelling stations available anywhere in Korea (and only ten government-owned stations for research purposes). So, despite its success in bringing a world-first product to market, Hyundai was unable to actually sell this product at home. The government's under-investment in refuelling infrastructure thus threatened to stymie Hyundai's first-mover advantage. Meanwhile, although Japan trailed Korea in the race to commercialize FCEVs, its government had the foresight to start investing in refuelling infrastructure back in 2009, in anticipation of commercialization. So, when Toyota announced that it had produced Japan's first FCEV for commercial use in 2014—one year after Korea—Toyota was immediately able to begin selling its vehicles domestically, giving it a considerable edge over Hyundai. Needless to say, the Korean government's lack of investment in FCEV refuelling infrastructure was the cause of considerable frustration for Hyundai, who believed it still had the lead over Japan in FCEV technologies, even after Japan had released its commercial version.[25]

In sum, despite significant policy commitments, institutional innovations, and investments under Korea's FYPGG, the lack of consensus over Korea's EV promotion strategy meant that Korea fell far short of its EV industry creation goals. For example, where Korea had intended for EVs to make up 21 per cent of all domestic car sales by 2015, they had achieved only two per cent.

Conflicts within the state over fossil fuel destruction initiatives: As noted previously, despite major ambitions in the 'creative' arena, the Korean government appeared far less ambitious and active on the 'destructive' front during the period in question. We identify a number of reasons for its reluctance to phase-out ICE vehicles more rapidly.

[25] In the words of one Hyundai representative in 2016: 'We have confidence that we have leading technologies for hydrogen cars as our developments began in the late 1990s ... If the appropriate infrastructure is established, we can top the hydrogen car markets' (Hyundai Motor Spokesperson cited in Lee 2016).

First, Korea's automakers relied heavily on income from ICE vehicle sales to fund their significant R&D investments in EVs. On this basis, automakers argued that if governments sought to reign in ICE vehicle sales before EVs reached cost-competitiveness (or at least closer to it), they would undermine auto companies' ability to invest in more aggressive EV development—and governments would have to pick up the slack. An early phase-out would hurt small- and medium-sized suppliers particularly hard, as they have far less financial wiggle room than the auto majors like Hyundai to invest in R&D to make the full EV transition.[26] At the same time, if governments signalled their intention to tax or restrict the sale of ICE vehicles too prematurely, they might discourage lower-income ICE vehicle owners (who could not afford to buy more expensive EVs) from trading in their older, less environmentally-friendly combustion engine vehicles for newer, lower-emissions ones—at a great environmental cost. So, unless the government wished to dramatically ramp-up its EV-related subsidies, a premature ICE vehicle phase-out policy might inadvertently have a *negative* environmental impact. Leaving the veracity of these arguments to one side, they provided Korean policymakers who were sceptical of more 'destructive' policies with logical reasons to delay.

Significantly, Korea's labour unions were also vigorously opposed to any proposal to scale back ICE vehicle production for fear of the impact on jobs. While the flip side of ICE vehicle phase-out would undoubtedly be EV-market expansion, the fact remained that manufacturing EVs requires about 30 per cent less labour than traditional ICE vehicles thanks to fewer parts.[27] So the idea that automakers should scale back ICE vehicle production to support EV production was particularly concerning to workers and their union representatives (and thus their political representatives in the government as well).

The government's clean diesel policy appeared a helpful workaround for these challenges, insofar as it would allow Korean automakers to continue producing combustion engine vehicles for the short-to-medium term—but ones with less of an environmental impact. Of course, in retrospect, from an environmental perspective, it is clear that the clean diesel policy was a disastrous misstep for Korea (and for other nations). For evidence now shows that while diesel vehicles may be more fuel efficient and produce less CO_2 than petrol cars, they still produce about nine times the amount of particulate pollution, and have thus become a leading cause of Korea's deteriorating air quality—a point we return to below.

[26] See for example the arguments made here: H. Nam. 'Will Korea end sales of combustion engine vehicles in 2035?', *The Korea Times*, 20 November 2020, https://www.koreatimes.co.kr/www/tech/2020/10/419_297838.html

[27] Indeed, this remains an issue in Korea; in 2020 Kia workers in Korea threatened to walk off the job thanks to the company's plans to produce electric vehicles. 'Kia Motors Workers in South Korea to stage Partial Strike Over Wages, EV plans', *Reuters*, 19 November 2020, https://www.reuters.com/article/us-kia-motors-strike/kia-motors-workers-in-south-korea-to-stage-partial-strike-over-wages-ev-plans-idUKKBN27Z0XO.

In sum, while efforts to phase-out some kinds of fossil fuels by promoting 'clean diesel' over gasoline proved somewhat effective—increasing the proportion of diesel vehicles on Korea's roads—the environmental assumptions underlying this policy approach proved disastrously flawed, contributing to worsening particulate pollution in Korea over the 2008-2015 period.

Part Three: Growing creative-destruction alignment (2015–present)

From 2015 onwards, we observe a growing alignment between the Korean state's 'creative' and 'destructive' ambitions and capabilities. This is evidenced by poli-cymakers' renewed momentum for the hydrogen FCEV push, and their growing efforts to dismantle fossil fuel incumbencies and promote a green energy shift more broadly. We attribute this growing alignment to three key factors, which we consider in turn: major external shocks and changing market dynamics; pres-idential orientation and ambition; and the emergence of local governments as 'creative-destructive' allies.

External shocks and changing market dynamics

In 2015–16, three major external developments converged to change the compet-itive dynamics of the global automobile industry: 'Dieselgate', the Paris Accord, and China's growing geostrategic ambitions and wholesale assault on the EV market (as we detail in Chapter 5). Taken together, these three external shocks had significant implications for Korea's 'creative' and 'destructive' ambitions and actions.

In 2015, the automobile world was shaken by revelations that European car manufacturer VW had, since 2006, been systematically falsifying its diesel car emissions data, and that most of its diesel cars were in fact spewing dangerous levels of ultrafine dust and nitrogen dioxide into the air. The so-called 'Dieselgate' scandal soon widened to encompass other manufacturers, helping to undermine faith in so-called 'clean' fossil fuel alternatives, and to increase the appeal of EVs across the board. Dieselgate was soon followed by the 2016 Paris Accord, which marked growing global action on climate change. Under the Accord, many govern-ments around the globe embraced ambitious new carbon reduction commitments. By prompting governments to embrace tougher vehicle emissions standards, the Accord also paved the way for the exponential expansion of the global EV market.

Taken together, Dieselgate and the Paris Accord sparked a major transition in international automotive markets. From 2017, a number of major economies announced their intention to ban the sale of new internal combustion engine vehicles within a specified period of time. France was one of the first countries off the mark, announcing in July 2017 that it would ban the registration of ICE vehicles by 2040. The United Kingdom (UK) soon followed, announcing a similar ban (which was brought forward to 2030 under the UK's 2020 Green New Deal). France and the UK were soon joined by a swathe of smaller European and Nordic countries announcing even more ambitious goals; Austria for example pledged no new ICE vehicle sales from 2020. Taiwan took the Northeast Asian lead, announcing in December 2017 no sales of fossil fuel powered vehicles from 2040. For the first time, governments in major advanced economies—some of Korea's key export markets—demonstrated a willingness to draw a clear line under the ICE vehicle era. This could mean only one thing for the future of EVs—rapid market expansion, and rapidly expanding export opportunities.

From 2015 onwards, China's growing geostrategic ambitions also served to transform global EV market dynamics, leading to expectations of massive market growth—and of intense new competitive pressures for Korea. By 2015, China had already established itself as a serious new competitor in the EV space, and in that year actually leapfrogged Korea as the world's number two provider of EV batteries (Japan has long ranked number one). Batteries are by far the most valuable component of BEVs, and the component in which Korea had become hyper-competitive globally, thanks to Samsung's and LG's long-standing experience in consumer batteries.

As Figures 4.1 and 4.2 show, China's rapidly expanding share of the global EV market—and the battery market in particular—was built on the growth of its domestic market under dedicated government sponsorship. That is, China's EV battery makers were supplying Chinese auto manufacturers who were supplying Chinese consumers. Korean firms on the other hand were mainly supplying Japanese, American, and European car manufacturers—and thus still retained a significant technological advantage over their Chinese counterparts. Nevertheless, China's rapid rise in the BEV space was confronting for Korea, and gave new momentum to Korea's 'creative' ambitions and actions in the EV arena, as we elaborate shortly.

However, as we discuss in detail in Chapter 5, 2015 marked a strategic turning point for China, and for its EV ambitions. The country's *Made in China 2025* strategy—released in 2015—made China's economic ambitions in the EV arena clear and set aggressive targets for technological upgrading and localization. The *Made in China* strategy was interpreted by the US as signalling China's intention to compete for geo-economic primacy both in Northeast Asia and more broadly (as we discuss in detail in Chapter 9). The EV aspect of the Made in China strategy was lent further support in 2016 with the announcement that the government would not grant approval for any new ICE vehicle producers. But it was in 2017 that China's EV plans were seriously turbocharged with the announcement of the

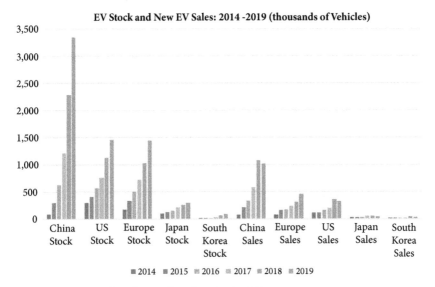

Figure 4.1 EV stock and new EV sales, 2014–2019
Data: IEA

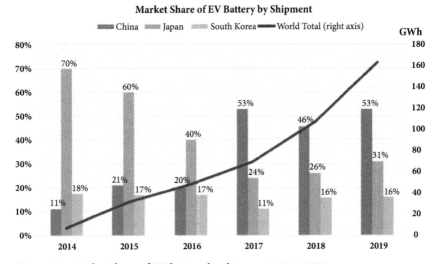

Figure 4.2 Market share of EV battery by shipment, 2014–2019
Data: Collated by the authors, sources include insideev.com, koreajoongangdaily.com, Forbes.com, reneweconomy.com

Auto Industry Medium and Long Term Plan, which set unprecedentedly ambitious growth and upgrading targets for the EV industry (see Chapter 5 for details).

The point we emphasize here is that from 2015 onwards, the combined effect of Dieselgate, the Paris Accord, and China's growing ambition was to enliven the

Korean state's 'creative' and 'destructive' ambitions and actions in the automobile arena.

Enlivened destructive actions: On the destructive front, Dieselgate was significant in that it marked the beginning of the end of the Korean government's support for so-called 'clean' diesel as an acceptable alternative to EVs. The Korean government's response to Dieselgate was swift and strong. In October 2015 it demanded that VW recall more than 125,000 of its diesel cars in Korea and revoked the certification of over 80,000 cars across various diesel models. It also slapped large fines on VW and arrested the senior local executive involved in the scandal, who was later jailed for more than a year. Having dealt with VW, the government then cast a wider net, ordering emissions tests for all diesel car models in the market in Korea. Upon finding that all except BMW's failed to meet emissions standards, the government ordered another major round of recalls while slapping widespread restrictions on diesel vehicle imports. The government's strong reaction to the scandal and its rapid about-face on the environmental benefits of diesel had a visible effect on domestic market sales. In the first half of 2016, sales of imported diesel models dropped by 2.2 per cent while domestic purchases of EVs increased by 42 per cent compared to the previous year.[28]

To be sure, the government's response to Dieselgate could have been stronger from a 'destructive' perspective. Policymakers could have slapped a tax on diesel cars. They could have formally abandoned the government's longstanding 'clean diesel policy'. They could have identified a timeframe for the full national phase-out of diesel vehicles. In 2015–16 however, Korean policymakers did none of those things. Nevertheless, we see Dieselgate as significant insofar as it marked a major change in the government's 'clean diesel' tune and paved the way for the more substantive 'destructive' steps that followed, including President Moon Jae-In's 2017 pledge to get all diesel vehicles off Korean roads by 2030 (discussed in the section that follows).

Enlivened creative ambitions: Insofar as they signalled the dramatic expansion of EV markets and presented Korea with exceptional new export opportunities, the collective external shocks associated with Dieselgate, the Paris Accord, and China's new positioning also lent significant momentum to the government's 'creative' ambitions. These ambitions were reflected in the government's launch of Korea's second FYPGG of 2014 and its new Green Car Plan of 2015. The bold nature of these plans revealed that the 'creative' ambitions that had emerged under President Lee Myung-bak would not only be sustained, but be deepened under President Park Geun-hye, who replaced Lee in 2013. Intensifying competition from China also sharpened the state's strategic focus on FCEVs as a frontier

[28] Y. Kang. 'South Korea shuns diesel following emissions scandal', *Nikkei Asia*, 29 June 2016, https://asia.nikkei.com/Economy/South-Korea-shuns-diesel-following-emissions-scandal.

technology arena in which Korea might actually retain a long-term competitive advantage over its new rival. While the 2014 and 2015 plans pledged to support both BEVs and FCEVs, FCEVs soon took centre stage in the government's future car plans.

Korea's drive to dominate the FCEV frontier was first articulated under the Park administration's five-year Green Car Plan of December 2015. The plan's stated aim was to significantly reduce GHG emissions by dramatically expanding the production and local uptake of EVs.[29] At the same time, Hyundai announced its own aggressive Green Car Plan, aiming to dramatically increase its EV offerings and local sales volumes. Then in 2016 the Park administration made it clear that it would put FCEVs at the centre of its efforts. To this end, in April that year, the government announced the establishment of what we view as the first dedicated hybridized industrial ecosystem in the FCEV space: the Hydrogen Fusion Alliance (since re-named H2Korea). Trade Minister Joo Hyung-hwan articulated the DE ambitions that lay behind the government's FCEV push and its establishment of H2Korea thus:

> The importance of hydrogen fuel cell vehicles has risen not only as a centre of the nation's future car plans but also as a countermeasure for environmental issues such as emissions and fine dust ... The alliance will push ahead with its plans for promoting the nation's hydrogen auto industry.[30]

As a genuine fusion of public and private actors and interests, H2Korea brings together representatives from national and local governments, large auto firms (namely, Hyundai Motor) and their small suppliers, hydrogen producers and suppliers, energy companies, and learned societies. Its primary purpose is to serve as a 'control tower' to facilitate the creation, commercialization, and distribution of FCEVs and their infrastructure. One of its most important functions is to coordinate the creation of special purpose companies (SPC) charged with developing and building hydrogen refuelling stations. This initiative came to fruition in 2019 with the creation of Hydrogen Energy Network (HyNet), Korea's first FCEV SPC dedicated to executing the government's hydrogen refuelling infrastructure ambitions by building 100 refuelling stations across Korea by 2022. The first of these—in Sejong City—was opened to the public in September 2020.

---

[29] The plan sought to: boost domestic production of EVs from just under 80,000 per annum (p/a) in 2015 to 920,000 p/a in 2020; increase domestic market share of EVs from two per cent in 2015 to nearly 20 per cent of all new vehicles sold by 2020; reduce the amount of GHG released into the atmosphere by 3.8 million tonnes p/a (up from the previously planned 200,000-tonne reduction p/a).

[30] Cited in D. Jhoo. 'Government, private sector team up for more hydrogen cars', *The Korea Times*, 24 August 2016, https://www.koreatimes.co.kr/www/tech/2020/06/693_212621.html.

Presidential orientation and ambition

The second factor driving greater alignment between the Korean state's 'creative' and 'destructive' ambitions and capabilities since 2015 was the strong developmental-environmental orientation and ambition of President Moon Jae-In, elected in May 2017. As previous studies have shown, the presidential office in Korea has, since the 1960s, been endowed with distinctive status and authority. This has meant that the orientations and ambitions of Korean presidents have often served as a hinge-factor when it comes to the momentum behind and execution of developmental initiatives, even in the democratic era (Thurbon 2016: 5–7). As briefly noted above and discussed in detail in Chapter 6, President Park Geun-hye was less personally invested in developmental-environmental ideas than her predecessor Lee Myung-bak. While supportive of the 'creative' (industry-building) aspects of Lee's green growth initiative, President Park was far from ambitious on the 'destructive' front. The same cannot be said of President Moon. Our argument is that Moon's election was crucial to enlivening not just the 'creative' but also the 'destructive' (read: fossil fuel exit) aspect of Korea's green energy shift.

Moon came to power on a platform of clean energy action, pledging not only to phase-out coal and nuclear power plants (which we discuss in Chapter 6), but also to get diesel cars off the road by 2030 and make a swift transition to a full-EV future. One of his first actions was to appoint Hangyang University professor of energy engineering, Paik Un-gyu, as the minister for trade, industry and energy. An expert in renewable energy (RE), Paik was a well-known advocate of a clean energy transition and had advised Moon on his election commitments for nuclear and coal exit. As minister, Paik was responsible for the development of Korea's Eighth Basic Plan for Long-Term Electricity Supply and Demand (2017–2031). As we discuss at greater length in Chapter 6, that plan introduced an Energy Transition Roadmap to phase-out nuclear, dramatically reduce coal, and increase the share of RE to 20 per cent of generation output by 2030 (since increased to 37 per cent by 2030). These measures would reduce Korea's GHG emissions by 26 per cent by 2030 (MOTIE 2017: 45).

Moon also dramatically stepped up support for the FCEV industry, working closely and collaboratively with long-time fossil fuel incumbent Hyundai Motors to ensure that it maintains its competitive national and global position in the green car arena. In June 2018, the Moon administration announced a plan to thrust Korea into world leadership in the rapidly growing FCEV industry. As a Business Korea analyst put it: 'The government and the industry plan to strategically cooperate to pre-empt the global hydrogen car market. They are going to establish a hydrogen car industry ecosystem, involving all stakeholders ranging from hydrogen car producers and hydrogen filling station operators to hydrogen energy suppliers.'[31] The plan, led by MOTIE, set ambitious targets across three key areas: the technological and cost competitiveness of FCEVs; the technological competitiveness and availability of refuelling stations; and localizing and expanding hydrogen production.

Moon's FCEV promotion plan was backed by the world's most ambitious funding package for FCEVs; 2.6 trillion won (USD 2.34 billion) was committed to FCEV development by 2022, putting Korea far ahead of its two key competitors—Japan and the US (read: California)—in terms of financial support. To meet these goals, the government announced the most ambitious funding package for FCEVs seen anywhere in the world.[32] Specifically, the government pledged to invest 2.6 trillion won (USD 2.34 billion) in FCEV industry development by 2022.

As 2018 progressed, President Moon took an increasingly high-profile interest in the future of Korea's FCEV industry and the idea of a green hydrogen economy, throwing his personal weight behind efforts to increase the profile of Korean FCEVs in domestic and international markets. For example, in February 2018, President Moon publicly test drove Hyundai's Nexo FCEV in Seoul. Then, in October 2018, Moon travelled to France to publicly test drive Hyundai's Nexo on the streets of Paris and to mark the signing of a Memorandum of Understanding (MOU) between Hyundai, French industrial gas supplier Air Liquide, and ENGIE, a French electric utility company. The purpose of the MOU was to increase the number of hydrogen chargers and FCEVs in France, with a view of Hyundai exporting 5,000 FCEVs to France by 2025.

In 2019, Moon elevated FCEVs to one of *the* flagship economic issues of his presidency, situating the ambition to dominate the global FCEV market in the context of a broader vision to transform Korea into a 'Hydrogen Economy'. Moon announced this vision in a landmark speech in Ulsan, the industrial capital of Korea (Moon 2019). The location (emphasized by Moon) was deeply symbolic: the birthplace of Korea's first industrial revolution in 1962. Ulsan is also home to Korea's automobile, shipbuilding, and petrochemical yards—three traditional fossil fuelled strategic industries that stand to be transformed and reborn under a hydrogen economy revolution. In this landmark speech, Moon launched Korea's Hydrogen Economy Roadmap, with FCEVs as the centrepiece; by 2040

---

[31] M. Herh. 'South Korea Makes a Fresh Push for Hydrogen Vehicles', *BusinessKorea*, 25 June 2018, http://www.businesskorea.co.kr/news/articleView.html?idxno=23248

[32] While Japan also has ambitious plans to expand FCEV production and sales over the next decade (i.e., 40,000 FCEVs in 2020, 200,000 in 2025, and 800,000 in 2030), it plans to spend less than a third on FCEV subsidies per annum than Korea. Moreover, Japan has planned to roll out only 160 fuelling stations by 2020, compared with Korea's 310. While California does not have distinct targets for FCEVs (only for EVs more broadly), by 2025 its government proposes to spend as much on EV development as a whole as Korea does on FCEVs alone. California also only plans to install 200 refuelling stations (compared with Korea's 310). S. Crolius. 'South Korea to Launch Major Fuel Cell Initiative', *Ammonia Energy*, 26 July 2018, https://www.ammoniaenergy.org/articles/south-korea-to-launch-major-fuel-cell-vehicle-initiative/

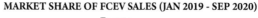

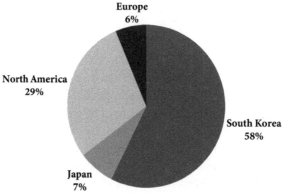

Figure 4.3 Market share of FCEV sales, January 2019–September 2020

Data: Hyundai Motor Group

Korea would emerge as a global technological leader in FCEVs, produce 6.2 million hydrogen cars, and distribute 15 GW fuel cells for power generation.[33] As Figure 4.4 reveals, Korea's 'creative' efforts in the FCEV arena have paid off, with Korea now dominating the world in market share.

It is worth examining Moon's speech at length as it so clearly illuminates the developmental-environmental underpinnings of Korea's current FCEV strategy.[34] To begin, Moon located Korea's FCEV strategy within the context of broader energy security concerns:

> In the carbon economy age, Korea had to import all of its oil and natural gas. This frequently posed difficulties as global price fluctuations impacted our country significantly. The hydrogen economy era is different. Available anywhere, hydrogen is an inexhaustible resource ... If the country is able to be relatively energy self-sufficient through the hydrogen economy, it will be possible to steer our economic growth more stably and safeguard our energy security more steadfastly.

Moon also articulated the desirability of FCEVs from both a 'new growth engine' and frontier technology perspective; by promoting FCEVs, Moon argued that Korea would advance the goal of transitioning from fast-follower to innovator:

---

[33] See J. Shin. 'Korea picks Hydrogen Industry as first point of deregulation', *Korea Herald*, 11 February 2019, http://www.koreaherald.com/view.php?ud=20190211000809

[34] For the full speech see: 'Remarks by President Moon Jae-in at Presentation for Hydrogen Economic Roadmap and Ulsan's Future Energy Strategy'. 17 January 2019, http://english1.president.go.kr/briefingspeeches/speeches/110

Now, while the hydrogen economy is in its infancy, it is important to pre-empt global markets. Many countries are already in competition, jockeying for a leading position. Fortunately, our strength and potential are boundless ... The hydrogen economy roadmap is a blueprint for making the leap to a global pace-setting country based on our strengths. Korea aims to hold the largest global market shares for both hydrogen-powered vehicles and fuel cells by 2030 ... We are already equipped with world-class technology for utilizing hydrogen. We were the first country to succeed in mass-producing hydrogen-fuelled cars, and 99 per cent of its core components are supplied domestically ... Now when the hydrogen economy is about to take off worldwide, the hydrogen cars manufactured in Korea have a global market share reaching 50 per cent. Korea is also staying at the forefront in the field of fuel cells, another pillar of the hydrogen economy.

Perhaps most importantly, Moon emphasized the developmental-environmental ambitions that underpin the FCEV push; by promoting FCEVs, Moon believes that Korea will be able to green and grow its economy at the same time. This belief is clearly reflected in the epigraph at the start of this chapter, which ends with the following statement:

As of now, [Hydrogen] is commonly extracted from fossil fuels, but it will become commonplace to produce it while utilizing renewable solar, wind, and bio energies ...

We view Moon's emphasis in his speech on *renewable* hydrogen as important in the context of wider concerns and criticisms that hydrogen generally, and FCEVs in particular, are not really 'green'. Critics point to the fact that currently, hydrogen is mainly derived from fossil fuel by-products (i.e., extracted from petrochemical plants or gas plants). But as Moon's statements—and a growing body of evidence—indicate, Korea is committed to rapidly making the shift from fossil-fuelled to emissions-free 'green hydrogen' (created by renewables-powered electrolysis). The government also pledged to source at least 70 per cent of all hydrogen from renewable sources by 2040, and 100 per cent by 2050. This commitment was made prior to the landslide election win of Moon's party in the national assembly election of April 2020, and the announcement of his government's even more ambitious Green New Deal, discussed below.

The sincerity of this commitment was reflected in high-level discussions between Korean and Australian government officials. While Australia has long supplied Korea with a secure and stable supply of coal and liquified natural gas (LNG), Korea now sees Australia as a reliable future supplier of renewable hydrogen. Korea's hydrogen society ambitions have thus sparked a wave of Korean investment in green hydrogen projects in Australia, which is seeking to transform itself into a renewable hydrogen superpower (Australian Government 2019; Garnaut 2019). In recent discussions, Korean officials made it clear that they expect their hydrogen imports from Australia to be emissions-free (ASTE-NAEK 2020). Korea is also pioneering the development of a green hydrogen certification system to guarantee that its hydrogen imports are truly green (Kim 2021).

In sum, by pursuing the rapid development of Korea's green hydrogen industry alongside nuclear and coal-exit plans, Moon has demonstrated commitment to expediting both the 'creative' and 'destructive' aspects of Korea's clean energy shift. Moon's 'destructive' ambitions have certainly raised the ire of some domestic fossil fuel (FF) interests. However, the emergence of renewable hydrogen as a viable coal and nuclear alternative helped Moon articulate a clear economic vision for Korea as a future renewable energy power—and a central role for erstwhile FF incumbents (namely, Hyundai and KEPCO) in that order. This again highlights our point that while the government is seeking to expedite the destruction of the existing fossil-fuelled economic order, this does not involve the 'destruction' of FF incumbents. Rather, the government is seeking to work collaboratively with incumbents to ensure that they can survive and thrive in the new green era.

In the final indication of the developmental-environmental underpinnings of Moon's FCEV strategy, the president made clear his view that the government can and should play a key role in strategically supporting FCEVs, and creating an industrial ecosystem centred on local technology and production:

> The Korean Government is strongly determined to promote the hydrogen economy. On the supply side, related laws will be modified to form an industrial ecosystem ... On the demand side, the Government will prime the pump to create a bigger market. Subsidies now provided only for hydrogen-powered cars and buses will be applied to taxis and trucks as well ... Regulations governing hydrogen fuel stations will be streamlined, and support for setting up stations will be strengthened. New industries will be expanded and the size of related markets will be enlarged by expanding the distribution of fuel cells for power generation and the adoption of fuel cells by public institutions.

In a step that revealed the president's commitment to these promises, the Moon administration swiftly followed up this announcement with deregulation efforts to allow refuelling stations to be built in regulatory sand-pits—getting around the objections that had made rapid roll-out difficult.[35] However, perhaps the most significant step in the execution of these plans—and in the development of hybridized industrial ecosystems in Korea—has been the creation of special purpose companies, to which we now turn.

[35] For a discussion of Korea's regulatory sandbox program under President Moon see Malyshev et al. (2021). See also J. Shin. 'Korea picks Hydrogen Industry as first point of deregulation', *Korea Herald*, 11 February 2019, http://www.koreaherald.com/view.php?ud=20190211000809.

From vision to execution: The role of special purpose companies: In terms of the execution of the Moon government's FCEV promotion plan, special purpose companies (SPCs) emerged as the most significant institutional innovation. SPCs are public–private entities with time-bound aims and clear funding commitments. They can be created for a variety of reasons, but in the case of FCEVs they are an effective way of sharing the risks and rewards of very expensive projects—especially the development and roll-out of hydrogen fuelling stations. As previously noted, hydrogen refuelling stations are extremely expensive to both build and operate, and this cost had been a critical factor constraining the development of the industry. Until recently, because of this cost, hydrogen fuelling stations have been built exclusively by local governments and research centres for research purposes only. To meet their ambitious goal of installing 310 hydrogen refuelling stations by 2022, Korean policymakers had to find a way of bringing the private sector on board, and of sharing not only the risks but also the rewards of building a national hydrogen refuelling infrastructure. An SPC was the perfect vehicle for such a purpose.

Korea's first FCEV-focused SPC—the HyNet—was established in March 2019 under the auspices of H2Korea for the specific purpose of expediting the government's ambitious refuelling infrastructure development goals. HyNet represents a true fusion of public and private actors and interests and brings together all aspects of the hydrogen fuelling station production-innovation chain (which itself makes up just one part of the much larger FCEV production-innovation chain—see Table 4.1).

Specifically, HyNet takes in the key environment, transport and industry ministries, a publicly-owned energy company (Korean Gas Corporation (KOGAS)),

Table 4.1 FCEV production-innovation chain

Hydrogen production	Fuel Cell production	FCEV Parts and materials production	Hydrogen Refuelling Stations (The primary focus of HyNet)
Increasingly involves the creation and production of renewable-hydrogen fuel and the transportation of that hydrogen fuel.	Involves the creation and production of new kinds of fuel cells and stacks.	Involves the manufacture of FCEV vehicles (cars, trucks, buses, trains and ships).	Involves developing and installing hydrogen fuelling stations.

Source: Authors' own elaboration

and 12 private firms, including a number of foreign-owned energy firms. The key public and private investors are KOGAS (the largest investor),[36] and Hyundai (the second largest investor) respectively. The 13 participating companies have contributed a combined initial investment of USD 118.7 million.[37] HyNet's CEO is You Jong-Soo, formerly the managing director of KOGAS. As an SPC, HyNet has a limited life span and is anticipated to operate until 2028. Its specific aim is to develop a private sector-led hydrogen station and operation model. This is in line with the broader aim of Korea's second Five-Year Plan for Green Growth, which aimed to ensure that Korea's green growth projects were led by private actors and were thus financially sustainable over the long term. Because HyNet draws fuel cell vehicle (FCV) manufacturers, hydrogen suppliers, and refuelling installation companies into a collaborative relationship, industry insiders anticipate that the group will be able to reduce by one-third the investment volume required for the installation of hydrogen refuelling stations by sharing technological expertise.[38] This cost reduction will be critical to a viable, private sector-led business model. In the words of the MOTIE representative who announced the intention to create HyNet in 2018:

> Until now, hydrogen fuelling stations have been built by local municipalities or research centres rather than private enterprises because of high installation and operating costs. Having lower initial risks due to joint investment by various organizations, SPCs will develop a business model that allows the private sector to construct and maintain hydrogen fuelling stations on its own.[39]

The inclusion of foreign-owned energy companies in HyNet is significant, as it highlights the ultimately export-oriented ambitions that underpin the domestically-oriented objectives of HyNet (which are to deliver no less than 30 per cent or 100 of the government's planned 310 hydrogen refuelling stations

---

[36] Korea Gas Corp is majority government owned (Govt. of South Korea 34 per cent, KEPCO 20.5 per cent, National Pension Service 8.25 per cent). See 'Korea Gas Corporation', *MarketScreener*, 2021, https://www.marketscreener.com/KOREA-GAS-CORP-6494959/company/

[37] See interview with HyNet CEO Lee Jongsu at *Monthly Hydrogen Economy*. http://www.h2news.kr/news/article.html?no=7389. See also 'South Korean Government Launches Company to Grow its Hydrogen Fuel Cell Vehicle Infrastructure', *FuelCellWorks*, 11 March 2019, https://fuelcellsworks.com/news/south-korean-government-launches-company-to-grow-its-hydrogen-fuel-cell-vehicle-infrastructure/. See also: K. Choi. 'Hyundai joins gov't-led hydrogen charging infra SPC', *Yonhap News*, 10 March 2019, https://en.yna.co.kr/view/AEN20190308012800320

[38] C. Hampel. 'South Korea forms HyNet for hydrogen charging', *Electrive*, 11 March 2019, https://www.electrive.com/2019/03/11/south-korea-forms-hynet-for-hydrogen-charging-infrastructure/

[39] 'Korea to promote the spread of hydrogen fueling stations'. Press Release. *Ministry of Trade, Industry and Energy*. 25 March 2018. Following this announcement, a call for interested parties to participate in the SPC followed, and then a selection process overseen by MOTIE. An MOU for the SPC was signed a month later, and the SPC finally established in March 2019.

by 2022).[40] Indeed, Hyundai has already entered into MOUs with French Company Air Liquide (also a member of HyNet) to increase the number of hydrogen chargers across France.[41]

Equally importantly from a developmental-environmental perspective, Hyundai's MOUs with foreign companies include the commitment to securing an adequate supply chain for renewable hydrogen. For example, Hyundai's 2018 MOU with Swiss hydrogen company H2E to provide 1,000 heavy-duty fuel cell electric trucks also included an agreement to secure an adequate supply chain for renewable hydrogen.[42]

In 2020, Moon's renewable energy ambitions were lent fresh momentum by his party's landslide National Assembly election win of April and the global COVID-19 pandemic, which saw governments across the globe embrace green stimulus packages and ambitious new clean energy targets, at the urging of global bodies including the International Energy Agency (IEA) (IEA 2020). Under Korea's Green New Deal, Moon wrote into law Korea's commitment to a net zero emissions target by 2050, and turbo-charged the nation's hydrogen development plans (Stangarone 2020).

Importantly, Moon also found crucial support for his politically contentious 'destructive' ambitions in local governments, which are now helping to enliven both the 'destructive' and 'creative' aspects of Korea's green energy shift.

The emergent role of local governments as creative-destructive allies

We identify the newfound activism of local governments as the third key factor helping to enliven the crucial 'destructive' aspect of Korea's green energy shift. As we show in Chapter 6, this is particularly evident in efforts of local governments to 'get fossil fuels out of the grid' by closing down coalfired power stations and replacing coal-fired energy with renewable sources, including from renewable hydrogen. However, it is equally evident in efforts by municipal governments to get fossil-fuelled cars off the road in order to combat the nation's intensifying pollution problems.

---

[40] In addition to delivering 100 fuelling stations, HyNet is also charged with enhancing the efficiency of hydrogen stations, improving regulations, and raising the quality of services, see: J. Sampson, 'HyNet Officially Established in South Korea', *Gasworld*, 15 March 2019, https://www.gasworld.com/hynet-officially-established-in-south-korea/2016825.article

[41] B. Kim. 'President Moon test rides Hyundai Nexo FCEV in Paris', *The Korea Herald*. 15 October 2018, http://www.koreaherald.com/view.php?ud=20181014000218

[42] See Hyundai press release of 19 September announcing the MOU here: https://www.hyundai.news/eu/articles/press-releases/hyundai-motor-and-h2-energy-will-bring-the-worlds-first-fleet-of-fuel-cell-electric-truck-into-commercial-operation.html. For industry coverage see 'Hyundai Motor enters MoU with H2 Energy for 1,000 heavy-duty fuel-cell trucks and renewable hydrogen'. *Green Car Congress*, 21 September 2018, https://www.greencarcongress.com/2018/09/20180921-hyundaih2.html

As noted previously, while campaigning for president in 2017, Moon pledged to place taxes on diesel vehicles and to get all diesel cars off Korea's roads by 2030, and to expedite the transition to a full-EV future. Moon's pledge followed decades of worsening smog issues in Korea—especially in Seoul—where air quality continues to rank amongst the worst in both the developed and developing world. Between 2014 and 2017, Korea slipped dramatically in the world's air quality rankings and in 2017 was ranked the last in the OECD for air quality.[43] Historically, there had been a tendency for the Korean government to shift blame for Korea's dreadful smog issues to trans-boundary pollution emanating from China, as that country turbocharged its industrialization efforts. There is no question that transboundary pollution from China has been—and continues to be—a major problem for Korea. Moreover, pollution from China has often been exacerbated by dust storms from the Gobi Desert in Mongolia, which shrouds the country in a thick yellow haze. However, the Dieselgate crisis of 2015 shone a light on the central role of diesel vehicles in contributing to Korea's air quality problems, which then became impossible for the government to ignore.

In 2017, a study conducted jointly between South Korea and the National Aeronautics and Space Administration (NASA) found that while China was a major source of air pollution in Korea, local sources accounted for around 52 per cent of harmful particulate emissions (Trnka 2020). And in the Seoul Metropolitan area, vehicle emissions (mostly diesel) were the largest contributor to PM emissions, accounting for close to a quarter of the total (Trnka 2020). In 2017—Moon's election year—the smog situation in Seoul had become so bad that the government introduced a host of emergency measures that included ordering public servants not to drive to work, offering free public transport, and ordering the temporary closure of parking stations in an effort to get cars off the road. This was the context in which Moon made his election pledge to remove all diesel vehicles from Korean streets by 2030 and to introduce a diesel tax, with the ultimate goal of reducing fine dust by a massive 30 per cent by 2022 from 2017 levels. Upon assuming power Moon also formally terminated Korea's previously discussed 'clean diesel' policy, which had incentivized the purchase of diesel cars under the false assumption that they were environmentally-friendly.

However, Moon's diesel tax plan faced obstacles on numerous fronts. Representatives of small businesses and low-income earners depicted it as a tax on the poor—many of whom relied on diesel vehicles for their work in the transport and construction industries and who could ill afford a tax hike. Korea's domestic oil refineries also opposed the move; diesel constituted between 25 and 30 per cent of their total annual production.[44] A lack of consensus within the government

---

[43] Measured in terms of the percentage of population exposed to dangerous levels of PM2.5.
[44] W. Shim. 'Industry calls for cautious approach in cutting diesel vehicles', *The Korea Herald*, 25 May 2017, http://www.koreaherald.com/view.php?ud=20170524000890&ACE_SEARCH=1

also made action difficult; while the ministry of environment strongly supported a diesel tax, the ministry of finance and economy and segments of the ministry of trade and industry remained sceptical, fearing the short-term economic impact. Faced with this opposition and spiralling crises, the Moon government took a different tack, delegating significant new powers to local governments to deal directly with the problem of diesel emissions.

In August 2018, the Moon government's Special Act on Particulate Matter Reduction and Management gave provincial governments special enforcement powers and obliged them to enact emergency measures when particulate matter exceeded a certain limit within their jurisdictions. These measures included banning diesel cars from the roads, closing parking stations, and ordering public officials not to drive to work. Local governments are also required to strictly regulate the operations of coal-fired power stations and limit work on construction sites. By empowering local governments in this way, the central government has created powerful allies in its efforts to get diesel vehicles off the roads and to transition swiftly to a fully-EV future.

Seemingly emboldened by its new powers, in November 2019 the Seoul Metropolitan government announced a ban on all old diesel cars from entering central Seoul between 6am and 9pm. Then in August 2020, the Seoul government announced its 'no diesel' initiative which aims to phase-out diesel cars from public sector and public transit fleets by 2025 and to replace them with green car alternatives (a mix of EVs and FCEVs). This is significant because in 2020 approximately 65 per cent of all government vehicles were diesel. Seoul is one of the largest cities in the world to introduce a diesel ban for public fleets.[45] At the same time, the Seoul government pledged to ban the registration of all ICE vehicles (diesel and gasoline) by 2035 and to ban all ICEs from the city centre by 2050.[46]

In April 2021, Seoul's move to ban ICEs from public fleets was replicated by the central government which announced that going forward, public institutions would be prohibited from purchasing anything other than environmentally-friendly vehicles (i.e., BEVs or FCEVs). By the end of 2021, then president Moon had also thrown his support behind the introduction of a full ban on new ICE vehicles by 2035, one of the key recommendations of the National Council on Climate and Air Quality (NCCA).[47] The NCCA was a presidential committee established in 2019 at the behest of President Moon, and former United Nations

---

[45] Z. Shahan. 'Seoul: Dirty Diesel Vehicles Banned From Public Fleets In 2025', *CleanTechnnica*, 11 August 2020, https://cleantechnica.com/2020/08/11/seoul-dirty-diesel-vehicles-banned-from-public-fleets-in-2025/.

[46] 'Seoul will ban ICE vehicles in 2035', *Inside*, 7 August 2020, https://inside.com/campaigns/inside-electric-vehicles-2020-08-07-24023/sections/202530; S-e. Lee, 'Mayor announces Seoul's Green New Deal goals', *Korea JoongAng Daily*, 8. 'Mayor announces Seoul's Green New Deal'. July 2020, https://koreajoongangdaily.joins.com/2020/07/08/national/socialAffairs/green-new-deal-seoul-electric-car/20200708183500332.html.

[47] The other key recommendation was to raise the diesel tax.

(UN) Secretary General Ban Ki Moon. The council was tasked with developing a concrete set of recommendations to help address particulate pollution and climate change. In this sense, by the end of Moon's presidency, the end of Korea's ICE era was also clearly in sight.

Concluding remarks

At the end of 2021, the three factors we identify herein: external shocks and growing competitive pressures; presidential orientation and ambition; and local government activism, were continuing to enliven, and to drive the growing alignment between the state's 'creative' and 'destructive' ambitions and actions.

On the international front, the COVID-crisis spurred many national governments to turbocharge their investments in the green energy shift and relatedly to bring forward their efforts to phase-out ICEs. For example, in September 2020 the British government brought forward its ICE-vehicle phase-out ban by a decade and announced the mass roll-out of charging and refuelling infrastructure, while the EU announced tough new vehicle emissions standards.[48] Then perhaps more dramatically, in November 2020, the Chinese government declared that it would ban the sale of new ICE vehicles from 2035 in an effort to make a full EV transition. Already, these decisions have prompted some major automakers to announce that they will stop producing ICEs within a specified time frame (see Figure 4.4). In early 2021 for example, both Audi and VW announced that they would no longer develop new combustion engines, and that they would make the full transition to electric offerings by 2032. In light of these trends, it is reasonable to assume that other automakers—including Korea's—will soon follow suit. In fact, in May 2021, Hyundai revealed that it planned to slash the number of ICE vehicles models it offers by 50 per cent in order to plough its resources into R&D for EVs. Hyundai now plans to be selling only EVs in the EU, the US, and now China, by 2040.[49]

At the same time, over the course of 2021, international competition in the EV market intensified, eliciting a host of major new collaborative responses from the Korean government and business. Perhaps the most significant collaborative efforts came in response to Tesla's recent and very successful foray into Korea's domestic BEV market with its smaller, cheaper Model-3 BEV offering. Tesla's rapid penetration of the Korean BEV market took Hyundai—and very possibly the Korean government—by surprise. As noted previously, until recently, Hyundai had put most of its eggs into the FCEV basket, on the assumption that concerns about cost and range anxiety would eventually make FCEVs more popular than

[48] H. Edwardes-Evans. 'UK government brings forward ban on new ICE cars 10 years to 2030', S&P Global Platts, 18 November 2020, https://www.spglobal.com/platts/en/market-insights/latest-news/electric-power/111820-uk-government-brings-forward-ban-on-new-ice-cars-10-years-to-2030

[49] G. Guillaume and H. Yang. 'Hyundai to slash combustion engine line-up, invest in EVs – sources', Reuters, 28 May 2021, https://www.reuters.com/business/finance/exclusive-hyundai-slash-combustion-engine-line-up-invest-evs-sources-2021-05-27/.

More than 20 countries have electrification targets or ICE bans for cars, and 8 countries plus the EU have announced net-zero pledges (as of 20 April 2021)

YEAR	2025	2030	2035	2040	2045	2050
100% Electrified Sales		UK	China and Japan			
100% ZEV Sales	Norway	Denmark, Iceland, Ireland, Israel, Netherlands, Scotland, Singapore, Slovenia and Sweden	Cabo Verde and UK	France, Canada, Portugal and Spain		Costa Rica and Germany
100% ZEV Stocks				Sri Lanka		
Net-zero Pledge					Sweden	Canada, Chile, Eu, Fiji, Korea, New Zealand, Norway and UK

Notes: Only countries that have either an ICE ban or electrification target or with net-zero emission in law or proposed legislation have been included. Electrified vehicles here include BEVs, PHEVs, FCEVs, and HEVs. ZEV (Zero-emission vehicles) include BEVs, PHEVs and FCEVs.

Figure 4.4 Timeline for ICE phase-out

Source: Adapted from IEA (2020) https://iea.blob.core.windows.net/assets/ed5f4484-f556-4110-8c5c-4ede8bcba637/GlobalEVOutlook2021.pdf

EVs. Moreover, Hyundai had not seen Tesla as a potential threat in Korea's mass BEV market because the US behemoth had originally focused on more prestige offerings. For these reasons, Tesla's recent assault on the Korean domestic market with its more affordable model came as a shock to Hyundai, and Tesla is now challenging Hyundai for market dominance on its own home turf.

Intensifying competition from China has only added to Korea's competitiveness concerns in the BEV space. For the past decade, Korea's top three battery makers (LG Chem, Samsung's SDI, and SK Innovation) have collectively captured up to 35 per cent of global battery sales. However, in the space of just a year, Chinese battery firms have emerged as serious contenders for global battery market dominance. Between 2019 and 2020, Chinese battery producer CATL doubled its global market share, which jumped from 17 per cent to a massive 31.6 per cent in just twelve months (compared with Korea's combined share of 34 per cent).[50] Moreover, massive global demand for BEVs has given rise to concerns about battery (read: critical material) shortages. Indeed, in recent years, Hyundai has had to limit the number of vehicles it sells in some markets because of battery supply constraints.[51] Over the past year, such battery supply issues have led many automakers to announce their intentions to bring their battery supply arrangements in-house, further compounding concerns about Korea's market share.

[50] Reporting based on findings by Seoul-based market tracker SNE Research, available at https://www.sneresearch.com/kr/business/tracker/

[51] R. Jennings. 'Inside Hyundai's $7.4 Billion U.S. Investment: Electric Vehicles And Hydrogen Stations', *Forbes*, 17 May 2021, https://www.forbes.com/sites/ralphjennings/2021/05/17/inside-hyundais-74-billion-us-investment-electric-vehicles-and-hydrogen-stations/?sh=643e66a74b08

This combination of new global competitive pressures lit a fire under the Korean government and its automakers and battery producers. The collective response came in the shape of the 'K-Battery Alliance'—intended to usher in a new era of cooperation between Korea's major conglomerates (Hyundai, Samsung SDI, LG Chem, and SK Innovation) in pursuit of global EV-market domination (with the full support of the Korean government). Between May and July 2020, the chair of Hyundai Motors held a series of meetings with the chairpersons of each of Korea's battery producers and entered into agreements to collaborate on the production of next generation batteries for Hyundai's future EVs; Hyundai seeks to release 23 brand new models of all EVs by 2025—and for all to be powered by next-generation Korean batteries. The Moon government pledged its full support to the K-Battery Alliance, inviting members of the Battery Alliance to the Blue House where President Moon declared batteries as 'the next semiconductors' for Korea.[52]

In support of the alliance, both President Moon and his prime minister publicly intervened in a longstanding and high-profile legal dispute between LG and SK centred on intellectual property violations that in 2021 threatened to derail cooperation. In a public statement, PM Chung called on these companies to settle their differences swiftly for the sake of Korea's global competitiveness: 'Simply, can I say you don't have to fight for small stakes. I hope the two companies settle the issue immediately and join forces for the global market'.[53] When a settlement was finally reached, President Moon tweeted his gratitude and encouraged the companies to kickstart their cooperation for global market share: 'The agreement between the two companies is very meaningful in that it is both in the national interests and the long term interests of individual companies for domestic members of the industrial ecosystem to cooperate based on mutual trust, while competing with each other'.[54] For its part, the government also pledged serious financial support for firms developing next generation EV batteries.

To help meet the domestic Tesla challenge head on, the government also made strategic changes to its EV subsidy schemes. In 2021, it revised its generous subsidies for BEV purchases which had seen 43 per cent of subsidies go to the purchase of Tesla vehicles in 2020. From 2021 onwards, subsidies will be limited to the purchase of only the cheapest BEVs, effectively meaning that only Korean-made EVs will qualify for the subsidy (Randall 2021). Korea's local governments have also stepped up to the mark, ramping up their subsidy schemes for EV purchases to match the central government.

---

[52] See 'Remarks by President Moon Jae-In at K-Battery Development Strategy Presentation'. 8 July 2021. https://www.korea.net/Government/Briefing-Room/Presidential-Speeches/view?articleId=200817

[53] 'Korea's Prime Minister urges LG, SK to settle battery dispute', *The Korea Times*, 28 January 2021, https://www.koreatimes.co.kr/www/tech/2021/02/515_303248.html

[54] 'Moon calls LG-SK deal on EV battery trade fortunate, meaningful', *Yonhap News*, 12 April 2021, https://en.yna.co.kr/view/AEN20210412005500315

But while the Tesla challenge has certainly tested the developmental-environmental resolve of the Korean government in recent years, it is the challenge from China's dramatic incursion into the EV space that has predominantly driven—and will continue to drive—Korea EV DE-initiatives to higher levels of intensity. It is to China's strategic embrace of EVs—and the motivations and ambitions informing that embrace—to which we now turn.

5

Creative-Destruction in China's Electric Vehicle Industry

The China Central Television 'Dialogue' Program Host: I have to raise this question with you, Party Secretary, based on concerns I came across on the Internet. People say that if the [city] government thinks of the return of your investment [in companies like Nio] all the time, you seem to lose focus on your own job.

The municipal head of Hefei City (CCP Party Secretary): It is not a shameful thing for the [city] government to make money. The more, the better, because this is money made for the people [of the city]. There are many things the government is supposed to do, including to improve people's livelihood, to improve infrastructure, and to make efforts on technological innovation. [...] But there is always a basic condition—that you need to have financial resources. So where do financial resources come from? You must rely on [economic] development, you must rely on projects, and you must focus on new industries. [Only by doing so] you would have a future, otherwise you have no future. So, some people think that [it is risky] the government in Hefei jumps into the water and swims [with the companies]. But it is precisely because of this action of the government that many companies have fewer worries. If you only watch and do not pull them out even if the company is drowning, what do we need a government for?

(China Central Television 'Dialogue' Program, 12 June 2021)[1]

The pattern

In the early 2010s, the electric vehicle (EV) industry barely existed in China, despite government efforts to promote EV-related R&D from the early 1990s. It is

---

[1] To view the full program (in Chinese) see: '合肥市委书记虞爱华深度解密为何投资蔚来' [Yu Aihua, Secretary of the Hefei Municipal Party Committee, explains the decision (of the Hefei government) to invest in NIO Inc. (a Chinese EV company)], *Sohu*, 13 June 2016, see https://www.sohu.com/a/471968278_574698

Developmental Environmentalism. Elizabeth Thurbon et al., Oxford University Press. © Elizabeth Thurbon, Sung-Young Kim, Hao Tan, and John Mathews (2023). DOI: 10.1093/oso/9780192897794.003.0005

thus almost unfathomable that in the space of just a decade, China has emerged not just as the world's largest EV market, but as one of the world's undisputed leaders in the production and export of EVs and related equipment, including batteries.

While BYD—one of the pioneers of EV technologies in China—launched the world's first plug-in hybrid car in 2008, most of China's leading EV companies today such as Nio (the subject of the epigraph above) only started their EV business in the mid-2010s (2014 in Nio's case). Nevertheless, a number of China's fresh local firms like Nio are now competing alongside established foreign players such as Tesla in China's booming domestic EV market. The word 'booming' seems entirely accurate in the Chinese context; in 2020, EV sales in China recorded a 60 per cent increase. This was despite the automobile market in China shrinking by two per cent in overall sales, and by six per cent in the sale of passenger cars.

The striking rise of China's EV industry has been driven by strong central and local government policies from the outset, and this support has only intensified as time has passed. For example, in 2019, China's Nio—just 5 years old at the time— faced tremendous challenges as battery failures forced it to recall one quarter of total sales of its most popular model, shaking consumer confidence and leading institutional investors to abandon the company. As a result, shares of Nio on the New York Stock Exchange dropped to around one dollar, and the company faced delisting. Luckily for Nio, the government of Hefei came to the rescue, injecting a total of 11.26 billion yuan to acquire a 24.1 per cent stake in the embattled firm. In this regard, the investment arm of the city government, Hefei Construction Investment and Holding Co., Ltd, acted as a venture capital firm: it enlisted several independent, professional teams to carry out a comprehensive assessment of the company's technological capabilities and market potential as well as legal and financial due diligence before making a decision to invest. In return for this much-needed lifeline, Nio agreed to reallocate its headquarters to Hefei, the capital city of Anhui province where automobile manufacturing is designated as a pillar industry. The company has now started developing a smart electric car industry park in Hefei which it claims to be the largest of its kind in the world. By June 2021, the stock price of Nio had climbed to over 40 USD. Consequently, the Hefei government has not only achieved a remarkable return on its initial investment, but facilitated the development of an industry cluster around EV manufacturing in the city.

This kind of dedicated government support—which has evolved in focus and substance over time—underpinned the phenomenal growth of China's EV industry throughout the 2010s. By 2020, 1.3 million electric cars were sold in China, nearly 1,000 times as many as in 2010 (Figure 5.1) (IEA 2020). There were about 3.3 million EVs in use in China by the end of 2019, accounting for 46 per cent of the global EV stock (IEA 2020). According to the country's Auto Industry Medium- and Long-Term Development Plan released in 2017 and the New Energy Automobile Industry Development Plan (2021–2035) in October 2020,

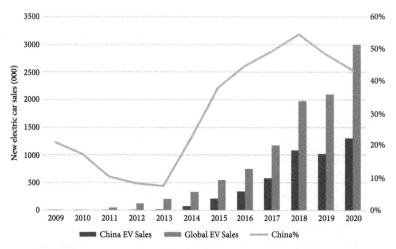

Figure 5.1 The sales of EVs in China and the world, 2009–2020

Sources of primary data: The 2009–2019 data is from IEA (2020) Global EV Outlook; the 2020 China EV sales data is from a news report based on an estimate of the Ministry of Industry and Information Technology; the 2020 global EV sales data is from IEA

new energy vehicles (NEV),[2] amongst which EVs take the lion's share, will account for 20 per cent of all vehicles sold annually by 2025. These two plans have also established other targets, such as breakthroughs in major technological areas, internationalization of Chinese EV firms, and the formation of a strong indigenous supply chain of EVs.

China is now not only a major EV market but also a manufacturing powerhouse for EVs. In 2019, ten Chinese firms were ranked among the top 20 EV manufacturers in the world; and three of these Chinese firms achieved more than five per cent of the global market share each (Ren 2020). Further, indigenous Chinese auto makers appear to have moved faster in electrification compared with their foreign peers (ChinaEV100 2020). China has also rapidly increased its production capacity in the upstream EV battery industry. It has been the largest EV battery producer in the world since overtaking Japan in 2017, and currently accounts for 53 per cent of the global EV battery shipment (Thurbon et al. 2021).

---

[2] According to the official definition of the Chinese government, NEVs in China include plug-in hybrid EVs (PHEV), BEVs, and FCVs, see: '国务院关于印发节能与新能源汽车产业发展规划(2012—2020年)的通知, [The State Council on Issuing the Energy-Saving and New Energy Automobile Industry, Notice of Development Plan (2012–2020)], *The Central People's Government of the People's Republic of China*, 28 June 2012, http://www.gov.cn/zwgk/2012-07/09/content_2179032. htm. However, only 1,170 FCVs were produced in China in 2019, accounting for a very small proportion of the NEV market compared with EVs, see: Y. Liu, 'China on track to increase production of hydrogen fuel-cell vehicles by 53% in 2019', *Renewable Energy World*, 25 November 2019, https://www.renewableenergyworld.com/hydrogen/china-on-track-to-increase-production-of-hydrogen-fuel-cell-vehicles-by-53-in-2019/)

However, China's EV industry is also facing considerable challenges. Despite its rapid growth over the past decade, new energy vehicles accounted for only about five per cent of the total cars sold in the Chinese auto market in 2020. Although China beat its target for producing 500,000 NEVs annually by 2015, it failed to meet the 2020 target it set for itself in the 2017 Auto Industry Medium- and Long-Term Development Plan, that is, selling two million EVs annually. While the global market shock caused by the COVID-19 pandemic goes some way towards explaining this shortfall, China's EV industry also suffers from more deep-seated challenges. These include price competitiveness limitations vis-à-vis conventional combustion engine vehicles, and thus an over-reliance on government subsidies that have been rapidly diminishing for strategic reasons; central government subsidies were reduced six times during the six-year span of 2014–2020 to keep domestic competitive forces alive.[3] Technological bottlenecks and related concerns over 'range anxiety' have also kept a cap on consumer adoption. And like the wider auto industry, the EV industry is highly fragmented; by 2018, there were 487 EV makers in China, many of which joined the race recently.[4] Chinese EVs also continue to be sold predominantly in the domestic market.

Despite these challenges however, EVs are becoming increasingly established in specific market niches in China including taxis, buses, ride-hiring and car-sharing fleets, and in small cities and rural areas (Huang and Li 2020).[5] In these markets, EV technology has emerged as a serious contender, threatening to destabilize the conventional gasoline vehicles-based regime. As the costs of EVs fall rapidly thanks to the learning curve effects driven by improvement in the manufacturing process and economies of scale, the industry is starting to stand on its own feet in the broader market, as evidenced by a growing proportion of personal purchases of EVs in the absence of subsidies. Overall, the penetration rate of NEVs in China, as measured with the share of sales of NEVs in the total sales of passenger cars, is highest among major economies, including the EU, the US, and Japan. According to data from the Chinese customs authorities, EV exports from China have recently started rising, increasing by 40 per cent in 2018, and by more than 70 per cent in 2019, before a fall by 13 per cent in 2020 associated with the COVID-19 pandemic. The increase in EV exports indicates the growing international competitiveness of the Chinese EV industry.

[3] See: H. Cui, D. Hall, N. Lutsey, 'Update on the global transition to electric vehicles through 2019', *International Council on Clean Transportation*, 13 July 2020, https://theicct.org/publications/update-global-ev-transition-2019

[4] See a *Wall Street Journal* article: M. Trefor, 'China Has 487 Electric-Car Makers, and Local Governments Are Clamoring for More', *Wall Street Journal*, 19 July 2018, https://www.wsj.com/articles/china-has-487-electric-car-makers-and-local-governments-are-clamoring-for-more-1531992601 We see a similar pattern historically in the US auto industry, which was also highly fragmented prior to the consolidation to three majors—GM, Ford, and Chrysler.

[5] See: H. Cui and H. He, 'Liuzhou: A New Model for the Transition to Electric Vehicles?', *International Council on Clean Transportation*, 18 December 2019, https://theicct.org/blog/staff/liuzhou-new-model-transition-electric-vehicles

As China's ambitious industry building and technology upgrading policies have begun to pay off in terms of growing exports, so the government appears to have become more willing to adopt policies designed to shrink and eventually displace the market for conventional (read: fossil-fuelled) internal combustion engine vehicles (ICEVs). Beyond China's recent macro-level commitment to reach Net Zero by 2060 (discussed in more detail in Chapter 7), since 2015 Chinese governments at both central and local levels have—amongst other things—moved to tighten air quality requirements, to stop granting approvals to new producers of ICEVs, and to mandate that all auto firms produce a minimum percentage of EVs per annum, thereby displacing ICEVs. So, while obstacles to a full transition clearly remain, the end of the ICE vehicles era in China now appears to have dawned.

The puzzle

In this chapter, we examine China's push to promote EVs in the context of the state's emerging developmental-environmental orientation and its evolving 'creative' and 'destructive' ambitions and capabilities. We ask: (1) What has motivated the Chinese state to seek to create and develop the NEV industry so ambitiously, and with its particular focus on battery electric vehicles (BEVs)? (2) How have Chinese policymakers, at both the central and local levels, pursued their 'creative' ambitions? (3) Why has the government appeared more ambitious and active in 'green car' industry creation than in 'dirty car' industry destruction? (4) To what extent is this 'creative-destructive' misalignment now resolving? And (5) What factors are now driving this realignment, and what obstacles to a fully green shift remain? To address these questions, as with Chapter 4, we divide the case study into four parts, structured temporally. A linear temporal structure allows us to both demonstrate and explain the varying degrees of alignment between the state's 'creative' and 'destructive' ambitions and capabilities over time, and to anticipate the most likely future trajectory.

In Part One, we provide an overview of the historical development of the Chinese auto industry in the pre-EV era, starting in the mid-1980s. We show that—as with other new industries in China (and elsewhere in Northeast Asia)—the state's early efforts to build a local automobile industry were informed by quintessentially 'developmental' ambitions.

In Part Two, we turn our attention to the government's decision to embrace EVs as a strategic industry in the early 1990s, and to the emerging 'developmental-environmental' logic informing that decision. We show that, in addition to traditional developmental considerations, China's first wave of EV promotion policies from the early 1990s to 2008 also strongly reflected the government's growing concerns about environmental challenges and resource constraints. So, in contrast to the Korean case (Chapter 5), we find that both developmental *and* environmental considerations informed the embrace of EV promotion policies from outset. In this sense, China's EV industry was 'born green'.

In Part Three, we examine the take-off of China's EV industry in the 2009–2017 period, a period also characterized by the clear misalignment between the state's 'creative' and 'destructive' ambitions and actions. We link the intensification of the government's EV industry creation efforts to the 2008 global financial crisis (GFC) and the government's desire to stave off an economic downturn through the creation of new industries and domestic demand. Thanks to strong policy supports in the forms of subsidies, tax exemptions, direct investment in R&D, special government procurement programs, easier access to licence plates, and waivers from traffic restrictions, the EV market in China expanded rapidly during this period. However, the market for traditional ICE vehicles also expanded at the same time. Moreover, strong resistance from ICE-related interests combined with uncertainty around EV technology to create a clear misalignment between the state's 'creative' and 'destructive' ambitions and actions in this period, slowing the transition towards a NEV regime.

In Part Four, we examine the growing alignment between the state's 'creative' and 'destructive' ambitions and capabilities in the EV arena from the mid-2010s to the present. As the EV market and technological capabilities of EV firms have grown in recent years, so competition between EV and ICE producers has intensified. Nevertheless, we argue that the actions taken by central and local governments since the mid-2010s—and particularly since 2017—are strongly suggestive of growing 'creative-destructive' alignment. We attribute this growing alignment to three main factors: intensifying international competition in strategic technological areas, growing local government activism, and the personal ambitions and orientation of President Xi Jinping.

Part One: The developmental origins of China's auto industry focus in the pre-EV era

Before China's reform and opening up in the late 1970s, the Chinese auto industry largely consisted of two state-owned enterprises (SoEs), the First Auto Works (FAW) and the Second Auto Works (SAW), which focused on truck production and produced only a small number of passenger cars (Chu 2011).[6] In the face of rising demand for passenger cars—as evident by rapid surge of car imports and widespread smuggling in the country in early 1980s—the Chinese government for the first time included the auto industry as a pillar industry in its seventh Five-Year Plan (FYP) (1986–1990). To grow and protect the domestic auto industry, the government set import tariffs as high as 250 per cent (Chen, Lin Lawell, and Wang 2020).

---

[6] Chu (2011) provides an excellent overview of Chinese policy and strategy in the automotive sector.

Following the central government's policy orientation, many local governments rushed to promote the auto industry as a pillar industry in their cities or regions. For a short period of time, over 100 auto manufacturers were established all over the country, many of which were deemed to be based on imported 'obsolete technologies' and were of unsustainable scale in production (Xu and Ou 2017). To address the so-called 'disorderly competition' among local governments and consequently the fragmentation of the auto industry, the central government issued a series of policies from 1985 to 1988 to prevent local governments and enterprises from establishing new auto manufacturing sites and importing foreign auto products and technologies. The central government also identified 'three majors' (FAW, SAW, Shanghai Auto Industry Corporation (SAIC)) and 'three minors' (Beijing, Tianjin, and Guangzhou auto firms) for focused policy support (Chu 2011). However, these policies were less effective due to rapidly rising demand for passenger cars in China and a low level of technological capabilities within domestic auto firms (Xu and Ou 2017).

Joint ventures (JVs) were formed between Chinese and foreign auto companies from the mid-1980s onwards. However, the central government placed substantial restrictions on the formation of JVs, such as capping foreign ownership at a level of 50 per cent, an increase in domestic content ratio over time, and capping the maximum number of JVs foreign auto companies could establish in China (Chu 2011). These policies aimed to drive import substitution and facilitate technology transfer. However, the performance of these JVs in their pursuit of localization varied substantially. In Shanghai, the municipal government's local developmental approach led to successful localization of car components within the JV between SAIC and Germany's VW, achieving a localization rate of over 90 per cent by the end of the 1990s. In Beijing and Guangzhou, the municipal governments adopted a local laissez-faire state model, while in Changchun and Wuhan, the auto JVs were characterized by an enterprise-leading local state model. These cities failed to produce substantial localization outcomes (Chu 2011).

In 1994, as one of the first industry-focused policies that have ever been introduced in China, the 1994 Auto Industry Policy was released by the State Council. The policy specified two main goals, including 1) an increase in the concentration level of the industry with an aim to develop a small number of large auto companies with international competitiveness; and 2) self-reliance in auto products and technologies (Xu and Ou 2017). Specifically, the policy called for 90 per cent of domestic demand for automobiles to be met by local production by 2000.[7] In each market segment, the top three Chinese car makers combined were to account for a market share of 70 per cent. The policy envisioned automobile manufacturing

---

[7] According to China Auto Industry Development Report (2009), a total of 2.08 million cars were sold in the Chinese market in 2000. In the same year, 2.07 million cars were locally produced (see http://www.gov.cn/jrzg/2005-12/21/content_133554.htm). Therefore, this objective as specified was reached.

to become a pillar industry in the national economy by 2010 and that it would substantially contribute to the development of other related industries.

Meanwhile, China faced pressures in its negotiations to enter the World Trade Organization (WTO) in the late 1990s. These environments led to a 'trade market access for technology' policy at the central government level that sought to improve the competitiveness of the Chinese auto industry and the localization of auto supply chains. This was realized mainly through forming JVs between major Chinese state-owned car makers and identified foreign auto companies, rather than relying on indigenous technological development (Chu 2011). Between the mid-1990s and 2000s, many large JVs were formed in the Chinese auto industry.

The 'trade market access for technology' policy had mixed outcomes. On the one hand, the policy seemed to have helped China build a globally competitive automobile industry. Even after China's accession into the WTO in 2001 with reduced tariffs and raised domestic content requirements, cars sold in China and their components were increasingly manufactured domestically (Nam 2011). In other words, one of the major policy goals—localization of the industry—was successfully achieved. On the other hand, the 'trade market access for technology' policy was criticized for failing to foster national brands and close technological gaps between Chinese and foreign auto firms (Chu 2011). Against this background, the success of some experiments by local governments to promote indigenous automobile firms, notably the state-owned Chery Auto based in Wuhu city in Anhui province, and privately owned Geely and BYD, were used to justify a revision of the policy towards more emphasis on indigenous technological development.

Ten years after the introduction of the first industry policy for the Chinese auto industry, the Chinese government replaced its 1994 Auto Industry Policy with a new Automotive Industry Development Policy released in 2004. To promote concentration in the industry and to foster several large Chinese auto firms with international competitiveness continued to be major goals of the policy. However, the 2004 policy placed a much greater emphasis on the development of Chinese indigenous technologies and brands. Further, the new Policy required the industry to develop technologies in line with China's energy saving and environmental protection strategy, including technologies relating to NEVs, such as EVs, EV battery, and hydrogen technologies. These policy objectives had not been included in the 1994 policy. In line with the new policy, the first fuel economy standards were introduced in the country in 2004. The fuel economy and pollutant emission standards were gradually strengthened in the following years, which have posed growing pressures on traditional ICE cars (Chen, Lin Lawell, and Wang 2020).

China's auto industry policy shared some commonalities with the industry policy in other Northeast Asian countries. Two features stand out according to Chu (2011). First, China's auto industry policy was developed and implemented through a multi-layered process, in which the ambitions and actions of central and local governments were mutually shaped. The resultant policy was more 'propelled by the catch-up [with the West] consensus' than driven by 'integrated central economic bureaucracy with embedded autonomy' (Chu 2011: 1267). Second, the legacy from the economic planning era in China played a role in the formulation and revision of the industry policy. For example, the Chinese bureaucracies and large state-owned enterprises have consistently undergone reforms, which created an unstable policy environment. As we will see below, these factors have played an important role in the creation and evolution of the Chinese EV industry and the destruction of the gasoline auto industry.

Part Two: From developmentalism to developmental environmentalism and the emergence of the EV industry in China (1990s–2008)

Notwithstanding the strong developmental logic underpinning the auto industry policy in China, many policies to support the initial creation of the new energy vehicle industry were introduced as part of the broader environmental and energy policies that aimed for objectives such as to ease local air pollution or reduce dependence on imported oil. This perhaps reflected scepticism towards NEVs on the part of many in the central ministry that directly oversaw the auto industry. To them, NEVs would serve to complement rather than substitute technologies of ICE vehicles. The worsening air quality in Chinese cities and alarming level of oil imports provided justification for an NEV segment within the automobile industry. Consequently, the development of NEV technologies gained further support. Policy support and initiatives for NEV technologies were embodied in policies designed and implemented by various ministries with different perspectives and priorities. Despite the fragmented policy regime in relation to NEVs, this period saw important developments in the knowledge base of EV-related technologies and created their initial market niches.

The development of EV technology in China can be traced to the late 1990s, when EVs were listed as one of the 238 key projects (including 104 projects in the area of energy and transport) in the ninth Five Year (1996–2000) National Key Technology R&D Program, together with other technologies in which China determined to achieve breakthroughs, such as large wind power generation system and high-speed rail (HSR). Those projects were overseen by the Ministry of Science and Technology (MoST). As part of the program, China set up an EV test and demonstration zone in Shantou, Guangdong Province (Gong, Wang, and Wang 2013). By the end of the 1990s, MoST (2001) estimated that the concept electric cars designed and manufactured as a result of the project were technologically comparable to those in foreign countries in the 1990s.

In the late 1990s, the rapid growth in the automotive market in China caused considerable air pollution, especially in major cities, as well as concerns over the supply security of oil. For example, five Chinese cities—Beijing, Xi'an, Shenyang, Shanghai, and Guangzhou—were among the top ten cities with the worst air quality in the world (Booz & Co. 2014). Meanwhile, China became a net importer of oil in 1994, and the gap between oil consumption and domestic production has been widening ever since (Figure 5.2). As a response, the Chinese government launched the 'Clean Auto Action Program' in 1999, which was designed with two main objectives, namely to reduce air pollution caused by emissions by vehicles and to lower the level of fuel imports. The program outlined both immediate measures and mid- to long-term measures for achieving these goals. As immediate measures, the program focused on implementation of new, more stringent emission standards for vehicles, and the development and promotion of compressed natural gas (CNG) and liquified petroleum gas (LPG) vehicles as alternatives to gasoline vehicles. For the mid- to long-term measures, the program identified EV as a major national technology-industry project, and highlighted the importance of developing critical EV technologies, such as nickel-metal hydride batteries, lithium-ion batteries, fuel cells, and hybrid vehicle technologies. EVs were seen as meeting the twin problems of reducing air pollution in cities and reducing oil imports at the national level. The aim of the mid- to long-term measures was to 'achieve leapfrog

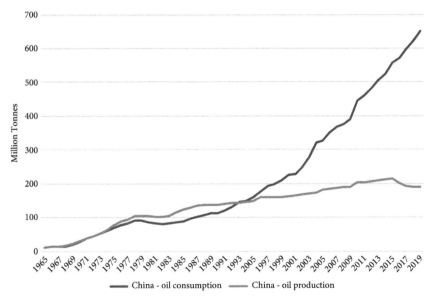

Figure 5.2 Oil consumption and production in China, 1965–2019

Source: Authors based on data available from *BP Statistical Review of World Energy*

development and establish a new environmentally-friendly automobile industry with Chinese characteristics'[8].

A major development of the EV technology in China saw the inclusion of the technology in the *863 Program* during the country's tenth Five-Year Plan (FYP) period (2001–2005). The 863 Program, or the *State High-Tech Development Plan*, was to develop 'strategic, cutting-edge and forward-looking' technologies that 'matter to the country's long-term development and national security' (State Council 2001). The development of EV technologies in the 863 Program was based on a 'Three by Three' R&D framework, which highlighted not only the three key EV technologies (fuel cell electric vehicles (FCEV), hybrid electric vehicles (HEV) and BEV), but also the three main EV components (powertrain control systems, electric drive motor, and battery) (Figure 5.3).[9] In this framework, no preference was specified over FCEV, HEV, or BEV technologies, suggesting that the state placed the same level of priority on various technological options at the time. The Chinese central government invested RMB 880 million (~USD 100 million) of funding on those technologies under the 863 Program. Six cities were chosen as EV demonstration cities. Taken together with the funds matched by local governments and enterprises, it is estimated that a total of RMB 2.4 billion (~USD three billion) was invested in these technologies during the tenth Five-Year Plan period (2001–2005). The R&D activities resulted in prototypes and production at small scale of EVs of different technologies, the establishment of 26 national standards,

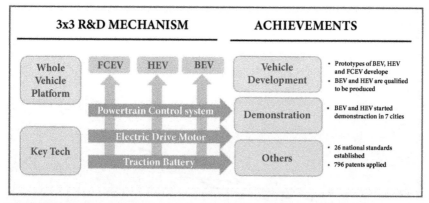

Figure 5.3 The 3×3 R&D framework for EVs under the 863 Program

Source: Adapted from Booz & Co. (2014)

---

[8] Ministry of Science and Technology et al. 1999. Several Opinions on the Implementation of the Air Cleaning Program - Clean Auto Action Plan. https://www.chinacourt.org/law/detail/1999/12/id/36059.shtml. (in Chinese) accessed 28 Nov 2022.

[9] For discussion on this point, see the report by Booz & Co. (2014).

and 796 patent applications in relation to both EVs and their components. However, by the end of the tenth Five-Year Plan period, no EV project had achieved production at a commercial scale.

In 2004, the National Development and Reform Commission (NDRC) issued two important policies in relation to China's automobile industry. The 2004 *Auto Industry Development Policy*, which replaced the 1994 auto industry policy, required the industry to actively undertake R&D and commercialization of EV and EV battery technologies, to align with the shift of the national energy strategy and continuously upgrading emission standards. The policy placed an emphasis on the fuel economics of ICE cars, requiring fuel consumption per 100 km to reduce by more than 15 per cent from 2003 to 2010. The NDRC also released the *Medium- and Long-Term Plan for Energy Saving* in the same year. The plan called for favourable fiscal and taxation policies to encourage development of hybrid and pure EVs, and meanwhile to accelerate the phase-out of vehicles with high fuel consumption. The plan suggested a strategy to implement a fuel tax reform.

In 2006, the State Council released China's *Science and Technology Medium- and Long-Term Development Plan (2006–2020)*. The plan highlighted 'energy efficient and new energy vehicles' as a science and technology (S&T) priority in transport, with the development of indigenous innovation capabilities as one of the key goals. The plan also identified a number of key transport technologies, including design, integration, and manufacturing of hybrid vehicles, alternative fuel vehicles and FCEVs; key component technologies such as integrated power control systems, auto computing platform technology, high-efficiency, low-emission ICE, fuel cell engine, power batteries, and drive motors; and NEV testing techniques and infrastructure technology.

A series of policies were introduced in the following years to implement these high-level policies and plans. For example, in a new consumption tax system introduced in 2006, the Ministry of Finance significantly increased the valued-added tax (VAT) rate on the purchase of high emission ICE, and granted VAT discounts for hybrid vehicles. In 2007, in an effort to develop clearer industry standards, NDRC established several rules for granting production and market access of NEVs based on the enterprise's R&D and production capacities. This document officially defined NEVs, which include HEVs, BEVs, FCEVs, hydrogen internal-combustion engine vehicles, and other vehicles with new fuels. Finally, continuing with the efforts in the tenth Five-Year Plan, MOST again included 'energy saving and NEV' as a major project in its 863 Program in the eleventh FYP (2006–2010). With an investment of RMB 7.5 billion (~USD 0.9 billion), the project included a total of 270 research topics covering technologies relating to key components, power systems, vehicle integration, test platforms, technology demonstration and promotion, and policy research. The project led to applications for 2,011 patents. It has been one of the most successful R&D projects launched by the Chinese government.

During this initial period of EV development, the policies were largely focused on building a platform of EV technological capabilities in China. Meanwhile, the policy environment started to place pressures on ICE technologies, mainly due to concerns over energy security (and thus the need for energy saving) and air pollution. In addition to conventional developmental considerations, such as the need for technological leapfrog, the emergence of the Chinese EV industry was therefore featured with strong environmental considerations. China's EV industry was thus 'born green'.

Part Three: The rapid growth of EVs in China and growing creative-destructive misalignment (2008–2017)

Despite those developments, an EV market in China barely existed by the end of the first decade of the new century. However, in the face of the GFC in 2008, the Chinese government issued ten 'industry adjustment and revitalization plans' in 2009 for ten key industries respectively, including the auto industry. The overall goal of those plans was to maintain growth (*Bao Zhen Zhang*), expand domestic demand (*Kuo Nei Xu*), and improve the economic structure (*Tiao Jie Gou*). As a specific plan for the automobile industry, the *Auto Industry Restructuring and Revitalisation Plan* set explicit targets for the sales of automobiles in China in 2009 (ten million vehicles), as well as a target growth rate for the next three years (10 per cent annual average growth). The plan also set objectives to develop a production capacity of 500,000 EVs, and to achieve a market share of five per cent by NEVs among passenger cars sold in China by 2011. The plan required major auto companies in China to introduce NEV models.

Various financial and tax incentives were introduced to achieve those objectives. As part of the stimulus plan, for example, the purchase of EVs for buses, taxis, waste collection, and government fleets in a number of cities received heavy subsidies (Gong, Wang, and Wang 2013). This period saw a take-off of the EV market in China. Sales of EVs in China soared from less than 500 vehicles in 2008 to 1,400 in 2009, and again 5,000 in 2010. Meanwhile, the overall Chinese automobile market also jumped in those years, with annual growth at 50 per cent in 2009 and 30 per cent in 2010 (Figure 5.4). China overtook the US and became the world's largest car market in 2009.

Locally-oriented policies and inter-regional competition for opportunities related to EV technologies started emerging. In 2009, four ministries in the central government jointly launched an NEV demonstration and promotion initiative, which was widely known as the *Ten Cities, Thousand Vehicles* program as the initial objective of the program was for ten pilot cities to launch 1,000 EVs each within three years. The number of pilot cities increased to 25 by 2011. This program was supported by funding from the central government, but selected pilot cities had

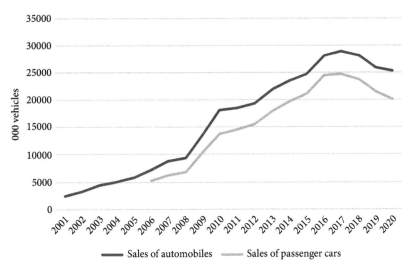

Figure 5.4 The sales of automobiles in China, 2000–2020

Source: Authors based on data from China Association of Automobile Manufacturers

significant leeway to choose their models for promoting EVs in their cities (Marquis, Zhang, and Zhou 2013). In this it was typical of Chinese programs, which experiment with different policies for different cities and choose the most successful to roll out the program nationwide. The program also caused concerns, such as inflation of the success of their EV projects by city leaders, local protectionism, and increased obstacles for the development of national standardization in the industry.

At the central government level, policies were increasingly enhanced to support the creation of an NEV industry, especially the EVs segment, not only for their short-term economic benefits but more importantly for their long-term industrial development potential. In 2010, the State Council published a policy document, the *Decision to Accelerate the Development of Strategic and Emerging Industries*. Those industries were considered by the Chinese government to play a major leading role in the economic and social development of the country in the long run (State Council of China 2010). NEVs were identified as one of the seven strategic industries, in addition to the 'new energy industry' which was also closely related to EVs.

Following the identification of NEVs as a strategic industry in China, the State Council issued an *Energy Saving and NEV Industry Development Plan (2012–2020)* in 2012. While different technologies including hybrid, plug-in, and FCVs were all covered in the plan, BEVs (also variously termed as 'all-electric vehicle', 'pure electric cars', etc.) were now being formally recognized as the main focus among NEV technologies in China (with important implications for Korea's EV strategy, see Chapter 4). Further, the technology was regarded as providing a main strategic direction for the entire Chinese auto industry. A principal target set in the plan was to sell a cumulative number of 500,000 battery and plug-in hybrid EVs (PHEV) by 2015, and five million by 2020. Two considerations—technological simplicity and competitive advantage—appear to have contributed to the decision to prioritize BEVs, as we now discuss.

An important advantage of the BEV technology over other NEV technologies lay in the fact that BEVs are simpler technology-wise, sometimes described as 'batteries on wheels', thus eliminating the need for complex transmission systems. This makes technological catch-up easier. Perhaps more importantly, the selection of BEVs as a priority area of development was because Chinese firms were well positioned in EV battery technologies. Unlike ICE-related technologies, EV batteries were seen as a sector where Chinese companies such as BYD, CATL, and Lishen have little technological gap between themselves and foreign companies such as Panasonic, Samsung SDI, and LG Chem, because all those players entered the field around the same time (Rengarajan 2019; Jiang and Lu 2018). Chinese firms have surged ahead in EV battery production capacity, accounting for over 70 per cent of the global EV battery production capacity (Rengarajan 2019). Through aggressive investments in the upstream resource sectors, Chinese firms are increasingly dominant in the EV battery supply chain, controlling about 85 per cent of the global supply of cobalt, and nearly half of global lithium production.

A comprehensive industry policy to promote EVs was rolled out over the next few years. For example, a new pilot program was introduced jointly by four ministries in 2013. The program aimed to deploy a total of 300,000 vehicles in 39 select cities and city groups (such as Beijing-Tianjin-Hebei, Yangtze River Delta, and Pearl River Delta) over the period 2013–2015. The program focused on both public and private procurement. Similar to its precedent, subsidies were provided to encourage procurement of EVs. Other forms of financial incentives, including subsidies, rebates, and tax exemptions were offered to facilitate R&D, production, and use of BEVs (Li, Yang, and Sandu 2018). Most provinces in China have also introduced non-subsidy EV promotion policies, such as easier access to licence plates, waivers from traffic restrictions, and/or reductions in parking fees (IEA 2020).

This period saw a rapid take-up of EVs from a low basis as well as a steep decrease in prices due to a combination of factors based on technology improvement, economies of scale, and competition among manufacturers. In this sense, China began to see state ambition and market forces pushing in the same direction. According to a survey by Bloomberg New Energy Finance (BNEF) (2017), the price of lithium-ion batteries, the major component which accounts for 30 per cent to 50 per cent of the total cost of an EV, dropped by 73 per cent during the period between 2010 and 2016. BNEF (2017) further estimated the learning rate of batteries in BEVs to be 19 per cent over the next decade. These cost reductions are systemic, related to the fact that EVs are products of manufacturing, and are thereby benefiting from the learning curve (Mathews and Tan 2014b).

The rapid growth of the EV market driven by the initial BEV strategy also had unintended outcomes. From 2009 to 2015, the Chinese government offered 33.4 billion yuan (USD 4.87 billion) of subsidies to EV manufacturers and users. Driven by direct cash subsidies, a large number of companies rushed into the industry. The EV segment became highly fragmented. By 2018, there were 487 EV makers in China, most of which had few technological capabilities and relied on government support for their business models.[10] Many EVs produced by these companies were deemed to be of low quality and sometimes caused serious safety concerns. A national investigation in 2016 found that a total of 12 companies were involved in subsidy fraud.[11]

The increasing market share of EVs also prompted strong resistance from the ICE regime both in the technology and policy arenas. As previously mentioned, in the technological arena, the costs of BEVs, especially those of batteries as core components of BEVs, have fallen considerably thanks to the learning curve effects driven by improvement in the manufacturing process and economies of scale during the past decade. The costs of batteries for BEVs dropped from over USD 900 per kWh in 2010 to around USD 200 per kWh in 2018 (Rengarajan 2019). However, the cost reduction of batteries is also subject to other market dynamics, especially the prices of the key raw metals in the global market. EVs also face pressures arising from technological developments of ICE vehicles such as improvements in fuel economy. In other words, EVs faced a moving target in seeking to oust ICE vehicles from the market.

Prompted by resistance from ICEs, a misalignment in the policy arena also became evident during this period. Facing growing sales of EVs and their direct threats in the market, interests associated with ICE technologies increasingly challenged the state support to EVs in a bid to influence the policy. For example, some have argued that ICE-based vehicles have longer value chains; and, thus, the production and use of ICE cars can lead to more jobs in the upstream auto parts industries than those of EVs (Wang 2019). As we saw in Chapter 4, similar arguments were mobilized in South Korea. Opponents of EVs have also disputed their environmental benefits, arguing that improvements in ICE technologies and the increasingly stringent emission requirements for gasoline cars have reduced the gap between the two technologies in their levels of pollutant emissions. The role of EVs in enhancing national economic security has also been

---

[10] See a *Wall Street Journal* report: M. Trefor, 'China Has 487 Electric-Car Makers, and Local Governments Are Clamoring for More', *Wall Street Journal*, 19 July 2018, https://www.wsj.com/articles/china-has-487-electric-car-makers-and-local-governments-are-clamoring-for-more-1531992601

[11] See: H. Cui, 'Subsidy Fraud Leads to Reforms for China's EV Market', *The International Council on Clean Transportation*, 30 May 2017, accessed 27 June 2020, https://theicct.org/blogs/staff/subsidy-fraud-reforms-china-ev-market

questioned, for the demands arising from production of EV batteries for key minerals cannot be fully supplied from domestic sources, such as nickel and cobalt (ChinaEV100 2020).

Political and business actors associated with the automobile industry consistently defend ICE-based vehicles from an economic perspective. The Chinese automotive industry, in which ICE cars were dominant, contributed over five per cent of the Chinese GDP in 2014 in terms of its industry added value. In 2020, over 250 million vehicles were sold in the Chinese market, including 200 million passenger cars (Figure 5.4). Despite a decline in sales since 2018, the total value of the Chinese automotive manufacturing industry reached USD 426 billion in 2019 (Marketline 2020). The economic significance of the automobile industry goes beyond the industry added value generated by the industry per se. According to the same report, seven new jobs in the upstream and downstream industries are created for every additional job in the auto industry.

Consequently, while the 'creative' ambitions of the state successfully helped create an EV industry, the progress was not accompanied by the decline or destruction of the ICE sector. Since 2015, many European countries announced plans for phasing out ICE vehicles. However, no official document confirmed that China would consider such a plan until 2019.[12] In 2017, the vice-minister of the Ministry of industry and Information Technology (MIIT) told a forum that the ministry had started relevant research on possible timetables of phase-out of 'traditional energy vehicles'.[13] Although this remark did not suggest any timetable for a phase-out of ICEVs, nor was any implementation plan mentioned, this remark still attracted strong backlash.[14] For the next two years, little discussion within the government on the phase-out of ICE technologies in the automobile industry was revealed.

---

[12] In its response to an enquiry raised in the National People's Congress annual meeting in 2019, the Ministry of Industry and Information Technology for the first time confirmed the ministry was working with NDRC and other government agencies to develop an ICE vehicle phase-out policy, see: '工信部答复 "关于研究制定禁售燃油车时间表加快建设汽车强国的建议"'[The Ministry of Industry and Information Technology responds to 'Recommendations on Studying and Formulating a Timetable for Banning the Sale of Fuel Vehicles to Speed up the Building of a Powerful Automobile Country'], *People's Daily Online*, 22 August 2019, http://auto.people.com.cn/n1/2019/0822/c1005-31310122.html

[13] See: 'China studying when to ban sales of traditional fuel cars: Xinhua', *Reuters*, September 10 2017, https://www.reuters.com/article/us-china-autos/china-studying-when-to-ban-sales-of-traditional-fuel-cars-xinhua-idUKKCN1BL01U

[14] For example, Fu Chenwu, the chairman of the China Automobile Engineering Society, has reportedly stated in a China Automotive Brand Development Forum in September 2017 that 'phase-out of gasoline vehicles is a matter with utmost significance. Our country needs to be very, very careful on this matter. We need to follow scientifical and market principles, rather than blindly follow [other countries who made such policies]'. (See news report at: '传统燃油车禁售时间表起争议 新能源发展将多元化?'[Controversy over the timetable for the ban on the sale of traditional fuel vehicles. Will the development of new energy be diversified?], Nbd, 28 September 2017, http://www.nbd.com.cn/articles/2017-09-28/1151212.html).

The lack of alignment between 'creative' and 'destructive' transition efforts was also reflected in the behaviour of individual automobile firms. Three types of EV producers emerged in this period. These include: 1) incumbent ICE car makers that have diversified into the EV business; 2) battery manufacturers that have entered the EV industry through vertical integration; and 3) internet giant-invested EV companies. Most auto makers in the first two categories continued to invest in both incumbent ICE technologies and new NEV technologies. Even BYD, which is a world leader in EV battery technologies, produced and sold 231,700 ICE cars in 2020 compared with 162,900 NEV cars it produced in the same year.[15] Meanwhile, many EV technologies have been invested or supported by Chinese internet companies. For example, the EV car maker Nio was founded in late 2014 with venture capital backing from Baidu and Tencent. These companies are particularly interested in areas where China has an advantage, such as internet-connected cars, because the technologies are based on big data in real time equipped with 5G technology.

In the face of uncertainties over the 'creative' and 'destructive' dynamics in the industry, Chinese auto companies publicly or implicitly pursue 'strategic flexibility' and many are committed to diversifying their products and markets. For many incumbent ICE car makers, their targets of electrification tend to be shorter-term (typically for the next five to ten years) and more conservative than those of the government (ICET 2019). Vague terminologies have been used by auto makers in their communications with stakeholders to deal with the paradox. For example, when being asked about an announcement of the company regarding completely stopping production of 'ICE cars' by 2025, the president of Changan Automobile, one of the major auto manufacturers in China, stated that the company in fact was to abandon the 'traditional' ICE technologies, but would continue to invest and utilize 'high-efficiency' ICE technologies in their vehicles. Auto makers have also attempted to form a coalition with oil companies to influence major policy changes, such as for lobbying the government not to commit to the phase-out of ICE. In short, auto makers play a paradoxical role in both stabilizing and destabilizing the current ICE technology regime.

Part Four: Growing creative-destructive alignment (2018—present)

As discussed in the last section, a significant level of 'creative' efforts made by the state was critical to the rapid development and deployment of EV technologies

---

[15] See the news report: '退步的比亚迪, 留给王传福的时间不多了'[The regressive BYD has run out of time for Wang Chuanfu], *Sina*, 6 April 2021, https://finance.sina.com.cn/tech/2021-04-06/doc-ikmyaawa7724907.shtml

in China. Yet, the government and individual auto firms seemed to have little motivation and actions to phase-out traditional ICE cars during a good part of the 2010s. Instead, the ICE output and sales continued to grow. A complete displacement of ICE cars by EVs seemed far from reality.

However, a trend that started in the mid-2010s, and in particular, became evident since 2018, saw the emergence of intertwined 'creative' and 'destructive' actions in the auto industry. On the one hand, more targeted 'creative' policies were implemented by the government at both the central and local levels, aiming to promote not only the quantity but also the quality of development of the EV industry, especially in terms of its technological capabilities. On the other hand, policies have placed increasing pressures on the traditional ICE-based technological regimes, resulting in the start of substantial structural change of the automobile industry. After ten years of uninterrupted growth, the auto market in China saw a fall in its total sales for the first time in 2018, dropping 2.8 per cent from the level in 2017 (CAAM 2020). The domestic auto market has further shrunk in 2019 and 2020, by eight per cent and two per cent, respectively. Nevertheless, EV sales increased by 124 per cent from 2017 to 2020.

The growing alignment of the 'creative' and 'destructive' ambitions and actions in the Chinese auto industry may be attributed to several factors. These factors include: i) the increasing emphasis on technological capability building induced by the new international environment facing China, ii) the growing role of local governments in the design and implementation of economic and environment policies, and iii) the new domestic political environment together with the top leader's personal commitment. We elaborate on each of these factors in turn.

Changing international environment and the quest for tech-supremacy

The pursuit of technological catch-up and possible technological leadership have always underpinned policies relating to the Chinese automobile industry. However, this goal has become paramount in the new international environment in which China now finds itself—an environment that China, through its own actions, has also helped to create. This environment is characterized principally by growing competition—not only economic, but also geostrategic—with the West, and especially with the US. It is now widely accepted in Western scholarship that China's foreign economic policy approach has transformed significantly under President Xi. As we discuss in more detail below, since the mid-2010s especially, Xi has adopted a far more assertive foreign policy stance than his predecessors. This has included the frequent deployment of economic statecraft in the traditional sense of the word, with China proactively seeking to shape the behaviour of other nations by, for example, attempting to rewrite the rules of the international economic game, or by engaging in strategic foreign investment initiatives, not least the Belt and Road Initiative.[16] In this context, it seems reasonable to speculate that since 2015, China has also been engaging in a less conventional kind of economic statecraft: 'domestically oriented economic statecraft', by which is meant 'government initiatives designed to reach for or push the high-tech frontier in order to fend off, outflank, or move in step with clearly defined rival powers—whether such rivalry is primarily economic or military' (Weiss and Thurbon 2020: 474. See also Thurbon and Weiss 2019). This would seem a reasonable interpretation of the motivations underpinning the Xi government's 2015 *Made in China 2025* strategy, which we discuss in more detail below. But whatever China's motivations, that particular strategy—and China's engagement in broader statecraft efforts—have elicited a clear response from many developed nations, not least the US, to the extent that increasingly China finds itself in a *tech cold war* with the West.[17] As a result, China now faces tremendous pressures to compete in strategic new technology areas—including new energy vehicles—with both developed western countries and newly industrialized countries such as Korea (see Chapter 4).

Reflecting this reality, EV development policies since the mid-2010s have leaned more towards the need to build technological autonomy and international competitiveness than to deliver short-term economic benefits. From this perspective, resources need to be mobilized for supporting identified priority technological areas, which in the automobile industry are EV-related technologies. Meanwhile, traditional ICE technologies are deemed as technologies of yesterday and their role in the competition facing China in the new international landscape has become less important. This notion was reflected in the aforementioned *Made in China 2025* policy, released by the State Council in 2015. As stated at the outset, the policy was developed to respond to the 'dual pressures' arisen from the reindustrialization of developed countries and takeover of industrial activities by other developing countries in global value chains. Under this framework, not only was the EV industry identified as one of the ten key technology areas, but also—with other identified areas—was to play important roles for the transition and upgrading of China's manufacturing sector. In 2016, under the name of 'reducing excess capacity', China decided to no longer approve new producers of traditional ICE vehicles.

The motivation to align between the 'creative' and 'destructive' dynamics driven by this thinking became clearer in the *Auto Industry Medium- and Long-Term*

[16] A significant and growing body of literature is now devoted to examining China's externally-oriented economic statecraft and its intensification over time, and offers rich insights into the origins, contours, effectiveness, and implications of this phenomenon. See for example Norris (2016), Lampton (2008), Bremmer (2009), Reilly (2021), Helleiner and Kirshner (2014), Goh (2016), Shirk (2008), Li (2017). However, this strategy also faces backlashes, such as a 'new liability of origin' as experienced by Chinese-invested enterprises overseas (Tan and Yang, 2021).

[17] See e.g., Segal, A. 2020. 'The coming tech cold war with China', *Foreign Affairs*, 9 September, and Yellen 2020.

Plan, released by the MIIT in 2017. In this policy, the Chinese government has further articulated the need for the auto industry to be transformed from a 'large' industry to a 'strong' industry. The plan recognizes that 'opportunities arising from the NEV technologies provides the country a path to catch up and even move ahead of other major auto producing countries', supported by 'a market with massive potential and various levels of demand'. On the 'creative' side, the plan set several growth targets for NEVs, including an annual sale of two million NEVs by 2020, and for NEVs to account for 20 per cent of all vehicles sold in China by 2025. The industry fell short of the target for NEV sales in 2020. The plan not only specified these demanding growth targets for EVs, but also put forward principles that would have destructive effects to ICE technologies, including a control of the output volume of the auto industry, optimization of the industry structure, and transition and upgrading of technologies. Specifically, the plan called for the establishment of more stringent and comprehensive mechanisms for the business exit of auto firms, and punitive and compensation systems for non-compliance. While technically these mechanisms apply to both the manufacturing and use of NEVs and ICE cars, the punitive mechanism has greater effects on ICE cars as they are more subject to requirements and standards on emissions and fuel economics. For example, for the first time since the revised Air Pollution Prevention and Control Law took effect in 2015, two Chinese car manufacturers were fined more than 38 million yuan by the Ministry of Environmental Protection in January 2018 for producing motor vehicles with their emissions above the standards and installing fraudulent pollution control devices.[18]

The emphasis on technological development was reflected in the revision of subsidy policies for NEVs since 2016 under the name of a 'dynamic adjustment mechanism'. Since 2009, the development of the EV market in China had been strongly supported by subsidies, first applied to public procurement in select cities, and later extended to private use of EVs in the whole country. Figure 5.5 compares the levels of subsidies to EVs in China and those in other countries, revealing that total subsidies supporting EVs in China amount to 23 per cent of the purchase price (lower than for European countries like Denmark and Norway, and for Korea). The Chinese government first included a plan to cut back EV subsidy in a policy in 2013, with a modest rate of five per cent reduction per year for 2014 and 2015. In 2015, the government announced a plan with more substantial reduction of subsidies for EVs by 20 per cent and 40 per cent in 2017–2018 and 2019–2020 respectively compared to the 2016 level. In the following years, the subsidy policy was regularly reviewed and adjusted to respond to issues that emerged in the EV market, including overcapacity, fragmentation, and insufficient attention to tech competitiveness. In recent years, the objectives of the subsidy policy have been more towards the facilitation of advanced technologies through a closer

---

[18] See news report at https://www.sohu.com/a/215933534_526255 (in Chinese).

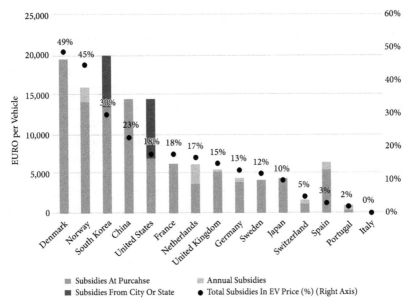

Figure 5.5 Subsidies to EVs by country

Source: Adapted from McKinsey & Co. (2017)

linkage between the level of subsidies and the technological level, as reflected in indicators such as travel range per charging. In 2020, for the purpose of 'reducing the subsidies at a steady intensity and pace', the government announced that the subsidies for EVs would be extended for two further years despite its previous announcement to completely phase-out the subsidy by 2020.[19]

The NEV mandate policy introduced in 2017 was a significant move in enabling both 'creative' effects (on EVs) and 'destructive' effects (on ICE vehicles) simultaneously. According to the policy, automakers that produce more than 30,000 vehicles per year need to obtain a NEV credit of at least ten per cent in 2019, a threshold which will be increased to 12 per cent in 2020. According to an update of the policy in 2020, this policy in its revised version has been extended to 2023, by which the threshold will be further lifted to 18 per cent. For example, a car manufacturer needs to earn 1,800 credits if it produces 10,000 ICE vehicles in 2023, which can be achieved through, for example, producing 600 NEV cars at three credits each. The calculation of NEV credit scores is based on the green credentials of the NEVs, such as recharge mileage, and the number of NEVs the firm produces relative to its total output of vehicles. BEVs will be granted higher credit

---

[19] See: '关于完善新能源汽车推广应用财政补贴政策的通知'[Notice on Improving the Financial Subsidy Policy for the Promotion of New Energy Vehicles], *The Central People's Government of the People's Republic of China*, 23 April 2020, http://www.gov.cn/zhengce/zhengceku/2020-04/23/content_5505502.htm

scores than other types of NEVs, reflecting a continuous focus on the technology in the policy context. The policy also introduced a cap-and-trade system, in the sense that a firm could buy credits from other automakers to meet its credit requirement. The firm will face sanctions such as production halts on its gasoline cars if it fails to obtain enough credits either based on its own production of NEVs or through the NEV credits market. This policy has strongly spurred the market dynamics in the industry and has put firms with EV technological capabilities in a better position than their competitors. For example, it was reported that Ford Motors had to team up with a local EV company, Zotye, in order to produce cars eligible for the credits in China, due to its large volume of production of ICE powered vehicles in China. According to this NEV credit policy, car makers in China need to increase their NEV outputs by 80 per cent from 2019 to 2023 if they wish to keep the same production level of ICE vehicles. This NEV credit policy suggests the state's growing ambitions and capabilities to align its 'creative' policy to develop the NEV industry with the 'destructive' policy to suppress the gasoline vehicle industry.

Growing activism of local governments

Local governments have traditionally played an important role in EV industry creation and development, but in recent years some local governments have also led some of the destruction efforts by proactively phasing out the production and use of gasoline vehicles in their cities or regions, as in the Korean case (see Chapter 4). On their 'creative' efforts, a study by the International Council on Clean Transportation (ICCT) (2018) shows that there is a strong correlation between the monetarized benefits provided by a local government to NEV buyers and the overall share of NEVs in the local auto market. The study has also found that EVs have achieved a high market share in several cities in the absence of high monetarized benefits provided by local governments.

In these cities, the local governments have instead focused on promoting locally produced EVs for the use of large fleets such as taxis and rental cars (ICCT 2018). From 2009 to 2019, a national NEV demonstration program has covered 88 cities and regions (ICET 2019). These demonstration cities and regions are prioritized in accessing financial incentives provided by the central government for NEVs. As a condition of the program, the demonstration cities are expected to establish complementary policies and mobilize resources to achieve more ambitious objectives of developing EVs than the national targets. For example, Huang and Li (2020) reveal that the designation of Shenzhen as a national NEV demonstration city in 2009 was a key trigger for the municipal government to introduce a number of proactive measures in promoting EVs, including the establishment of an 'NEV Implementation Leading Group' headed by the mayor. The demonstration program acted as an important mechanism to align and connect the central and local governments' efforts in promoting EVs.

In recent years, the role of local governments goes beyond creating new EV industry but also involving the facilitation of the exit from the ICE industry, as they increasingly face dual pressures of economic growth and environment protection. Serious air pollution has frequently caused public outrage and undermined the legitimacy of the ruling party. As part of the response, a shift from ICE cars to EVs has been included in increasingly stringent measures and key performance indicators (KPIs) introduced in 'Air Pollution Action Plans' for and by local governments in recent years. These measures include the development of NEVs, control of ICE car stocks, traffic restrictions on ICE vehicles, and development of alternative, clean fuels. At the national level, the *Action Plan for Winning the Blue Sky War for 2018–2020* by the State Council required the percentage of NEVs in the newly added auto stocks in focused regions to reach at least 80 per cent in areas such as public transportation, taxis, and vehicles for logistics by 2020; and buses in capital cities and major cities in the focused regions need to be 100 per cent powered by clean energy sources by 2020. At the local level, measures and targets related to supporting EVs and suppressing ICE cars have been included in the Air Pollution Action Plans of almost all Chinese provinces. Similar to those in Korea (Chapter 4) these initiatives, driven by local governments, have supported the expansion of local EV markets in China.

At the same time, economic performance continues to be the most important performance indicator for local government officials. Economic growth is also critical for other activities at the local level for which local governments have responsibilities or interests. As the remarks by the municipal head (CCP party secretary) of Hefei City indicate (see epigraph of this chapter), economic growth provides the necessary financial resources for the government to carry out other activities of interest. The creation and development of a NEV industry seems to simultaneously meet the two major objectives of local governments.

Local governments' policies support, and sometime direct investments, such as that made by the Wuhu government in the Nio project (mentioned at the head of the chapter), and have led to the emergence of a number of industry clusters around EVs, and more recently FCVs. The specific drivers and developmental paths of NEV industry clusters in different regions vary according to the local contexts, in particular the initial industrial conditions in the city or the region. Some EV clusters focus on enhancing the market positions of established car makers from the region, while others aim to attract emerging technologies and establish more complete value chains; yet there are EV clusters that strive for achieving both goals (Table 5.1). In these processes, local governments have engaged in competition for investments, technologies, and human capital. According to an estimate of the MIIT, over 500 policies were introduced by various local governments in China between 2012 and 2020 to promote NEVs. Many local

Table 5.1 Key NEV clusters in China

NEV industry clusters	Key industry players		Focus and coverage
	Passenger NEVs	Commercial NEVs	
Beijng-Tianjin Cluster	BAIC Group	BYD (Tianjin)	Leading players dominating the cluster; a relatively complete EV value chain available in the local area
Yangtze River Delta Cluster	SAIC Motor; BAIC Group (Zhenjiang); Zhejiang Geely; Zhidou; Kangdi	SAIC Motor	A high level of availabilities of components in the local area; a complete EV value chain available in the local area
Peal River Delta Cluster	GAC Group; BYD; BAIC Group (Guangzhou); Southeast Motor	BYD; BAIC Group (Guangzhou)	There is a dominant firm in both auto manufacturing and battery production respectively; a complete EV value chain available in the local area
Southwest Cluster	Changan; Lifan	Changan; Lifan	A less complete EV value chain available in the local area;
Central Cluster	Anhui Chery; JAC Motor; Dongfeng Motor	Anhui Chery; JAC Motor; Dongfeng Motor	A relatively complete EV value chain available in the local area; a focused market in the local area; a high level of overlapping of players in passenger and commercial NEVs

Source: ICET (2019)

governments have provided NEV manufacturers with cheap land, loans, and direct subsidies for every NEV produced. On some occasions, competition between local governments to attract NEV industrial activities resulted in overcapacity on the part of NEV producers. On other occasions, the involvement and actions of local governments contributed to the realignment of 'creative' and 'destructive' dynamics in the auto industry.

A notable example is Liuzhou City. Although not being included in the national NEV demonstration program, EVs achieved a market share of 30 per cent in the city in 2020, a penetration rate only behind Oslo worldwide.[20] More significant is the change in the share of gasoline vehicles vis-à-vis NEVs produced within the city during recent years. Auto manufacturing is the largest industry in the city, accounting for over one-third of GDP in 2010. In 2010, there were 415 automobile and parts manufacturing companies in the city, producing 1,400,000 cars. As one of the top three cities in China in terms of the volume of cars produced in 2010, the city barely produced any NEVs at that time. A decade later, in 2020, the city produced a total of 1,873,000 auto vehicles, of which NEVs accounted for ten per cent, or 187,000 vehicles. A major success factor of Liuzhou both in its adoption and production of EVs is the close collaboration between the municipal government and EV manufacturers driven by their shared interests (Cui and He 2019). The government has a strong motivation to promote local industries; meanwhile the local auto maker is keen for a transition towards electrification. The firm has specifically developed EV models designed for intra-city transportation, which are easy and cost-effective to drive and park.

Meanwhile, the local government has introduced a series of policies that fit the purchase and use of EV cars, such as vehicle purchase subsidies, free and reserved parking, and the rapid development of charging infrastructure in the city that suits these EVs.[21] Coordination between the municipal government and the EV firm at three levels has been established in the process of EV development, including that between the leaders, between various departments within the municipal government and those within the firm, and on daily operations.

Presidential orientation and ambition

President Xi Jinping's personal commitment to an energy transition in China, together with his centralization of power in recent years, has become an important enabling condition for the growing alignment of the 'creative' and 'destructive' efforts by the state as well as the private sector in the Chinese automobile industry. As in the case of Korea (Chapter 4), the ambition and actions of the political leader

---

[20] See 'China's electric car capital has lessons for the rest of the world', *Bloomberg News*, June 27 2021, at: https://www.bloomberg.com/news/features/2021-06-26/china-s-electric-car-capital-has-lessons-for-the-rest-of-world

[21] See: H. Cui and H. He, 'Liuzhou: A new model for the transition to Electric Vehicles?', *International Council on Clean Transportation*, 18 December 2019, https://theicct.org/blog/staff/liuzhou-new-model-transition-electric-vehicles

from the highest level in China make a significant, if not decisive, difference in the green energy transition process. While in some ways a continuation of the 'scientifical view of development' as devised by his predecessor, Hu Jingtao, Xi puts greater emphasis on environmental quality as a major political narrative of his leadership. As the party chief of Zhejiang Province in 2005, Xi first used the phrase 'clear waters and green mountains are as valuable as mountains of gold and silver'. This phrase has subsequently become a slogan of the party since Xi became the party leader in 2013. The so-called 'two mountain theory' derived from this slogan was highlighted in the report of the Nineteenth National Congress of the Communist Party of China as a key principle to guide the party and the country. Not long after he took the party leadership, in 2014 Xi delivered a major speech calling for 'a revolution of energy consumption and supply' for the country. In 2020, Xi unilaterally announced a 2060 target for carbon neutrality, surprising both international and domestic observers of climate policies in China.

On the automobile industry, Xi has showed personal support for the development of NEVs. Xi made a remark during his visit to SAIC Motor that the development of NEVs is the only pathway for China to move from a 'large' auto-producing country to that of a 'strong' auto-producing country. In his congratulatory letter to the 2019 World New Energy Vehicle Congress held in Boao, China, Xi once again emphasized the need to accelerate innovation in NEV technologies and development of related industries. In the letter, he states that the rapid development of NEVs has 'not only injected strong new momentum into the economic growth of different countries but also will help to reduce greenhouse gas (GHG) emissions, tackle climate change, and improve the global environment'.[22] More recently in 2021, Xi chaired a Politburo meeting which announced that the country is to support the accelerated development of NEVs.

In a sharp contrast to his predecessors, Jiang Zeming and Hu Jingtao, Xi has greatly elevated his personal power and enhanced control over economic and political systems. As a result, his personal commitment has been more effectively translated to policies. Further, his support to a transformation of the Chinese automobile industry towards EVs provides strong political legitimacy for overcoming resistance from the ICE-dominant regime.

Concluding remarks

In this chapter, we demonstrate notable features of China's policies towards EVs. Unlike those for the Korean FCEV industry which we examined in the last chapter, the EV-related industry policy in China incorporated environment and energy

---

[22] See: F. Li, Z. Liu, Q. Wang, 'Xi calls for accelerating new energy vehicle tech', *China Daily,* 3 July 2019, http://www.chinadaily.com.cn/a/201907/03/WS5d1baf60a3105895c2e7b42c.html

security considerations from the very beginning. However, as a more sizable EV market emerged, the industry's contribution to the national and local economies and industrial development were emphasized; as a result, the familiar developmental approach returned and dominated the policy design and implementation. Although the 'creative' ambitions and efforts based on the traditional DS approach did foster the rapid growth of the sector, unintended outcomes also emerged, such as overcapacity, a fragmented market, and a lack of progress in destabilizing the dominant gasoline vehicle regime. From the late 2010s, efforts have been made in the policy arena towards a growing alignment of the 'creative' and 'destructive' ambitions and efforts of the government.

The government at both central and local levels has played critical roles in the evolution of the industry. Their roles are complex. On the one hand, policies have been a major driving force for investments into sometimes seemingly immature technologies and flawed business models, causing chaotic market competition. On the other hand, they also enabled a rapid take-up of the EV market and manufacturing capacity. Consequently, EV technology has been increasingly established in some cities and niche markets. We submit that this precisely reflects a spirit of 'creative-destruction' as coined by Joseph Schumpeter—albeit in our case the state, especially at the local level, has become one of the key actors to drive the process. In her examination of the Chinese auto industry in the 1980s–2000s, Wan-Wen Chu (2011) concluded that, despite the flaws and failures in the industry policy that the Chinese state introduced for the auto industry in each stage, overall the policy process seems effective because 'each time, the policy was subsequently revised and improved, and the industry had moved closer toward the goal of building up the auto sector as a national industry' (2011: 1270). As we explored in this chapter, it seems this notion can also be applied to policy development in relation to the Chinese EV industry.

Finally, it is not only the development of individual NEV technologies or EV firms but more importantly emergence of hybridized industrial ecosystems around EVs that are placing increasing pressures on the ICE industry. For example, as an indication of efforts to draw greater input from the private sector into the state's policymaking apparatus, in 2014 the 'China EV100' association was created after a proposal by Li Lanqing, a former member of the top leadership of the Communist Party of China—the Politburo Standing Committee—in an effort to deepen links with the EV industry. The purpose of the association is to promote the development of the EV industry through boosting and coordinating the development of technologies, policies, and cooperation amongst the Chinese EV industry.[23] It has an encompassing membership of 178 domestic and 37 foreign members representing entities composed of manufacturers, upstream and downstream companies, and influential figures from government, industry, and

---

[23] See the association's website at https://www.chinaev100.com/

academia. The association has a number of prominent politicians serving on its advisory board, including leaders from the ministries of transportation, industry and information technology, finance, housing and urban-rural development, and China's special climate envoy. Indeed, the association's current president is Chen Qingtai, the former party secretary and deputy director of the Development Research Centre of the State Council. In addition to organizing many forums involving players from the whole EV supply chains, the association led a report in 2019 to spearhead the policy discussion on the timetable of full electrification of vehicles in China.

6

Creative-Destruction in Korea's Smart and Strong Grid Strategy

With the arrival of the era of resource shortages and intensifying environmental crises, developed nations recognized climate change and energy issues as their most dire problems and were required to focus all their strength on promoting the efficient use of energy and resources as well as minimizing environmental pollution. In particular, the limits of economic growth coming from the investment of elements such as capital and manpower have been overcome, while constant efforts have been made to turn these crises into opportunities such as the drafting of legislation to secure and promote new growth engines including renewable forms of energy, environmental industries, and a carbon-trading market among others. Several leading countries have set green growth as an important policy target and many of them have pursued green growth as their national development strategy for the purpose of breaking away from the carbon dependent economic paradigm and to pre-empt the world market in green technology and industry.

(Kim Sang-hyup, former Presidential Secretary for Green Growth and the Environment in the Lee Myung-bak administration, and Sang-Hyup and Choi 2013: 5)

The Green New Deal is the path the world seeks to simultaneously accomplish climate change response and economic growth. Europe and the United States have mobilized all of their national capabilities to launch a Green New Deal, and multinational companies are taking the initiative on environmental protection by pledging carbon neutrality ... We can also take the lead in the Green New Deal. With an extraordinary resolve that this is the only way for us to survive, we have to revamp politics, the economy, society and culture.

(President Moon Jae-In, 19 March 2021)[1]

[1] 'Remarks by President Moon Jae-in at Strategy Presentation for Chungcheongnam-do Province's Energy Transition and Green New Deal', *The Republic of Korea: Cheongwadae*, 19 March 2021, accessed on 1 October 2021, https://english1.president.go.kr/Briefingspeeches/Speeches/957

Developmental Environmentalism. Elizabeth Thurbon et al., Oxford University Press. © Elizabeth Thurbon, Sung-Young Kim, Hao Tan, and John Mathews (2023). DOI: 10.1093/oso/9780192897794.003.0006

Korea is a country with a very high degree of urbanization ... Now we are constructing 'smart cities' to meet the demand for future cities ... . Smart cities have become the inevitable urban future if not for anything else than creating eco-friendly municipalities that save energy and help mitigate climate change. The world will engage in yet another *fierce competition* over being the first to develop and proliferate smart cities ... The Government will accelerate the construction of smart cities as the Korean New Deal's core project which are based on *digital and green technologies*. We will come to experience smart cities in this leading example of Songdo, thereby getting a *head-start in spearheading* the era of smart cities worldwide.

(President Moon Jae-in, 22 October 2020, emphasis added)[2]

The pattern

The process of enabling the widespread uptake of renewable energy, thereby weaning a country off fossil fuels, is a herculean task involving countless complex steps. One of the most critical steps is the creation of smart and strong electricity grids—grids that can distribute green electricity to energy-hungry households, industries, and vehicle fleets swiftly, reliably, and efficiently. The Koreans recognized this challenge earlier than most and, over the past decade, the country has made rapid progress in the development of various smart grid (IT-enabled) and strong grid (power grid-enabled) technologies. Companies such as Samsung, LG Chem, LSIS, and Hyundai, and state-owned utility KEPCO are now at the cutting edge of core technologies related to smart grids. These include energy management systems (EMS), energy storage systems (ESS), virtual power plants (VPP), power conversion systems (PCS), and EV recharging infrastructure (including plug-in and online recharging). These technologies are being developed to enable the reliability, stability, resilience, and efficiency of power grids.

Korea's ascendency to the top of the smart grid technology pack has been characteristically swift by global standards. The Korean government and companies began focusing on smart grid projects in 2005 under the then Ministry of Commerce, Indusry and Energy's (MOCIE) 'Power IT' national projects. However, it was only upon the country's prioritization of 'green growth' in 2008 that a systematic and targeted approach to smart grid technology development came into being. Since that time, Korea has made rapid progress in developing core technologies to enable a smart grid, which will help achieve the government's

[2] 'Opening Remarks by President Moon Jae-in at Presentation of Smart City Strategy Associated with Korean New Deal', *The Republic of Korea: Cheongwadae*, 22 October 2020, accessed 23 February 2021, https://english1.president.go.kr/BriefingSpeeches/Economy/896

stated long-term goal of commercializing smart grids across the country from 2021 to 2030. Despite starting from behind, Korea is now a technological leader in many smart grid-related fields such as those mentioned above. However, in areas such as high voltage direct current (HVDC) grids, technologies where China has developed strong indigenous capabilities—and in technologically more advanced ultra-high voltage (UHV) grids (see Chapter 7)—Korean companies are still playing catch-up.

Yet despite the technological advances that Korea has made over the past decade or so, many challenges remain to the wholesale greening of the country's electricity grids. One of the most critical challenges is the slow pace of smart grid *commercialization*. While many smart grid technologies have been commercialized (e.g., ESS and EMS technologies), the pace of commercialization has fallen short of expectations, thanks in no small part to the *complexities* and *uncertainties* surrounding smart grid technologies. These complexities and uncertainties have served to slow the development of concrete and encompassing global standards—typically a prerequisite for the emergence of mass commercial markets (and the massive levels of public and private investment required to support them). Smart grids are technologically complex because they combine both the 'heavy' power equipment industry and the knowledge-intensive information and communications technologies industry. They are also complex from a business-model perspective because they require many different 'layers' of regulation and thus involve a multiplicity of stakeholders. In the context of these uncertainties, settling on global standards for smart grid technologies has proven a highly complex and somewhat fraught affair—although Korean public and private actors have been proactively seeking to influence global standards-setting processes in the relevant international organizations, as they have done so effectively in other technological arenas in the past (see Kim 2012). More generally however, governments and companies have preferred to adopt a 'wait and see' approach when it comes to the full-scale commercialization of smart grid technologies. This situation is likely to change significantly as technological uncertainties resolve, standardization efforts progress, and the costs of smart grid technologies fall accordingly.

However, even if smart grid commercialization were to progress more swiftly, Korea still faces a second major obstacle to the greening of its grids—be they smart and strong or conventional, that is, getting fossil fuels out of the grids and more renewable energy in. And it is here that Korea continues to struggle, despite its technological prowess on the smart grid front. Indeed by 2016, despite Korea's emergent leadership in smart grid technologies (and thus its strong renewables potential), the country's electricity was still overwhelmingly generated from coal (39.5 per cent), liquified natural gas (22.4 per cent), oil (2.6 per cent) and nuclear power (30 per cent) (KEPCO 2017: 62). Electricity generation from water, wind, and solar (WWS) resources accounted for a mere 5.4 per cent of total generation in the same year.

A key obstacle to getting more renewables into Korea's grids (both smart and conventional) has been the existence of a state-owned quasi-monopoly over electricity generation via the utility company KEPCO (mentioned above). Over the post-war era, KEPCO provided reliable electric power to Koreans at artificially low prices set by the government. It was this cheap electric power that fuelled Korea's remarkable post-WWII industrial transformation. And it is this cheap electric power that Korean industry (and financially-squeezed households) still expect from the government. According to a 2013 World Bank report, KEPCO retained 95 per cent market share over power generation and 100 per cent market share over the transmission and distribution of electricity (Vagliasindi and Besant-Jones 2013: 194). Given its critical role in the Korean energy (and socio-economic) system, efforts to drive meaningful competition against KEPCO in energy generation via the introduction of private players has had limited impact. Ironically, this is despite the fact that KEPCO is simultaneously leading green technology development efforts in fields including microgrids (Kim and Mathews 2016: 1). Korea's historic addiction to fossil fuels—which can be distributed by its already-existing vast network of conventional grids—has no doubt further slowed the commercialization of smart grids. As a result, the wider uptake of EVs (discussed in Chapter 4) and the increasing penetration of (intermittent) renewables into the national energy mix will put unprecedented new demands (e.g., during 'peak demand') on post-WWII power grids, which at present are simply ill-equipped to manage them.

Nevertheless, when it comes to both the commercialization of smart grids and getting more green energy into them, the tide does seem to be turning—if still slowly on some fronts. In the wake of the COVID-19 pandemic, then president Moon lit a fire under the country's smart grid commercialization efforts, placing a major emphasis on the creation of 'smart cities'—of which smart grids are a defining aspect. Moon also set in train a series of important new initiatives intended to phase-out fossil fuels and nuclear and to increase the uptake of renewables under the umbrella of his landmark Net Zero by 2050 commitment. Moon's efforts were soon mirrored by some key local governments like Chungnam province, home to the majority of Korea's coal-fired power plants. In 2018, Chungnam pledged to completely phase-out coal by 2050, and became the first Asian jurisdiction to join the global Powering Past Coal Alliance. Increasingly it seems, Korea's ambitious efforts to create, commercialize, and scale smart grids are being matched by efforts to displace fossil fuels and get more renewables into the grids.

The puzzle

The Korean state's approach to building a national smart grid industry—and to getting more green energy intro the grid—raise various questions. What has motivated the Korean state to become involved in smart grid industry creation initiatives, especially in smart grid technologies? How have Korean policymakers pursued their creative ambitions? Why has the government appeared more ambitious and active in smart grid industry creation than in getting fossil fuels out of energy systems more broadly (for example, by mandating the deployment of renewables in the grid, or by setting firm goals for fossil fuel exit?) To what extent is this 'creative-destructive' misalignment now resolving? What factors are driving attempts at realignment, and what obstacles to a fully green shift remain? To address these questions, we divide this chapter temporally into three main parts.

In Part One, we trace the origins of the 'creative' elements in Korea's smart grid initiatives formulated by the Lee Myung-bak administration (2008–2012) as part of the 'Low-Carbon, Green Growth' strategy (LCGG). We probe the developmental-environmental motivations and institutional set-up driving national green growth (GG) development plans amongst the policymaking elite, specifically programs related to smart grid development. We show that, for the first time, policymakers sought to *internalize* environmental goals within their industry creation initiatives. We do so by tracing creative-destructive efforts under President Lee and then President Park Geun-hye (2013–2017). As will be made clear, this timeline roughly coincides with the first phase of Korea's LCGG strategy (2009–2013) and the initiation of the second phase of the LCGG strategy (2008–2016).

However, notwithstanding the many successes during the 2008–2016 period, the commercialization of smart grids progressed more slowly than expected and there was little change to Korea's excessively high dependence on fossil fuels and nuclear energy. In Part Two of this chapter, we make sense of this *misalignment* between the 'creative' and 'destructive' forces in Korea's smart grid initiatives. We detail how the wider political environment under the Lee and Park administrations, especially with regards to the problem of *growing economic inequality*, made any change to the electricity system specifically over KEPCO's virtual monopoly, politically difficult.

In Part Three, we examine developments since the 2017 election of Korea's President Moon Jae-in (2017–2022), and his administration's efforts to achieve greater *alignment* between the state's 'creative' and 'destructive' ambitions and capabilities. We explore how various domestic and external events prompted President Moon to re-double the state's efforts to commercialize smart grids and to accelerate the phasing out of nuclear energy and the dirtiest fossil fuels like coal from the national energy mix. This includes Korea's growing environmental problem of fine dust particles, the economic and social impact of the global COVID-19 pandemic, and China's economic rise, especially in green industries.

The overall point we make in the pages below is that the state has pursued a sequential approach to its smart grids strategy, focusing on the creation of core technological capabilities as a necessary prelude to its emphasis on increasing the use of renewables, while phasing out the use of fossil fuels in the grid.

Part One: The emergence of the state's creative-destructive ambitions and capabilities (2008–2016)

Korea's efforts to develop a smart grid industry are linked to the 2008 Low-Carbon, Green Growth strategy, which emerged as a direct response by the Lee Myung-bak government to various international and domestic challenges. These concerns were laid bare in *Green Growth for a Greater Korea: White Book on Korean Green Growth Policy, 2008–2012*. One of the two authors of this White Book—Kim Sang-hyup—was the key architect behind Korea's GG initiative and the presidential secretary for Green Growth and the Environment in the Lee administration. According to Kim, there were three main factors driving the LCGG strategy: 1) the volatility in global fossil fuel (FF) energy supplies; 2) the limits of a manufacturing industrial structure based on exploiting FFs; and 3) national action on climate change throughout the OECD countries (Kim and Choi 2013: 2–9). All of these had a direct impact on Korea as will be made clear below.

In terms of the *first factor*, the authors highlight the volatility in global oil prices. By the second half of 2007, oil prices had skyrocketed from their long-term average of 40–50 USD to almost 150 USD per barrel, and the price of resources such as iron ore followed a similar trend (Kim and Choi 2013: 2, 7, 9). The prices of oil and other resources were also expected to grow exponentially with the enormous growth in demand expected from the rise of newly industrializing economies (NIEs) such as India and China. In terms of China alone and its burgeoning middle class, the country had grown ten times faster than the UK during its own industrial revolution. Citing the figures by the IEA's 2009 *World Energy Outlook*, the demand for oil was expected to grow from 12 billion tons in 2007 to roughly 16.8 billion tons by 2030. This represented a growth of 40 per cent in demand for oil by 2030 and was occurring in an era of increasingly scarce fossil fuel supplies. For Korea, which ranked as the fourth most dependent country on oil imports (at 96 per cent) and seventh internationally in terms of its oil consumption, this situation provided the impetus to strengthen the country's energy self-sufficiency through new and renewable energy sources.

With regard to the *second factor*, the volatility of energy and resource prices also heightened the vulnerabilities stemming from Korea's high energy-consuming industrial structure. Approximately 75 per cent of the nation's industrial output was related to energy hungry heavy manufacturing industries such as cement, steel, and chemicals. The nation's weakness was most evident when comparing the fact that the total cost of importing energy was USD 120 billion annually. Yet, this figure was equal to the total annual export value of Korea's mainstay industries including semiconductors, shipbuilding, and automobiles combined. For the key architect of Korea's Green Growth strategy, Kim Sang-hyup, the solution to this crisis was not only to increase the country's energy self-sufficiency but also to position the country away from fossil-fuel intensive industries towards new green technology industries such as solar, wind, green vehicles, and smart grids (Kim and Choi (2013: 8). In other words, the *nature* of manufacturing (not manufacturing itself) had to adapt to a world of unpredictable access to cheap and abundant fossil fuels.

The *third factor* highlighted by the former Presidential Secretary for Green Growth and the Environment and his co-author was the battery of national climate change action plans released by countries across the OECD including the EU, Japan, France, Germany, the US, and the UK (Kim and Choi 2013: 5–6). The efforts by the advanced industrial countries made clear that climate change was not only a challenge that needed to be confronted, but represented an enormous opportunity—and that Korea needed to catch-up or fall further behind in the global race towards green growth. The development of green technology industries was especially appealing for the Lee government as a means to drive new growth engines for the economy in the context of the low rates of economic growth, 'jobless growth', and increasing economic inequality in Korea (Kim and Choi 2013: 11). These were symptoms common to both Korea and other industrially mature economies, yet were in stark contrast to the decades of prosperity and growth-with-equity which has characterized Korea's five decades of rapid economic growth, and which ended with the 1997 Asian Financial Crisis.

These were the circumstances in which the Lee administration formulated the *National Strategy for Green Growth* (2009–2050)—the overarching national policy driving the development of smart grids and key green industries (PCGG 2009a: 5). Short- to medium-term plans for smart grid development were outlined in the first *Five-Year Plan for Green Growth* (FYPGG) (2009–2013). The Ministry of Trade, Industry and Energy (MOTIE)-affiliated Korea Smart Grid Association (KSGA) launched a dedicated *Smart Grid Roadmap 2030*, which laid out plans for the full commercialization of smart grids across the country by 2030 (Kim and Mathews 2016: 5). In the second FYPGG (2014–2018), it is notable that the explicit focus was on the targeted implementation of GG plans introduced under the first FYPGG. The first FYPGG sought to catalyze a government-led push for the building of the institutional infrastructure for governing GG. By contrast, the second FYPGG sought to encourage the *private sector* to lead greening efforts and to achieve concrete results.[3] In this sense, there was a clear evolution in strategy between the first and second FYPGGs.

---

[3] Kim, S. 'South Korea doubles down on Green Growth', *East Asia Forum*, 25 December 2015, accessed 21 June 2021, https://www.eastasiaforum.org/2015/12/25/south-korea-doubles-down-on-green-growth/

In 2012, the Presidential Committee on Green Growth (PCGG)—a high-level agency established to coordinate GG, headed by Soogil Young—finalized the First *Five-Year Master Plan for the Smart Grid* (2012–2016) in accordance with the *Special Act on Promoting Smart Grid Establishment and Usage*. The government pledged that a combined total of (KRW) 3.6 trillion (approximately USD 3.1 billion) would be invested in the plan, from a mix of public and private sources (KSGI 2015: 18). The *Five-Year Master Plan for the Smart Grid* set out clear technological and infrastructure deployment targets. Those targets would help drive a shift from testing the feasibility of new smart grid technologies to their eventual commercialization. It was expected that a total of eight proposed consortia involving 14 provinces, service providers, system integration firms, and device manufacturers would drive these pilot technology deployment projects (Kim and Mathews 2016).

It is important to mention these development plans as they provided a means of coordinating a multitude of smart grid initiatives launched by various governmental ministries and agencies. In the discussion below, we examine the numerous smart grid demonstration projects since the launch of the low-carbon, GG strategy, indicating the developmental-environmental ambitions and means in these technological initiatives. The core technologies targeted for development in the national smart grid projects include virtual power plants (VPPs), energy storage systems (ESS), energy management systems (EMS), advanced metering infrastructure (AMI) (including smart meters), power distribution and automation equipment, and renewable energy generation facilities.

The first major projects included the Jeju Island Smart Grid Test-bed and the Korea Micro Energy Grid (K-MEG). In December 2008, the government allocated investment funds of KRW 76.6 billion (USD 66 million) to the construction of a smart grid test-bed on Jeju Island. This was, at the time, the world's largest such test bed—with private sector investment totalling KRW 172.7 billion (USD 149 million). The government's aim in seed funding this project was to accelerate the commercialization and export of smart grids before foreign competitors (KSGI 2015: 10). Towards the conclusion of the Jeju Island test-bed project, the government launched building and community-based microgrids under the K-MEG project, which operated from 2011 to 2013 (Kim and Mathews 2016: 10). From 2014 to 2016, policymakers turned their attention to developing microgrids for energy self-sufficient islands and remote locations. Other initiatives include a focus on 'smart factories'.[4] To illustrate the Korean state's developmental-environmental ambitions and capabilities, we home in on one project, which has received less attention to date: the Smart Grid Distribution Project.

---

[4] 'Interview with Secretary Lee Gyu-Bong: Uniqueness of Korea's Industry 4.0', *BusinessKorea*, 23 November 2015, http://www.businesskorea.co.kr/news/articleView.html?idxno=13092

2013 Smart Grid Distribution Project

The development of a key technology used in smart grids, energy management systems, was the focus of MOTIE bureaucrats in the *Smart Grid Diffusion Project* launched in 2013. The major aim of this project was to develop an EMS for a wide range of applications such as factories (F-EMS), buildings (B-EMS), and larger districts through the Cloud (C-EMS).[5] However, unlike some previous projects, the aim was to involve consumers (energy users) from the outset in conjunction with manufacturers of smart grid systems. The MOTIE selected eight consortiums (with a total of 19 participating organizations in total) led by different conglomerates from various industrial sectors.[6]

With a total budget of USD 18.4 million, the MOTIE funded four consortia led by LSIS, Hyosung, Woojin Industrial Systems, and LG CNS to test energy storage system technologies. In the project led by LSIS, the company collaborated with small and medium-sized enterprises (SMEs), Kacon New Energy for PCS and software developer Maru System, to test a one-megawatt hour (MWh) ESS in Busan. Hyosung collaborated with SMEs Wells Telesis and Brenex to trial a 1.5MWh ESS in Chuncheon (Gangwon-do Province) and Jeju Island.

The ministry also used its budget to fund a further two consortia led by Lotte Information Communication and Wooam Corporation to construct and operate AMI technologies. The Wooam conglomerate collaborated with DM Power (a start-up specializing in EV and ESS equipment) and the Lotte Information and Communication group collaborated with Tide and YPP to construct an AMI system in various cities including the capital, Seoul.

The final two consortia funded by the MOTIE include those led by Byucksan Power (power systems manufacturer) and Hyundai Autoever (IT systems), which were supported by the ministry to trial the use of AMI in conjunction with ESS technologies. In the Byucksan Power Consortium, the company cooperated with IT equipment manufacturer Capus and a smart meter manufacturer, Sundo Electric. The Hyundai Autoever consortium involved a collaboration with smart meter manufacturer Namjeonsa, AMI manufacturer Nuri Telecom, and ESS company Kokam. This last consortium continued beyond the life of the project through a consortium starting in 2016 involving the Daegu City government.[7] Hyundai Autoever utilized its experience in developing C-EMS during the Smart Grid Distribution Project to install an automated energy management system for

---

[5] See: 'Homepage', *Korea Smart Grid Institute*, accessed 7 August 2020, https://www.smartgrid.or.kr/

[6] S-h. Lee, '스마트그리드 보급사업 참여기업 윤곽' [Outline of companies participating in the smart grid distribution project], *Electimes*, 23 September 2013, http://www.electimes.com/article.php?aid=1379294784106856007

[7] 'Daegu City, "Smart Grid Construction Project" in earnest', *Smart City Korea*, 1 July 2016, accessed 24 February 2021, Daegu City, 'Smart Grid Construction Project' Full-scale Promotion: Smart City Comprehensive Portal—SMART CITY KOREA

participating consumers including the city government's buildings—to be ready by 2025 as part of aspirations for Daegu to establish a smart city (see further below).

KEPCO's stronger grid projects: High voltage direct current technologies

While the main focus of Korean efforts has been on smartening-up its power grid, national efforts have also focused on building stronger grids, although at a pace and scale trailing China (see Chapter 7). Since 2012, KEPCO has collaborated with the American firm General Electric (GE) to utilize the company's technologies to construct high voltage direct current technologies (HVDC) transmission lines in Korea.[8] A joint venture between KEPCO (owning 51 per cent) and GE (49 per cent) which involved technology transfer of GE's core technologies in exchange for GE's involvement in the construction of nationwide grids was established in 2012 in the form of the KEPCO-Alstom (GE) Power Electronic Systems (KAPES) consortium. KAPES coordinates all aspects of the design, procurement, financing, and construction of HVDC grids. The company's goal is to establish a Korean presence in the HVDC industry through localizing the development of key technologies and by seeking new export opportunities through becoming a 'leader of North-east Asia super grid and global power grid market'.[9] This statement conveys the competitive pressures keenly felt by Korean authorities arising from China's efforts to drive a Global Energy Interconnection (GEI) and Japan's Asian Super Grid proposal (see further below).

To date, KAPES has coordinated the upgrading of existing (uni-directional) AC transmission lines to undersea HVDC (bi-directional) cables in various locations such as the Jindo Island-Jeju Island HVDC system. KEPCO owns and operates this grid, while the cables were designed and built by LS Cable and System (a subsidiary of the LS conglomerate), and the converter stations were designed and built by Alstom Grid (subsidiary of GE). Since 2014, KAPES has also coordinated the construction of a 33 km undersea HVDC link between Buk-Dangjin on the western coast of the Korean peninsula (the location of thermal power stations) to the Pyeongtaek Godeok Industrial Complex where Samsung Electronics will manufacture its next-generation semiconductors.[10] When completed, the new three-GW

---

[8] HVDC technologies enable more efficient bulk transfers of electricity over large distances through direct current electric power transmission after converting from alternating current (AC) to direct current (DC), or vice versa. Still, they fall significantly shorter in transmission capacity compared to Ultra High Voltage (UHV) technologies being pioneered in China.

[9] 'Global HVDC & Facts Leading Company', *KAPES: KEPCO and Grid Solutions Joint Venture*, accessed 22 February 2021, http://www.kapes.co.kr/eng/introduce/e_vision.asp

[10] 'Buk-Dangjin-Godeok: Transmitting Power to Cities', General Electric Grid Solutions, 2018, accessed 22 February 2021, https://www.gegridsolutions.com/products/applications/hvdc/bukdangjin-hvdc-lcc-casestudy-en-2018-04-grid-pea-0577.pdf

power capacity HVDC cable will provide greater reliability in electricity supply to the proposed industrial complex. KAPES is currently coordinating a second two-GW power capacity HVDC link, running 220 km between nuclear reactors and thermal power plants at Shinhanul (on the country's eastern coast) and Shingapyeong, to supply more reliable electricity to the country's major metropolitan centres including the capital Seoul.[11]

The motivations behind these projects are not explicitly 'green'. However, as KAPES's nationwide roll-out of HVDC plans indicate, the establishment of HVDC infrastructure is viewed as a *necessary precursor* to the growth of green electricity generated from renewables (e.g., through offshore wind farms)—although specific dates have yet to be determined.[12] The Korean government's support for the localization of HVDC technologies will also prepare KAPES's stated aim of participating in the construction of a Northeast Asian electricity grid linking up the energy markets of Russia, Mongolia, China, Japan, and Korea.[13] This reflects an impressive use of statecraft by the Korean government aimed at securing markets for domestic HVDC manufacturers in competition against Chinese companies (see related discussion of China's Global Energy Interconnection in Chapter 7). Indeed, construction plans published by KAPES reveal efforts to develop the grid over three phases (Figure 6.1)—although it is far from clear whether geopolitical tensions in the region can be overcome to enable the fruition of such plans.[14]

KEPCO's Smart Grid Station project

In addition to playing a leading role in the development and commercialization of HVDC grids, KEPCO has also directly coordinated its own smart grid initiatives since the mid-2010s. Under the *Smart Grid Station* project, KEPCO focused on developing self-sufficient power grids in buildings.[15] The aim of this project was to create energy-efficient buildings (ultimately, zero-emission buildings), the

---

[11] J. Kim, '신한울~신가평 HVDC송전선로 사업, 진통도 본격화?' [Shinhan Seoul~Shingapyeong HVDC transmission line business, labor in earnest?], *EcoTimes*, November 4 2021, accessed 22 March 2021, http://m.ecotiger.co.kr/news/articleView.html?idxno=25079

[12] 'Global HVDC & Facts Leading Company', *KAPES: KEPCO and Grid Solutions Joint Venture*, accessed 22 February 2021, http://kapes.co.kr/eng/business/e_technology1.asp

[13] 'Northeast Asia super grid' costs at least D6.2 billion: KEPCO', *The Korea Times*, 11 December 2018, and K-w Cho, 'South Korea and China hasten joint efforts toward Northeast Asian supergrid', *Hankyoreh*, 30 May 2018.

[14] Global HVDC & Facts Leading Company', *KAPES: KEPCO and Grid Solutions Joint Venture*, accessed 22 February 2021, http://kapes.co.kr/eng/business/e_technology1.asp; In phase one, a HVDC cable between Russia and Korea (near Seoul) will be established. In phase two, a HVDC link between Busan and Fukuoka (Japan) will be constructed and in phase three, the plan is to build a link between Korea and Yantai (China).

[15] See the mention of KEPCO's smart grid station project in the 2015 ISGAN Award of Excellence -Award Winners, at: 'Awards 2015', *International Smart Grid Action Network (ISGAN)*, 2015, http://www.iea-isgan.org/?c=395/397/403

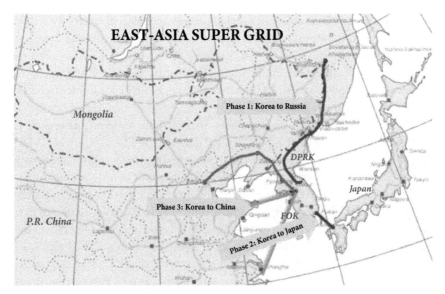

Figure 6.1 Interconnections to form a Northeast Asian super grid
Source: Adapted from KAPES website

reduction of energy costs, and the testing of core technologies from the use of renewable energy (RE) generators (Whang et al. 2018: 3). The long-term goal was to demonstrate the benefits to the private sector of using such a system—thereby encouraging investment in installing such systems in buildings across entire cities, to form the building blocks of 'Smart Cities' (more below) (Whang et al. 2018: 16). Launched in 2014, the project involved 39 SMEs and was aimed at developing an EMS capable of monitoring and controling RE resources (think solar modules, EV chargers, energy storage systems, and smart metering devices inside buildings). It also involved the development of hybrid power conversion systems (PCS). These systems convert stored (renewable) energy into electrical energy and vice versa—and as such constitute essential components of smart grids.

In 2014, KEPCO installed smart grid stations in 29 of its own offices and then in 2015, with a budget of USD 13.5 million, KEPCO launched a further 75 smart grid stations.[16] The projects demonstrated ten per cent reductions in power consumption (equalling ten GW) and five per cent cuts to peak demand (totalling four MW) for consumers. These reductions meant KEPCO was able to save USD 4.6 million in transmission, generation, and distribution costs as well as achieve five per cent reductions in CO_2 emissions. As of 2018, the system has been installed in 121 KEPCO-affiliated offices (Whang et al. 2018: 16).

---

[16] See 'KEPCO Smart Grid Station Project', *Global Smart Grid Federation Newsletter*, 6 July 2015, http://www.globalsmartgridfederation.org/2015/07/06/kepco-smart-grid-station-project/

In October 2015, KEPCO signed a USD three million construction project with the Dubai Electricity and Water Authority (DEWA) to pilot its smart grid station as part of national plans to turn Dubai into a Smart City by 2021.[17] The now completed KEPCO-designed smart grid station utilizes a 200 kW PV generator, a nine kW wind turbine, a 500 kW/H lithium-ion battery, a smart chiller system, and a 100-tonne thermal ESS (storing cooling energy).[18] The installation of 2,000 sensors monitoring power use and water demand provides real-time data to smart meters as part of an Internet-of-Things (IoT) platform. A building energy management system automates and manages electricity generated by the thermal cooling system and solar and wind generators.

These two projects—HVDC grids and Smart Grid Stations (in addition to the company's role in the Jeju Island Smart Grid project, Smart Grid Diffusion Project, and Island-based Microgrid project)—reveal genuine efforts on KEPCO's part to become a leading green innovator. At the same time, the further growth of these efforts into widely commercialized technologies in Korea (although evidently with greater success overseas) were hampered by the weak market for renewables in Korea. On this front, KEPCO has interestingly been one of the main stumbling blocks as we discuss below in Part Two.

Hybridized industrial ecosystems

A common trait in all of the projects discussed above is the existence of hybridized industrial ecosystems (HIEs)—a term which was coined to capture the organization of earlier Korean smart grid initiatives (Kim 2019; also see Chapter 4 for an extended discussion). Developmentally-oriented policymakers in government ministries such as the MOTIE and even officials in KEPCO have coordinated smart grid initiatives through creating a system of interactions between public and private actors involved in all segments of the production and innovation value chain. The MOTIE built a system of coordination involving government agencies such as the Korea Smart Grid Association and relied on large firms such as LSIS, Hyosung, LG CNS, and KT to help promote the creation of ecosystems of suppliers and co-innovators in smart grid technologies. The 2013 Smart Grid Distribution Project is another example of how MOTIE bureaucrats selected consortiums led by conglomerates to collaborate with SMEs including Kacon New Energy, Maru System, Wells Telesis, and Brenex to trial key smart grid technologies such

[17] See 'KEPCO to Build Smart Grid Systems in Dubai', *Business Korea*, 30 October 2015, http://www.businesskorea.co.kr/english/news/industry/12693-pilot-project-kepco-build-smart-grid-systems-dubai
[18] 'HH Sheikh Ahmed bin Saeed Al Maktoum inaugurates DEWA's Smart Grid Station in Al Ruwayyah', *Dubai Water and Electricity Authority*, 20 January 2019, https://www.dewa.gov.ae/en/about-us/media-publications/latest-news/2019/01/hh-sheikh-ahmed-bin-saeed-al-maktoum-inaugurates-dewas-smart-grid-station-in-al-ruwayyah

as energy storage systems. As mentioned above, KEPCO itself has pioneered the development of smart grid technologies such as UHV grids through HIEs involving 39 SMEs as part of the Smart Grid Station project. We discuss the extension of this development strategy in more recent initiatives over the construction of Smart Cities (more below).

The launch of Korea's smart grid initiatives—a key industry in the Low-Carbon, Green Growth strategy—led to many technological successes during the 2008–2016 period. As discussed in the previous section, President Lee's big bet on green growth was a direct response to new challenges in the external environment, all of which impacted Korea in unique ways. However, despite these efforts, Korea's attempts to commercialize smart grid technologies fell short of expectations and there was little change in the country's dependence on fossil fuels and nuclear energy. We make sense of this misalignment between creation and destruction in the following section.

Part Two: Misalignment between creative and destructive ambition and action in the 2008–2016 period

The official assessment of the second Five-Year Plan for Green Growth presented in the third FYPGG formulated by the Committee on Green Growth (CGG) (next section), highlights a number of notable achievements (CGG 2019b: 2). Korea established the institutions to adapt to climate change through national commitments contained in the Renewable Energy 3020 roadmap (*cf.* Kim 2021) and the national greenhouse gas (GHG) reduction target of 37 per cent by 2030 (compared to business-as-usual scenario) submitted to the UN in June 2015. The share of renewable energy generation apparently increased from 4.92 per cent in 2014 to 8.08 per cent in 2017 and there was growth in the use of EVs (from 1,075 in 2014 to 31,696 in 2018). The value of green industries in the country remained relatively consistent (KRW 107.9 trillion in 2014 to KRW 108.1 trillion in 2016).

However, the limitations of the second FYPGG were evident in a number of areas. To begin, while the supply of renewable energies may have increased, the underlying 'industrial ecosystem' remained weak—reflecting broader structural problems in Korea's *chaebol*-driven economy (CGG 2019b: 2). In particular, efforts to extend and deepen the green industrial value chain were hampered by the ongoing technological shortcomings of Korean SMEs; a problem that has long plagued the Korean economy.[19] At the same time, while Korean companies were powering ahead with the creation of new green technologies, the local uptake of those technologies was far more limited.

---

[19] See for example Park (2007).

As a consequence, total greenhouse gas emissions did not fall over the period in question, but in fact, *continued to increase* from 690.9 million tons CO_2eq. in 2014 to 694.1 in 2016.

To explain the shortcomings of the first phase of Korea's Low-Carbon, Green Growth strategy—especially the failure to get more renewables into the grid—it is important to examine KEPCO's complicated role in the country's green energy transition. On the one hand, as we have seen above, KEPCO had sought to reinvent itself as a green innovation leader. On the other hand, as we shall see below, KEPCO's virtual monopoly over the national electrical power grid system—and the entrenched governmental practice of power price capping through KEPCO—proved an impediment to the growth of the renewable energy market in Korea over the 2008–2016 period.

KEPCO as an obstacle to the growth of renewables[20]

As previously noted, KEPCO has long played a central role in Korea's rapid industrialization as a state-owned power provider enjoying quasi-monopoly status. Since the early 1960s, the company has stood at the centre of a tightly regulated power industry, and been charged with the task of providing abundant, reliable, and affordable electricity to households and businesses at artificially low prices capped by the government. The practice of price capping has long held an important developmental function, giving Korean firms a major cost advantage over foreign competitors (GGGI 2015: 88). Cheap electricity has also been politically popular with Korean households (as we discuss in further detail below). As such, even as Korea embarked upon its aggressive promotion of green energy industries over the 2008–2016 period, electricity prices were being kept at artificially low prices in global terms. For example, in 2013, according to data from the Korea Smart Grid Institute, electricity prices in Korea were half the average for OECD countries.[21] Korean power prices were even lower than the average in the shale-gas rich US (the US burns very little oil for power, so fracking's impact on electricity supply has primarily been via gas).[22] The unsurprising result of such a policy was the substantial increase in energy consumption by 56 per cent over the 2002–2010 period, or between three and four per cent a year, exceeding the rate of GDP growth, while the price of electricity grew by only 15 per cent (Global Green Growth Institute 2015: 338).

[20] The paragraphs in this section draw on Kim and Mathews (2016: 2–4).
[21] Standing at US six cents per kilowatt hour (c/kWh) for industry and eight c/kWh for domestic consumers, compared with 15 c/kWh for industry and 24 c/kWh for domestic consumers in Japan.
[22] In the US at that time, industrial consumers paid seven c/kWh and domestic consumers 11 c/kWh. The OECD average was 11 c/kWh for industrial consumers and 15 c/kWh for domestic consumers. See C. S. Jong, 'Smart grid in Korea', *IEA Conference, Bangkok*, 26 Nov 2013, www.iea.org/media/training/bangkoknov13/session_7c_ksgi_korea_smart_grids.pdf link does not work

The policy of keeping electricity prices low has long posed a barrier to regulatory reform in Korea.[23] During the period in question (2008–2016), it also had a major negative impact on KEPCO, which was burdened with increasing levels of debt (GGGI 2015: 88). This is because cheap electricity prices encouraged users to increase their energy usage, but at the same time, KEPCO was prevented from raising prices to reflect the actual (global) cost of energy. These financial constraints may also help to explain why KEPCO's generation of electricity from renewables has remained so small over the 2008–2015 period. Of the total 8,618 MW generation capacity utilizing renewable energy sources, privately-owned generators produced at 8,408 MW capacity. In other words, KEPCO's contribution to the generation of renewable energy was next-to-nothing. In these ways, the government's cap on electricity prices and its impact on KEPCO were key impediments to increasing renewable power generation in Korea during the period in question.

KEPCO's monopoly over the generation, distribution, and retail segments of the electricity industry also directly limited the growth of competitors providing renewable energy over the 2008–2016 period. Attempts since the early 2000s to introduce full competition through liberalization and privatization were only partially successful (Lee 2014: 117). For example, in 2001, control over the power market was granted to the non-profit body, Korea Power Exchange (KPX). The core function of KPX was (and remains) to oversee the bidding, metering, settlements, and monitoring of the electricity market. KPX is required to release market information on the volume and cost of electricity on a daily basis and then accept or decline power generation offers by KEPCO and the several private power generator companies. However, given KEPCO's monopoly over the retail aspect of the electricity industry (until at least 2016), KEPCO was KPX's sole buyer. Moreover, while KPX is legally an independent body, it is unclear just how impartial this agency is given that KEPCO and private power producers have permanent representation on KPX's executive board. For reasons such as these, while private companies were allowed to participate in the generation of electricity and were responsible for the majority of RE generation in Korea, by 2013 they had reached a mere five per cent share of total electricity generation (cf. Vagliasindi and Besant-Jones 2013: 196).[24]

The key point to note is that between 2008 and 2016, the 'destructive' aspects of Korea's smart grids strategy (i.e. efforts to phase out fossil fuels and nuclear energy) were limited, thanks largely to the government's developmental commitment to cheap and reliable electricity, and to KEPCO's central role in delivering on that commitment.

---

[23] See D. Kim, 'Cheap electricity backfires', *The Korea Times*, 30 June 2013, at: http://www.koreatimes.co.kr/www/news/nation/2013/06/328_138344.html
[24] See Vagliasindi and Besant-Jones (2013: 196).

Domestic political impediments to destruction of the fossil fuel energy system and KEPCO's role

Over the 2008–2016 period, intensifying levels of economic polarization also made it politically difficult—if not impossible—to drive any meaningful change in the nation's energy system—effectively ruling out the possibility of reforming electricity subsidies.[25] Income inequality is not a new phenomenon in Korea. It has, however, grown dramatically since the country's embroilment in the 1997 Asian Financial Crisis and continued an upward trend ever since (Koo 2021: 2–3). Long-time analyst of Korean politics Hagen Koo argues that the problem is not simply that inequality has grown since 1997 (2021:17). The more pressing issue has been the growing concentration of wealth at the top, which has coincided with a dramatic deepening of economic instability and insecurity among everyday working Koreans. The seriousness of this situation cannot be underestimated. Koo's analysis suggests that the composition of the so-called 'middle-class' (of which its existence and growth was central to the 'developmental citizenship' of post-war Korea, *cf.* Chang 2011) is undergoing profound changes where a small minority have benefited since 1997, while the quality of life for the majority has substantively deteriorated.

Koo is not alone; his conclusions are shared by many other Korea experts. From Choong-Yong Ahn's perspective, the post-war era of high growth and high employment is now a distant memory, replaced by extreme levels of economic uncertainty and socio-economic fragmentation. Indeed, the term 'Hell Choson' has become a popular phrase used by many younger demographics in the population, in part describing the seemingly perpetual cycle of limited economic opportunities for young people. Korea's rapidly ageing population, high levels of income inequality (especially between regular and non-regular workers), and disparities between occupations according to gender, have all contributed to the perception of Hell Choson. In terms of income inequality, the high paying, regular employment, and internationally *chaebol*-dominated parts of the economy can be contrasted against the significantly lower paying proliferation of non-regular contracts, and low productivity and international competitiveness of Korea's SMEs. Yet, SMEs are the largest source of employment in the country. In this context, therefore, it is unsurprising that Korea's 'creative' efforts were misaligned with 'destructive' efforts over the 2008 to 2016 period.

However, as we shall see in the next section, from 2017 onwards, a changing international environment and new domestic challenges have led to renewed efforts to achieve greater alignment between these two forces in Korea's smart grid strategy.

---

[25] Y. Choong, 'Rising inequalities in South Korea', *East Asia Forum*, 10 August 2016.

Part Three: Growing creative-destructive alignment
(2017—present)

When President Moon Jae-in assumed the presidential office in 2017, he faced a changed international environment stemming from heightened global competition over green technologies (especially from China). On the domestic political front, during his election campaign, Moon committed to responding urgently to the problem of significantly higher air pollution in recent years (caused by 'fine dust' particulates) believed by many to be caused by China's industrial cities and Korea's own coal-fired power generation plants, along with a growing reliance on diesel cars from 2000 onwards (see Chapter 4). The ongoing social problems caused by economic polarization evident in the 2008 to 2016 period also remained unresolved and exacerbated by the onset of the global pandemic in early 2020. This confluence of external and internal developments led the Moon administration to respond by redoubling the government's efforts to drive new technological advances and commercialization initiatives over smart grids. Even more interestingly, his administration was the first in the country's history to declare an 'energy transition' (Kim 2021), which would involve the reduced use of fossil fuels and nuclear energy while mandating significantly higher rates of renewable energy. We examine the Moon government's 'creative' and 'destructive' efforts below.

The new international competition in green technologies
and domestic environmental problems

From around 2015, international competition for green technologies had grown significantly with the entry of new players from Northeast Asia (NEA). This is most clearly evident in entry by key green technologies such as solar photovoltaic (PV) technologies. To briefly recall the discussion presented in Chapter 2, in 2010 the European market share for solar PV exports was 59 per cent and NEA's was 27 per cent (Figure 2.8, Chapter 2). But, by 2015, the tables were turned: the European countries' market share was reduced to 27 per cent and NEA's had risen to 47 per cent. By 2019, NEA cemented its lead even more, capturing 35 per cent of the global solar PV market while the share of the EU grew only slightly to 33 per cent. The largest player in NEA (and the world) is China, which averaged annual export values amounting to USD 25.6 billion from 2010 to 2019. This eclipses the figures for Japan (USD 4.7 billion) and Korea (USD 3.9 billion) during the same period. Even more startling are the figures for NEA's market share of solar PV production levels (Figure 2.7, Chapter 2). Since China surpassed the US in 1998, the country has dominated solar PV production to become the top producer in the region and the world. Taiwan is another important player in this market. The country's production exceeded that of the US in 2006 and the EU in 2010. By 2019, NEA's share of global solar PV production was 74 per cent.

This snapshot reveals the intensifying competition over green technologies and, of equal concern to Korean policymakers, China's dominance in the green technology industry. For Korean government officials, these conditions provided the impetus for the country to extend its technological autonomy—the long-recognized strategy of Korean catch-up efforts as seminal studies have documented (Mathews and Cho 2000; Lee and Lim 2001)—through driving innovation in green technological fields such as smart grids.

On the domestic front, since the early 2010s, everyday Koreans have contended with environmental problems at a very direct level. The country has experienced rising levels of air pollution. The problem is not simply 'smog' (which has become a permanent feature of Korean skies in the major industrial hubs of the nation e.g., Ulsan) but the blanketing of whole cities with 'fine dust' (*misae meonji*) particulates. For many, the blame lies with China's mega industrial coastal cities, sand from the deserts of Northern China and Mongolia, the use of high polluting vehicles, and Korea's own coal-fired power generation plants.[26] The air quality has deteriorated so much that an increasing number of people have reported the development of cancers and lung problems—caused by the carcinogens in the air (invisible nano particles known as PM2.5), which can penetrate deep into the respiratory system. According to the World Health Organization, 18,000 deaths are linked to high pollution levels in Korea each year. It is no surprise then that taking action against the problem of fine dust pollution was one of the pillars in President Moon's election campaign and his decision to categorize the problem of fine dust officially as a 'social disaster' in 2019.[27]

The Moon government's efforts to sustain Korea's technological leadership in the green technology industry and engage public calls to address pressing environmental problems, are reflected in the growing alignment between the 'creative' and 'destructive' priorities in the contents of the third FYPGG.

The creative and destructive elements of the third Five-Year Plan for Green Growth (2019–2023)

The third and current Five-Year Plan for Green Growth (FYPGG) (2019–2023) was finalized in May 2019 with the front cover of the official document denoting the term 'Green Growth 3.0'.[28] The third FYPGG emphasizes 'synergy between economic and environmental goals' through 'Inclusive Green Growth' (CGG 2019b: 3–4). The use of the term 'inclusive green growth' is a direct reference to

---

[26] L. Bicker, 'South Korea pollution: Is China the cause of "fine dust"?', *BBC News*, 6 June 2019, accessed 1 October 2021, https://www.bbc.com/news/world-asia-48346344

[27] 'Moon urges legal support for government's fight against fine dust', *Yonhap News Agency*, 3 December 2019, accessed 13 October 2021, https://en.yna.co.kr/view/AEN20191203005251315

[28] The terms Green Growth 1.0 and Green Growth 2.0 were coined by the former chairperson of the PCGG, Dr Soogil Young (2013). Dr Young first presented these terms in his speech entitled 'Korea's green growth: Looking back, looking forward' at the Global Green Growth Summit, held

the calls by international organizations such as the OECD (2012),[29] and the Asian Development Bank (ADB) (2018), with the latter's emphasis on 'social equity' and 'participation of a broad range of societal actors' (e.g., local civil society organizations) into the policy-making process over GG. In the words of the current chairperson of the CGG, Professor Kim JungWk, the overriding goal is to create a 'green society' (Kim 2021: 364).

There are five policy approaches in the third FYPGG (CGG 2019b: 4). The *first* is to implement *GHG reduction targets* especially through the Renewable Energy 3020 Roadmap i.e., to increase the share of electricity generated from renewables to 20 per cent by 2030. The *second* policy approach is to drive an *energy transition* in parallel with the decentralization of the energy system by enabling greater community participation. The *third* is the *development of green economy and industrial promotion* (more below). The *fourth* policy approach is *green land management* and the *fifth* concerns *international cooperation*, that is, through moving on from responding to the 2015 Paris Agreement to preparing for the 26th United Nations Climate Change Conference of the Parties (COP26) (held in late 2021).

To illuminate the government's efforts to address the growing competitive environment over renewables and the problem of fine dust, let us examine in detail the third and fourth policy approaches.

In terms of the development of a green economy and industrial promotion (third policy approach), the current FYPGG explicitly focuses on technologies to solve real-world social problems, such as fine dust particulates. This reflects an effort to *reframe* the R&D focus of earlier efforts i.e., the second FYPGG (a broad focus on 'green technology development in response to climate change') as 'the development and commercialization of convergent technologies combined with green innovations'. This group of technologies broadly refers to Artificial Intelligence, IoT, Cloud, Big Data and Mobile (AICBM) (CGG 2019b: 17). To this end, there are ten core technologies targeted for development by 2022, which fall under three categories: 1) carbon reduction (e.g., fuel cells, batteries), 2) carbon resource conversion (e.g., conversion of by-products of gas), and 3) climate change adaptation (e.g., predictive and monitoring capabilities). Importantly, the aim is to achieve the 'localization of core technologies and development of leading technologies' in newly emerging high-tech fields such as renewables-derived-hydrogen (CGG 2019a: 112–113).

---

at the Songdo Convensia, Incheon City, Korea, 10–11 June 2013. A link to the programme is available here: https://www.mofa.go.kr/www/brd/m_20152/down.do?brd_id=11642&seq=346843&data_tp=A&file_seq=1 [Accessed 12/7/22].

[29] The third FYPGG specifically refers to the OECD's 2018 Green Growth and Sustainable Development (GGSD) Forum on the theme of 'Inclusive solutions for the green transition: Competitiveness, jobs/skills and social dimensions'. See: 'Inclusive Growth for the Green Transition', *OECD*, November 2018, http://www.oecd.org/greengrowth/ggsd-2018/

As outlined in Chapter 4, the development of a local hydrogen industry—and indeed the creation of a Hydrogen Society—formed a central pillar of the Moon administration's greening plans. A focus on developing and significantly using renewable energy technologies like solar and wind to generate green hydrogen is viewed as an important step in reducing the problem of fine dust particles and rapidly reducing greenhouse gas emissions. Citing the *Hydrogen Economy Revitalisation Roadmap* (January, 2019) prepared by various ministries across the government, a shift to hydrogen is expected to result in a 17 per cent drop in GHG emissions by 2050 and a 30 per cent reduction in fine dust particles by 2050 (CGG 2019a: 113).

Another major R&D initiative under the third policy approach is to create 'green clusters' composed of demonstration sites to test new business models (CGG 2019a: 114). A total of nine strategic demonstration projects will be undertaken. These include: 1) Diversification of application sites for solar power generation; 2) Large-scale offshore wind power generation systems including fixed offshore wind power of five MW or higher, and the floating offshore of several MW; 3) Power grid stability systems through, for example, use of ESS; 4) Integration of distributed resources through the use of VPPs; 5) EV Vehicle-to-Grid (V2G) Operating Platform; 6) Energy 'harvesting' system for power supply of IoT smart sensors; 7) Large-scale gas turbine systems to support domestic power systems; 8) Facilities to reduce fine dust for 500MW standard coal-fired power plant substantiations; and 9) Commercialization of nuclear power reactor dismantling technologies.

How did these broader objectives in the third phase of Korea's Low-Carbon, Green Growth strategy impact smart grid promotion efforts? As will be seen below, the Korean government redoubled efforts to develop sophisticated smart grid technologies through a decentralized grid infrastructure (as opposed to China's large scale renewable generation sites linked up by UHV grids to major cities) and through efforts to reduce the use of fossil fuels and nuclear energy.

The Second Five-Year Master Plan for smart grids

As 2021 drew to a close, policymakers were focused on implementing the *Second Five-Year Master-Plan for the Intelligent Grid (2018–2022)* (MOTIE 2018) approved by the CGG. The official document examines the achievements of the earlier initiatives discussed above and carefully evaluates the national smart grid strategies in the EU, the US, and Japan (MOTIE 2018: 7–12). The Master Plan is explicitly focused on implementing President Moon Jae-in's stated vision of an 'energy transition'. This means expanding renewable energy markets and nurturing technological innovation through creating a power infrastructure, which is more *decentralized, digitalized, and electrified* (MOTIE 2018: 7, 13).

To operationalize the overall goal, the MOTIE's Second Master Plan articulates four main 'policy approaches' (MOTIE 2018: 13). The *first* policy approach is to activate new smart grid services by expanding new electricity pricing plans based for different seasons and use-by-hour, and the expansion of new electricity trading businesses based on new technologies related to the fusion of AICBM technologies (MOTIE 2018: 16). The *second* is to create 'Smart Grid Service Experience Complexes' by developing demonstrations of new service models such as *smart microgrids* for use in homes, campuses, offices (via energy management systems), and use of EVs as a source of energy for the power grid (i.e., cars-as-batteries) (via V2G) (MOTIE 2018: 19). The *third* policy approach is to further expand smart grid infrastructure and facilities by developing new power grid technologies through the conceiving of power grids as 'smart grid platforms' or technically referred to as 'extensible power grid management platforms with intelligence' (xGrids). This will also involve further deployment of key technologies such as 'Advanced Metering Infrastructure' (MOTIE 2018: 22). The *fourth and final* policy approach is to establish the institutional foundations to facilitate the expansion of smart grids. For example, strengthening the standardization of new technologies such as ESS and microgrids (MOTIE 2018: 25–29). In terms of the budget to advance these policy agendas, the government committed KRW 4.5 trillion (USD 3.8 billion) for investments between 2018–2022—representing an increase from the USD two billion budgeted under the First Master Plan (MOTIE 2018: 30).

Of course, the creation of high-quality jobs to address the pressing issue of economic inequality is implicit in the formulation of the development plans laid out in the third FYPGG and the Second Master Plan for Smart Grids discussed above. However, the government's job-creating and wealth-generating targets behind its LCGG strategy became explicitly clear in its response to the onset of the global COVID-19 pandemic in early 2020.

In July 2020, then president Moon announced the launch of a 'Green New Deal' as part of a larger 'Korean New Deal', which also involves a 'Digital New Deal' and the introduction of a 'Stronger (Social) Safety Net'. Moon's vision was to dramatically accelerate the country's green economic transformation already well underway. Like all countries, COVID-19 plunged the Korean economy into a severe economic recession, revealing the harsh impacts on the most vulnerable members of society. In April 2020, 392,000 more people were unemployed compared to a year earlier and exports dropped by 24 per cent in May 2020.[30] In response, President Moon committed to USD 135 billion investment in green and digital technology comprising USD 96.3 billion from the Treasury, USD 21.2 billion from local governments, and USD 17.3 billion from the private sector (MOEF

---

[30] M. Herh, 'COVID-19 Crisis Drags Down Auto Industry's Contribution to Korea's Exports', *BusinessKorea*, 8 June 2020, http://www.businesskorea.co.kr/news/articleView.html?idxno=47152; J-h. Choi, 'S. Korea suffers steepest job losses in 10 years amid pandemic', *The Korea Herald*, 10 June 2020, accessed 9 August 2020, http://www.koreaherald.com/view.php?ud=20200610000707

2020: 14–15). To attain tangible results quickly, the Korean New Deal involves ten key projects: Data Dam, AI Government, Smart Healthcare, Green and Smart Schools, Digital Twin, Digitalization of SOC (Social Overhead Capital), Smart and Green Industrial Complexes, Green Remodelling, Green Energy, and Eco-friendly Mobility of the Future (MOEF 2020: 46). The aim is to rapidly create 887,000 low-skilled and high-skilled jobs by 2022 and 1.9 million new jobs by 2025. While a deeper discussion of the targets and development plans under the Green New Deal is outside the scope of this chapter (due to space limitations), as we have argued elsewhere, the plan accelerates many of the targets set out in the third FYPGG and the Second Smart Grid Master Plan.[31]

The 'creative' and 'destructive' impact of these plans is already visible through ambitious plans to scale-up the technologies and systems developed in earlier national R&D programs through the creation of Smart Cities and reductions in the use of fossil fuels and nuclear energy.

Smart cities: National pilot smart cities

Korea is of course no stranger to the term 'Smart Cities'. The former Ministry of Information and Communication (MIC) in conjunction with the Ministry of Land, Infrastructure and Transport (MOLIT) had promoted the development of 'Ubiquitous Cities' (U-Cities) since the mid-2000s. While there are clearly similarities between the two concepts in terms of the application of ICT networks to the design, operation, and delivery of city services (e.g., water management), the current focus on Smart Cities carries with it a more explicit focus on customising such technologies to the needs of users or consumers (Lim et al. 2019: 5–6). The idea of Smart Cities emerged in the context of President Moon Jae-in's focus on a national 'energy transition' towards the use of *cleaner and greener energy sources*. As such, the application of ICT to energy networks is another major point of difference with the broader focus on utility services in the earlier concept of U-Cities.

In 2018 the Moon government launched the *National Strategic Smart City Program*. This project is coordinated by the MOLIT-affiliated Korea Agency for Infrastructure Technology Advancement (KAIA) with involvement by the Ministry of Science and ICT (MSIT). The public and private organizations involved in this project have focused on three core focus areas (Yang et al. 2021: 7198–7199). The first is the development of fundamental technologies for smart cities such as 'xEMS'—energy management systems for a wide range of applications such as commercial buildings, residential homes, and factories to enable the

---

[31] S. Kim et al. 'South Korea's Green New Deal shows the world what a smart economic recovery looks like', *The Conversation*, 9 September 2020, at: https://theconversation.com/south-koreas-green-new-deal-shows-the-world-what-a-smart-economic-recovery-looks-like-145032

monitoring and automation of energy production and usage (Yang et al. 2021: 7202). Technologies associated with xEMS such as AI and blockchain technologies are expected to enable the creation of energy trading and new energy markets. The second and third focus areas involve the test-bedding of these technologies and business models at two sites: Daegu City and Siheung City (Gyeonggi-do).

As one of his key initiatives to cope with the COVID-induced recession, President Moon focused on the construction of Smart Cities as one of the core focus areas in the 2020 Korean New Deal as a means to overcome the challenges of the COVID-19 induced recession.[32]

There are currently two major smart city projects being pursued under the *National Pilot Smart Cities* project: Sejong City and Busan City. While the MOLIT has taken the lead in the construction of the smart cities, the MOTIE, MSIT, and Ministry of the Interior and Safety (MOIS) are also intimately involved (Intralink Limited 2019).

Hybridized industrial ecosystems

In 2020, the MOLIT announced a tender for the construction of a smart city capable of gathering data and automating the operation of finance, traffic, safety, security, health, and energy services at Sejong 5-1 Neighbourhood (one of six neighbourhoods in the Sejong New Town development area).[33] Interestingly, the decision to appoint the 'Master Planner' for the Sejong Smart City was not determined by the MOLIT but by the 'Special Committee on Smart City' established under a government body personally chaired by President Moon known as the 'Presidential Committee on the Fourth Industrial Revolution' (PCFIR) (Choi and Kim 2020: 61). At the committee's determination, Professor Jaeseung Jeong, a neural networks expert based at Korea Advanced Institute of Science and Technology (KAIST) was appointed to lead the project. This somewhat surprising process was indicative of the technological nature of the goals driving the smart cities project. While there were many sectors targeted under the Sejong Smart City Project, approximately 88.5 per cent of the total budget has been planned to be invested into the application of ICTs including AI and Big Data to four core sectors: Mobility, Healthcare, Education, and Energy and the Environment.

A good example of the Energy and Environment initiatives in the *Sejong Smart City Project* (Choi and Kim 2020: 64–65). The aim is to create a self-sufficient and 'zero-energy' city connected through heat grids for a targeted population of 22,600 (equivalent to 9,000 households). Renewable energy generation facilities will be

---

[32] 'Opening Remarks by President Moon Jae-in at Presentation of Smart City Strategy Associated with Korean New Deal', *The Republic of Korea: Cheong Wa Dae*, 22 October 2020, accessed 23 February 2021, https://english1.president.go.kr/BriefingSpeeches/Economy/896

[33] Where some of the offices of ministries have been located since 2012 after President Roh Moohyun's failure to relocate the capital (Seoul) to Sejong City.

established on public buildings (including vertical solar panels), public roads, and 'energy trading' (selling excess electricity back to the grid) will be enabled through the use of virtual power plant technologies. Plans also included recharging facilities for EVs and hydrogen-powered FCEVs. A city-scale energy management system will be used to gather, analyse, and automate the supply, distribution, and consumption of energy—enough to cut energy consumption by up to 25 per cent per year.

In terms of how state officials have promoted Smart Cities, the Korean government opened a tender and two consortia submitted proposals to construct the Sejong Smart City. One consortium led by KT (Korea's largest telecommunication company) and Hyundai prioritized the development of autonomous vehicles through 5G networks and FCEVs. The other and winning consortium was led by LG CNS (a digital IT solutions company and subsidiary of the LG Corporation) and included the participation of LG U+, LG Electronics, KB Financial Group, Shinhan Financial Group, CJ OliveNetworks (an IT solutions company and subsidiary of the CJ conglomerate), and Naver Business Platform (Korea's largest Internet search engine provider).[34] The LG CNS-led consortium is expected to utilize its Smart City platform technologies (using AI, Big Data, and building-centred microgrids) gained from its participation in earlier national smart grid and U-City projects.[35] This massive project is set for completion in 2023 at a total cost of KRW 2.5 trillion (USD 2.2 billion). The company's expertise has been recognized in export markets such as Vietnam, where efforts to construct smart cities is attracting interest from Korean firms such as LG CNS.[36]

The second National Pilot Smart City will be constructed at Busan.[37] The project will be called the *Busan Eco Delta Smart City*, the main idea being to replace the district's use of fossil fuels for heating and cooling within buildings (catering to 3,380 households) with the storage and recovery of thermal energy through groundwater wells. In addition to testing hydrothermal energy systems, the smart city will also utilize AI and Big Data to monitor and automate the use, buying, and selling of energy. In December 2020, the MOLIT and its affiliate, the Korea Water Resources Corporation, awarded the contract to a consortium led by Hanhwa Energy (the 'Grand Consortium')—one of Korea's largest solar manufacturers and steam energy systems manufacturers. The project is expected to cost a total of USD 2.7 billion and a special purpose company (SPC) will be set up to establish and operate the Busan Eco Delta Smart City for at least

[34] W. Shim, 'South Korea's first-ever smart project soon to be in action', *The Korea Herald*, 2 October 2020, http://www.koreaherald.com/view.php?ud=20200928001014

[35] E. Kim, 'LG CNS to Lead Smart City Development in Sejong', *BusinessKorea*, 12 October 2020. http://www.businesskorea.co.kr/news/articleView.html?idxno=52991

[36] E. Kim, 'Vietnam Seeking to Atract LG CNS's Investment in Smart City Projects', *BusinessKorea*, 19 January 2021. http://www.businesskorea.co.kr/news/articleView.html?idxno=58780

[37] 'Selected as the preferred negotiator for national pilot smart city SPC contest in Busan', *Smart City Korea*, 1 December 2020, accessed 3 January 2021, https://smartcity.go.kr/en/

15 years (see Chapter 4 for a discussion of special purpose companies in Korea's greening strategies more broadly). The Grand Consortium involves more than 20 companies, including Hanwha Energy (leader), Hanwha General Insurance, NH Investment and Securities.[38] These large firms will collaborate with various SMEs including Naver Cloud, Daelim E&C, and RMS Consulting.[39] Plans are underway to establish an SPC composed of the Grand Consortium, the MOLIT, Busan Metropolitan City, Busan City Corporation, and the Korea Water Resources Corporation.

As we can see, the aim of the cross-governmental Smart Cities initiatives is to build innovation and industrial value chains of all the major public and private players in the ecosystem for smart cities, features aligned with the concept of hybridized industrial ecosystems (see the introductory chapter and Chapter 3 for a more detailed discussion).

Importantly for our purposes, these 'creative' endeavours have been met by an equal level of ambition to drive 'destructive' initiatives, and nowhere is this more evident that in the efforts to phase-out coal.

Destructive ambitions in action: Korea's efforts to phase out coal

In 2018, the provincial government of South Chungcheong (Chungnam Province) announced plans to exit the use of coal.[40] This was surprising because Chungnam represents some of Korea's largest coal assets (discussed below). Nevertheless, in October 2018, Chungnam became the first region in Asia to announce its intention to exit coal by 2050. Under its 2050 Energy Vision, the province will close 14 coal fired plants (18 GW of capacity) by 2026 and increase renewable energy from eight to 48 per cent of the local power mix. To guard against policy reversal, the Chungnam provincial government sought to link its domestic pledges to international commitments, officially joining the global Powering Past Coal Alliance (PPCA)—becoming the very first Asian jurisdiction to do so (Kang 2018). Chungnam is significant to the Moon administration's coal exit ambitions because Chungnam is home to 50 per cent (or 30/61) of Korea's coal-fired power plants, including the second and third largest plants in the world (Kang 2018). Chungnam's announcement coincided with the announcement by two of Korea's Pension

---

[38] C-w. Lim, 'Consortium led by Hanwha Energy selected for state project to build smart city in S. Korean port city', *Aju Business Daily*, 2 December 2020, accessed 23 February 2021, https://www.ajudaily.com/view/20201202103952221

[39] Other SMEs include Wins, Tirayutech, Geumgang Industrial, Data Alliance, Crocent, Jellyx, Detonic, Autonomous AXNUMXG, Cresfree, Atori Search, Radius Lab, Darae Park Tech, Clawbot, AST Holdings, Owner Information System, IDware, Vincen, GI Tech, ICT Way. See 'Selected as the preferred negotiator for National pilot smart city SPC contest in Busan', *Smart City Korea*, 1 December 2020, accessed 3 January 2021, https://smartcity.go.kr/en/

[40] This section draws on Thurbon et al. 2021.

Funds (Teachers Fund and Government Employees Pension Fund) that they would boycott any future coal financing.[41]

To explain this somewhat dramatic shift at the local level, one must consider the growing importance of civil society movements, and the growing responsiveness of local governments to their concerns. As noted above, President Park's decision to expand the number of coal-fired power stations elicited an unprecedented wave of public opposition, not least in Chungnam province. The primary concerns were environmental—terrible air quality was proving a major health risk to the community, and a major headache to the government. Sensitive to the political implications, the governor of Chungnam was responsive to this growing local discontent, lending his voice to locals arguing for the suspension of coal expansion plans. Kim Hongjang, the mayor of one of Chungnam's largest cities, Dangjin, even joined the 2016 hunger strike against the proposed coal plant in his region. The national government eventually suspended the coal plant in late 2016. The mayor's participation in the hunger strike was reported to have been crucial in the Park government's decision to suspend the plant indefinitely (Burton, 2016).

These efforts have been matched by efforts since 2019 to turn Chungnam into a fuel cell electric vehicle 'Mecca' (see Chapter 4) through construction (by a consortium of domestic firms) of what will be the world's largest hydrogen fuel cell power plant, and developing the FCEV parts and components industry under a dedicated five-year industrial development planning initiative. More recently, Governor Choi Moon-soon of Gangwon Province and Mayor Kwon Young-jin of Daegu City have also announced their intentions to close coal generation facilities in their jurisdictions. Following Chungnam's example, these two leaders also joined the PPCA in March 2021 as a sign of their commitments.[42]

Concluding remarks

The Korean government's approach to the promotion of smart grids provides an ideal case to examine the *sequencing* of the Korea's smart grids strategy ambitions, and the state's *evolving* 'creative' and 'destructive' capabilities. From 2008 to 2016, developmentally(-environmentally) oriented policymakers helped create new domestic capabilities in key smart grid technologies such as ESS, EMS, VPPs, and HVDC grids through a range of initiatives including by KEPCO itself (a point to which we return in our discussion of the paradoxical role of incumbents in Chapter 8). However, for all the achievements in Korea's 'creative' efforts, the

---

[41] J. Shin, 'Two Korean pension funds to boycott coal finance', *The Korea Herald*, 4 October 2018, http://www.koreaherald.com/view.php?ud=20181004000615

[42] 'South Korea's cities and provinces pave the way for faster coal phase-out', *Powering Past Coal Alliance*, 18 May 2021, https://www.poweringpastcoal.org/news/member-news/south-koreas-cities-and-provinces-pave-the-way-for-faster-coal-phase-out

commercialization of these technologies fell short of expectations. There was little, if any, meaningful growth in the use of renewables, and the high reliance on the use of fossil fuels and nuclear energy remained unchanged—and so too KEPCO's virtual monopoly at the centre of the energy system.

We have shown why the *misalignment* between the state's 'creative' and 'destructive' efforts was unsurprising. As the bedrock of the nation's rapid industrialization over the post-war era, KEPCO provided cheap (subsidized) and reliable access to energy for industry. The significant economic and social pressures facing Korea over the 2008–2016 period—not least growing levels of inequality—provided major political reasons to resist any changes to the dominant energy structure centred on the provision of cheap, fossil-fuelled electricity.

However, after Moon Jae-in assumed the presidency in 2017, we witnessed efforts at greater *alignment* between Korea's 'creative' and 'destructive' smart grid endeavours. As a response to heightening global competition over green technologies (especially China) and domestic political pressures to respond urgently to worsening environmental problems (i.e., fine dust particulates), Korean policymakers have redoubled their focus on developing and commercializing decentralized smart-microgrid communities integrating green energies. The post-COVID Green New Deal launched by Moon in July 2020 has helped to accelerate the targets set out earlier and to focus explicitly on addressing the nation's ongoing problem of economic inequality. The greater alignment between 'creation' and 'destruction' in the smart grid strategy is no more evident than that in the construction of National Pilot Smart Cities and the phasing out of fossil fuel generation facilities.

It is notable that all of the technology development initiatives discussed above have exhibited features of hybridized industrial ecosystems (Kim 2019). Developmentally-oriented policymakers in government ministries such as the MOTIE and sometimes officials in KEPCO have coordinated smart grid initiatives through creating a system of interactions between public and private actors involved in all segments of the production and innovation value chain. We revisit the role of HIEs when we discuss the institutional commonalities between Korea and China in Chapter 8.

In the next chapter, we examine China's 'strong' and smart grid initiatives, integrating large-scale renewable energy projects, which stand in contrast to Korea's 'smarter' and more decentralized quality of smart grid development and commercialization.

7

Creative-Destruction in China's Strong and Smart Grid Initiatives: The Shift to Ultra-High Voltage

> UHV tech has become a symbol of Chinese innovation.
>
> (Liu Zhenya, ex-chairman of State Grid Corporation of China, speaking at Harvard University, April 2018)[1]

The pattern

In the early 2000s, China's electric power system was well on the way to becoming the largest coal-burning system on the planet, serving as the engine of China's fast growing manufacturing system. But the larger the system grew, through steady incremental expansion year on year, the more pressure this placed on China's fossil fuel imports (particularly coal), and on the rail system for transporting the coal needed from eastern seaboard ports to inland power stations. That the system was reaching its limits was evident in the growing number of blackouts and brownouts (i.e., partial electricity outages), which impacted severely on China's industrial economy.

At this point, in December 2004, a remarkable meeting took place between Mr Liu Zhenya, newly appointed head of the State Grid Corporation of China (SGCC) and Mr Ma Kai, cabinet member with responsibility for the National Development and Reform Commission (NDRC). The two men found themselves sharing a car ride, during which they launched straight into a discussion of China's power difficulties and powering the anticipated expansion of the electric power grid. Ma Kai explained that the NDRC was facing the challenge of preventing blackouts and brownouts, while tackling the problem of transporting coal to more and more distant points for power generation. Liu seized the opportunity to canvass ultra-high voltage (UHV) grid technology as a novel solution—enabling China to generate power in distant western regions, largely from renewable sources, and transmit the

---

[1] See report on speech: C. Simon, 'Harvard talk outlines plan for global energy sharing', *The Harvard Gazette*, 19 April 2021, https://news.harvard.edu/gazette/story/2018/04/harvard-talk-outlines-plan-for-global-energy-sharing/

Developmental Environmentalism. Elizabeth Thurbon et al., Oxford University Press. © Elizabeth Thurbon, Sung-Young Kim, Hao Tan, and John Mathews (2023). DOI: 10.1093/oso/9780192897794.003.0007

power with minimal losses to the load centres on the eastern seaboard. This argument was accepted, and an understanding was thereby created which has served China well.[2]

Liu Zhenya had been newly appointed to the position of CEO of State Grid Corporation of China, China's largest utility, in October 2004, succeeding the previous CEO when he retired. He had followed an illustrious career through the electric power industry in China. Having captured the attention of the NDRC, Liu then embarked on a rapid process of converting SGCC in pursuit of UHV technology. In early 2005 a series of conferences were staged, bringing national and international experts together to explore the technical and economic options involved in China's leapfrogging to UHV technology. Bear in mind that there were no commercial UHV power lines operating at this time, anywhere in the world. Japan had some experimental lines operating at 500 kV, but nowhere were lines at 1,000 kV AC or 800 kV DC operating commercially. Yet this is the technology frontier that Liu and SGCC tackled directly.

An important victory for the strategy was the naming of UHV as a target technology for Chinese leadership in the 2006 *Medium to Long-Term Plan for Science and Technology* (MLP for S&T) launched by the NDRC as a means of lifting China beyond mere imitation to indigenous technological innovation.[3] This was to be achieved largely through raising R&D levels across the board and focusing on certain key projects like hydroelectric dams, high-speed rail (HSR), and UHV power grids.

Flash-forward to the early 2020s and China has now leapfrogged to world leadership in installing UHV grid technology. As a state entrepreneur, SGCC has invested more than USD one trillion in the UHV grid and in the process has surged beyond even advanced regions in the US, the EU, and Japan, in building homegrown equipment value chains (or what we call hybridized industrial ecosystems (HIEs)) to produce the capital equipment involved. While the technology was first utilized by Swiss-Swedish power company ABB and German giant Siemens, it is China that has adopted and adapted the technology and now built a twenty-first century grid with its own indigenous technology, designed according to its own standards.

Debate in China turned on the question as to whether the UHV grid could provide an essential complement to the rising levels of power generated from renewable sources; without the grid upgrading, much of this power generated from renewable sources would remain unused (disconnected from the grid)— a phenomenon called *curtailment*. Critics of China's greening have cited rising

---

[2] For the cab ride story, see Xu (2016), and for further elaboration on China's UHV strategy, Xu (2019).

[3] For commentary at the time, see Cao et al. (2006).

curtailment levels as 'proof' that China is not serious in its greening efforts. But they ignore the enormous efforts being expended to upgrade the grid to UHV technology standards, and the impact these efforts are having in raising the capacity of the grid to carry higher and higher levels of renewable power, with consequent effects of reducing curtailment and in reducing carbon emissions.

The critics also ignore the government's intensifying efforts to green both the UHV grid and China's existing grids by setting more and more aggressive renewable energy acquisition targets for regional and national grid firms. As we demonstrate below, these fossil fuel phase-out targets initially lagged behind the government's ambitious 'strong and smart' grid-building efforts. But in recent years, the government has been ramping up its coal (and to some extent gas) displacement efforts through both general and specific policy measures. These include China's ambitious *Net zero by 2060* goal, announced in 2020, and its announcement in 2021 of a minimum 40 per cent renewables target by 2030 for all regional grid firms.[4] When coupled with the aggressive coal-exit policies of some of the country's largest coal producing local governments, it is clear that China's pattern of progress towards greening its grid systems is rapidly evolving: its ambitious 'strong and smart' grid-building initiatives are increasingly being matched by actions to rid the grid of fossil fuels.

The puzzle

In this chapter we examine China's efforts to build an electric power grid capable of powering the world's largest manufacturing system, with the emphasis initially on utilization of fossil fuels (as in all previous cases of industrialization) then moving to the 'creative' side of 'creative-destruction' (CD) in building new power sectors based on renewables and electric storage and hyper-modern grids, and now culminating in the 'destructive' side of CD as the fossil fuel power system is progressively phased back and dismantled, to make way for the green energy transition (GET). Along the way we observe how China has moved from being a latecomer engaged in catch-up to becoming an innovator in driving new levels of grid operation and new possibilities of grid interconnections, in what Liu Zhenya, driver of China's grid strategy, describes in his Harvard University talk in 2018 as a symbol of China's innovation.

China's 'strong and smart' grid initiatives need to be examined in the context of the state's emerging developmental-environmental orientation, and relatedly its

---

[4] M. Xu and D. Stanway, 'China plans to raise minimum renewable power purchase to 40% by 2030: government document', *Reuters*, 10 February 2021, https://www.reuters.com/article/us-china-climatechange-renewables-idUSKBN2AA0BA

evolving 'creative' and 'destructive' ambitions and capabilities. We will demonstrate that China's use of the state as economic driver far exceeds levels found in other jurisdictions, demanding an answer that might resolve this anomaly. We ask: What has motivated the Chinese state to become so involved in 'strong and smart' grid industry creation initiatives, especially in the UHV grid arena? How have Chinese policymakers pursued their 'creative' ambitions? Why has the government appeared more ambitious and active in 'strong and smart' grid industry creation than in getting fossil fuels out of the energy system more broadly (e.g., by mandating the deployment of renewables in the grid, or by setting firm goals for fossil fuel exit?) To what extent is this 'creative-destructive' misalignment now resolving? What factors are driving this realignment, and what obstacles to a fully green shift remain?

As in our previous cases, we examine the evolution of China's 'strong and smart' grid strategy in a linear temporal fashion, allowing us to highlight the emergent developmental-environmental ambitions informing that strategy, and to demonstrate and explain the varying degrees of alignment between the state's creative and destructive ambitions and capabilities from the mid-2000s to the present. However, it is important to preface our analysis with an examination of China's overall electrification strategy, which locates the electric power grid as a key instrument of modernization and industrialization, and the locus for China's major greening efforts.

China's electrification strategy

As a latecomer to industrialization, China has been able to seize latecomer advantages which enable the country to avoid the steps followed by the industrial pioneers. Whereas the early movers powered their industrial efforts with fossil fuels (FFs)—starting with coal in the nineteenth century and then moving to oil and gas in the twentieth century—the latecomers are able to build energy systems that utilize rising levels of electric power, drastically raising these levels as a matter of industrial policy. As shown in Figure 7.1, China's reliance on electrification as a source of energy rather than direct consumption of FFs has increased steadily in the twenty-first century, with China overtaking the level of electrification found in the US and the EU (a level of 16 per cent) in 2015, and then catching up with the Japanese level (just over 18 per cent) by 2019, reaching 18.6 per cent in 2020. Thus, we have seen China starting the new century with relatively low levels of electrification but raising these levels through a latecomer strategy to approach the highest level in the world—approximately 20 per cent—by the year 2020. The higher levels of electrification in China means that the Chinese grid can be utilized as an instrument of greening, via both the generation aspects of grid operation and upgrading the transmission and distribution aspects of the grid, via the leapfrog to UHV.

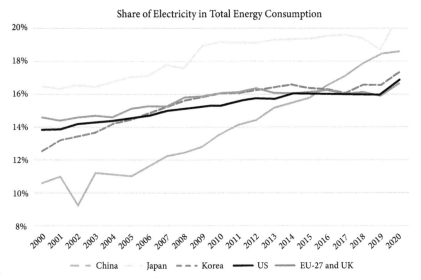

Figure 7.1 Share of electricity in total energy consumption, China, EU, US, Japan, 2000–2020

Data source: BP Statistical Review of World Energy

Through the early years of the twenty-first century, China was building an enormous electric power system to feed its enormous manufacturing system, now recognized as being the largest in the world. In terms of electric capacity, China's power grid has grown to exceed two trillion watts (TW) as compared with just over one TW for the US. In terms of electric energy generated, China reached over 7,780 billion kWh (or TWh) in 2020, almost doubling its output in the course of the past decade, as compared with the level generated in the US of just over 4,000 TWh.[5]

This enormous electric power grid is part of China's ambitious strategy to electrify its economy with a steadily rising contribution coming from green sources. The burning of coal in industry and the burning of oil in transport is anticipated to be superseded by the use of electric power in China's industry, transport, and in the power sector itself. And along with building the world's largest grid, China is leapfrogging to the lead in modernizing and updating the grid, from very high voltage (VHV) to ultra-high voltage status—earlier than any other country or region. So, while the EU is engaged in discussions on building a European high-voltage direct current (HVDC) grid, China has gone to the next level and is actually building a UHV grid, in both ultra-high voltage alternating-current (UHV-AC) and

---

[5] See: 'BP Statistical Review of world energy 2021', *BP*, July 2021, bp.com/content/dam/bp/business-sites/en/global/corporate/pdfs/energy-economics/statistical-review/bp-stats-review-2021-full-report.pdf; On the development and performance of China's power grid, see Mathews (2017b) and Mathews and Huang (2020).

ultra-high voltage direct-current (UHV-DC) versions. The aim is to create a grid that can carry vast amounts of electric power over vast distances, thus reducing the need for physical transport of oil, coal, and gas and raising the prospects for growing reliance on renewable sources of power generated in distant parts of the country. The UHV grid thus represents a fundamental technological advance for China's industrialization and electrification strategy, and one where traditional means of technological advancement such as 'forced borrowing'[6] are declining in favour of China's own technological innovation.

We will now review the development of China's 'strong and smart' grid through three distinct phases. In Part One we cover the first phase (the 1990s to the early 2000s), when traditional fossil-fuelled industrialization was pursued according to a traditional developmental logic, and tensions arising from growing fossil fuel use started to manifest themselves. In Part Two we examine the second phase (from the mid-2000s to mid-2010s) in which the state's emergent developmental-environmental ambitions became manifest in initiatives centred on both generation of power (a shift to renewables) and its distribution (the introduction of UHV). In Part Three, we examine the third and current phase (mid-2010s to the present) in which creative initiatives are now starting to be balanced by destructive initiatives aimed at the phase-out of coal and fossil fuels.

Part One: The developmental origins of China's 'strong and smart' grid focus (1990s–2006)

China's electric power grid is the backbone of the country's industrial develop-ment, with electrification as its central developmental driver. There have been twin aspects of China's grid development—its generation side (swinging from fossil fuels to renewables and battery energy storage) and its transmission side (leapfrogging from VHV to UHV in the second decade of the twenty-first century). As noted, we break the implementation of the greening of power generation into three phases—the initial push based on FFs, then the introduction of green sources of power, and finally the progressive destruction of the coal-burning infrastructure to complement the phasing in of green elements.

Manufacturing started up in a big way after the Tiananmen Square 'incident' of 1989, with energy production rising rapidly thereafter—indicating that the China leadership had made a clear choice between enhancing wealth generation and democratization. Wealth generation, via manufacturing at enormous scale, was to be given priority. The ramp-up in power generation was driven (as in all previ-ous cases of industrialization in Northeast Asia (NEA)) by fossil fuels. In the case

---

[6] 'Forced borrowing' refers to the practice of requiring foreign firms to transfer their technologies to Chinese firms as a condition of market entry.

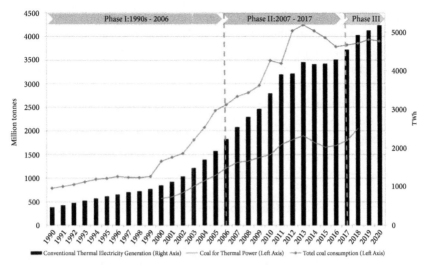

Figure 7.2 Coal power generation and consumption in China, three phases, 1990–2020

Data Source: CEC, NBS, and *BP Statistical Review of World Energy*

of the electric power grid, the FF of choice was coal. This created China's 'black' energy system, as shown in the first phase of Figure 7.2 (we discuss Phases Two and Three below).

Figure 7.2 reveals how China's electric power capacity rose steadily through the 1990s, fuelled by coal consumption. It really took off in 2001, the inflection point where China joined the WTO. This full-tilt, fossil-fuelled industrialization continued through the first decade of the twenty-first century, marked by successive Five-Year Plans (FYP) (tenth FYP 2001–2005; eleventh FYP 2006–2010) where rising targets set for power generation were successively exceeded. The central government set the growth targets, and the provincial governments then engaged in a series of 'industrial developmental' policies and strategies, learning from the prior success of the Northeast Asian economies—Japan, Korea, and Taiwan. Our interest lies in how this conventional developmental strategy was transformed into a developmental-environmental strategy, once problems with the conventional fossil-fuelled strategy started to emerge, in what we are describing as Phase Two of the transformation of China's electric power grid.

Part Two: Developmental-environmentalism and the emergent greening of China's electric power grid (2007–2015)

The full-tilt rush to fossil-fuelled industrialization that was reaching its zenith in the first decade of the twenty-first century was creating wealth, certainly—but also enormous problems for China. There were obvious physical environmental problems as the cities choked on particulate pollution from coal burning as well as the pollution smog from burning oil in transport vehicles. It was becoming clear that urban pollution could reach such dangerous levels that the public reaction could threaten the regime's legitimacy. There were also obstacles created by the scale of China's industrialization that called into question China's capacity to scour the world for the resources needed by its industrialization push. These are what we might call the *geopolitical limits* to China's growth—meaning obstacles encountered such as wars, revolutions, and revolts, as well as rising prices and supply shortages—as China's imports from exporting countries rose to unsustainable levels.

Visionaries pointed to these as problems endemic to fossil-fuelled industrialization and were calling for a fresh start with green power. The noted commentator Dr Hu Angang published an influential two-part essay in 2006 entitled 'Green development: The inevitable choice for China' (*China Dialogue*), where he developed an original argument that at China's scale of industrialization it would face insuperable obstacles if it continued with fossil-fuelled development. His arguments were echoed by the Chinese leadership. The Minister for Environmental Protection, Li Ganjie, went on the record in 2006 in Beijing stating that 'green development is an inevitable choice for China'—inevitable, meaning unavoidable.[7]

With its authoritarian governance structure, China was able to introduce green elements of its power system quickly and thoroughly. The build-up of wind power started in the middle of the first decade of the twenty-first century, and rose rapidly, doubling every two to three years—as shown in Figure 7.3. China was in this way demonstrating its capacity to introduce 'creative' initiatives in its green power transition.

We can also see the same green shift at work in the proportion of electric power sourced from renewable sources—from wind, solar, and hydro (water) (WWS). Figure 7.4 shows how the shift to WWS sources of electric power increased without interruption from 2007 onwards—right through to the present. This is our strongest evidence for the greening of China's electric power generation—an important aspect of the greening and modernization of the grid.

In terms of actual electricity generated, Figure 7.4 reveals that the proportion of electricity generated from WWS sources rose from 15 per cent in 2007 to 27 per cent in 2020, or a 12 per cent green shift in 13 years.[8] This greening of the electric power system has been fuelled by successive Five-Year Plans, with notable contributions made by the twelfth FYP (2011–2015) and the thirteenth FYP (2016–2020). Here the emphasis has been very much on the 'creative' side of

---

[7] See discussion of comparable arguments in Chapter 3, on the transition in China to an 'ecological civilization' strategy.

[8] The reason that the green shift is less pronounced in electricity generation is that the levels of generating efficiency vary across solar, wind, and hydro sources.

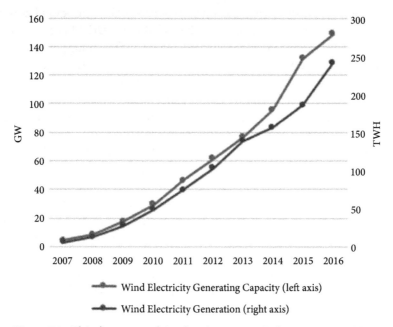

Figure 7.3 China's green push in electric power: wind energy, 2007–2016

Source of primary data: China Electricity Council

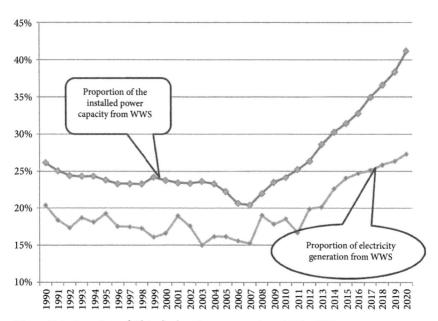

Figure 7.4 Greening of China's electric power system, 1990–2020

Data source: CEC and NBS China

'creative-destruction', that is, emphasizing new sources of electric power like wind and solar, and new means of engineering the grid, through UHV, in order to overcome problems like curtailment and accommodation of fluctuating power sources. The more that China built reliance on renewable sources of electrical energy, the more it became apparent that this would be consistent with an overall drive to electrify the economy (industry, transport, urban infrastructure) and would drive down costs, as China accelerated its own innovation efforts in hyper-modernizing the grid.

We locate China's intense interest in creating 'strong and smart' grids in growing concerns about the nation's energy security that emerged around the turn of the century—and of the implications of that energy insecurity for the viability of China's traditional developmental model. As in Korea, that model had been built on a fossil-fuelled, fast-follower industrialization strategy. And thanks to that strategy, by the early 2000s, China had emerged as a potential global competitor in a range of traditional manufacturing industries such as steel, automotive production, and chemicals. China's entry to the WTO in 2001 promised to lend new momentum to China's fossil-fuelled growth trajectory by dramatically expanding China's access to foreign capital and overseas markets—but at growing environmental costs.

It was becoming increasingly apparent that China's massive export-oriented manufacturing system was fast outgrowing the fossil-fuelled energy system upon which it ultimately depended. The manufacturing industry faced successive brownouts and blackouts, which acted to curtail output and reduce both domestic and export supplies. We point to the rising dependence on imports of materials from countries outside China, such as new sources of supply of oil from African countries or supplies of iron ore from Brazil. The growing levels of dependence on such unstable sources of materials we refer to as *geopolitical limits* to conventional, fossil-fuelled industrialization. An alternative pathway increasingly became identified as a strategic necessity.

Taken together, these factors led the Chinese government to embrace electrification as a national development strategy in the early 2000s. The scope of its ambitions, and its electrification compared with other global industrial powers, is shown in Figure 7.1 above. China has been expanding its electrical power system as a proportion of its total energy consumption, substituting electrical energy for direct combustion of fossil fuels (coal, oil, gas) in industry, transport, domestic, and other sectors as well. At the dawn of the 2020s, China stands alone in the proportion of its energy consumption supplied by electrical power. And importantly for our purposes, this level of electrification makes China the most open to greening through the contribution of power sourced from water, wind, and sun.[9]

---

[9] Another indication is 'Access to electricity (per cent of population)'. According to the data of World Bank, Japan, the US and the EU-28 had all achieved 100 per cent by 2000. China caught up from 96.91 per cent in 2000 to 100 per cent by 2013.

Indeed, it was at this time—in the early 2000s—that China began to ramp up its investments in renewables—as shown in Figures 7.3 and 7.4—but there was no real effort to insist upon renewable energy uptake (e.g., no mandated targets). It was not until after the global financial crisis (GFC) in 2008 when China really began to increase investments in renewable energies (as in Korea). But as China ramped up its building of renewables, at a scale never before attempted by other industrializing powers, so it faced obstacles and hurdles not encountered in other jurisdictions. Chief amongst these was the hyper-modernization of the electric power grid, to enable it to carry increasing quantities of renewable electric power to enhance its overall national energy security. This meant creating a power grid that could reduce levels of curtailment and could carry increasing levels of electric energy from the western sources of renewable generation to the eastern seaboard cities where consumption was focused. This entailed the shift to UHV.

The shift to a UHV grid

China has been leapfrogging the rest of the world in building both a 'strong and smart' grid as a principal nation-building project over the decade from 2010 to 2020. Such a grid is needed to carry the 7,000-plus billion kWh of electricity across the country, thereby displacing the transport of coal by rail to traditional sites where power is generated, and enabling the grid to accept rising levels of intermittent, renewable power generation. UHV-DC promises to enable China to carry enormous electricity loads the very great distances from western generation sources to eastern seaboard load centres, with minimal power losses. The UHV transmission lines will enable China to accept the rising levels of solar and wind power generation into the grid, and thereby reduce the curtailment levels that have constrained renewable power development.

The idea of creating a UHV grid formed a core part of the government's response to its growing energy security challenges—and the centrepiece of its national electrification strategy. The UHV grid would help solve a critical problem for China: the constraints of its rail-reliant energy system. One of the principal reasons driving the decision to embark on a massive UHV strategy on the part of China's leadership (in this case the NDRC and top management at SGCC) was to avoid having to ship huge quantities of coal across the country by rail to existing power stations located in the west. The upgraded grid instead allowed for generation of power from wind and sun in the western provinces and its transmission across the country along the UHV-AC and UHV-DC transmission lines, eliminating the need for rail transport of coal as well as enhancing prospects for generation of green electric power and its distribution.

The decision to embrace UHV must also be understood as an expression of China's evolving developmental strategy with growing emphasis on an environmental form of developmentalism (DE). As noted earlier, China's traditional fast-follower strategy had depended largely on technological imitation—and the aim was to 'catch up' with the leaders of the pack. But from the mid-2000s, China's ambitions changed. China's leaders were not satisfied with following behind—they wanted to overtake—to 'leapfrog' their competitors.

Economic and industrial catch-up has been the subject of intense scholarly endeavour ever since Japan achieved the first industrial breakthrough by a non-western country, followed by other Northeast Asian industrial success stories such as Korea and Taiwan. All these cases have brought attention to the role of state agencies interacting with private firms in facilitating technological learning and the acquisition of dynamic technological capabilities. Technological catch-up has been the focus, with cases like semiconductors, personal computers (PCs), and other ICT sectors, automotive, steel, and petrochemical all being subject to study. Then as the NEA countries consolidated their positions, and thrived in some sectors like flat panel displays (FPDs) and digital switches, while trailing in others like automobiles or PCs, the differences between learning as a catch-up process and learning as a leapfrogging strategy came to the fore, with studies in Korea, Taiwan, and Singapore again emphasizing these various strategies and their contingencies.[10]

Now in the twenty-first century, it is the turn of newly emerging industrial giants, led by China but also involving India and others eventually, like Brazil. These emerging giants are taking over all the acquired learning and strategies perfected by the prior firms and agencies in the NEA newly industrializing economies (NIEs), and doing so at enormous scale—becoming world-dominant competitors in many of the commoditizing sectors.[11] In an important article in *Sloan Management Review* (SMR), Willy Shih discusses how Chinese firms have learnt not only to catch-up with market leaders but leapfrog to the lead in one sector after another as they drive commoditization in the ICT industries.[12] China's adoption of a leapfrogging strategy in the case of its electric power grid and high-speed rail transport systems are signal cases of this strategy being put to work.

[10] The literature on leapfrogging as a development strategy can be traced to Soete and Perez (1988) and Amsden and Hikino (1994), the latter scholars pointing to the experience of the nineteenth century where leading American and German firms were able not just to catch-up with then leaders but leapfrog ahead of them. In more recent scholarship on the NIEs, Lee and Lim (2001) use the examples of six industries in Korea to discuss successful cases of 'stage-skipping' or leapfrogging strategies, particularly in the ICT and code-division multiple access (CDMA) industries. Early efforts to apply these insights to China can be found in the work of Wu and Zhang (2010) where three case studies of Chinese firms pursuing 'stage-skipping' strategies are discussed.

[11] The literature on China's 'catch-up and forging ahead' strategies, with a focus on technological leapfrogging (e.g., through development of homegrown standards) is now abundant. For prominent contributions, see Breznitz and Murphree (2013); Gao (2013; 2019); Wu and Zhang (2010).

[12] See Shih (2018).

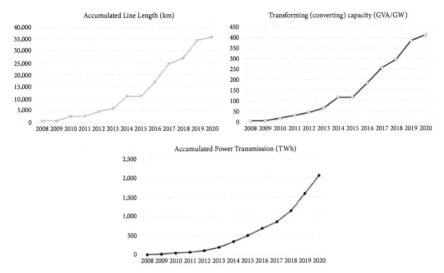

Figure 7.5 Progressive extension of China's UHV grid, 2008–2020
Source: Authors (based on SGCC website)

Executing the UHV strategic shift

So how did Chinese policymakers go about executing their 'creative' ambitions? As noted, from the outset China's UHV initiatives have been led by State Grid. At the beginning of 2005, the State Grid Corporation of China embarked on a major strategic entrepreneurial shift. This was the time when Liu Zhenya, newly appointed CEO of SGCC, had his famous cab ride with Ma Kai, minister in charge of the NDRC—as recounted above. Under the state entrepreneurial guidance of SGCC, the strategy of upgrading China's grid by leapfrogging to UHV status (in advance of the rest of the world) was supported and promoted strongly. The outcome was rapid growth in the extent of the UHV grid, as shown in Figure 7.5.

Part Three: Growing creative-destructive alignment (2015—present)

China's early years of greening, starting in the first decade of the twenty-first century, were characterized by innovations in power generation favouring renewable sources like wind and solar and grid upgrading to reduce curtailment, such as UHV transmission. These are what we call the 'creative' side of creative destruction. But as the greening trends became more secure, so the destruction of fossil fuel dependence started to be asserted. The building of coal-fired power was scaled back, as caps were placed on coal dependence. Here it was provincial governments that took the lead in reducing their coal dependence while allowing renewable sources of electric power to be scaled up.

China's build-up of coal-fired power means that it has an enormous problem in scaling back and winding down the use of coal as the swing to renewables gathers pace. Figure 7.2 above on the coal-fired power system, updated to 2020, reveals just how enormous it continues to be. The coal-fired plants generated 5,174 TWh power in 2020 (twice the level of the US), while total coal consumption is estimated to have dropped 0.8 per cent down to 3.9 billion tons in 2020.[13] The 'cap' on coal of four gigatonnes (billion tonnes, Gt) appears to be holding, more or less.

Figure 7.2 above reveals how China's scaling back of coal-fired power starts in the second decade of the twenty-first century. Coal consumption is capped at four billion tonnes per year. The chart reveals that serious efforts have been made in flattening the rise of coal-fired dependence, with a flattening of the growth curve registering from 2012/13, and the cap keeping coal consumption within a four Gt limit (with a small blip exceeding four Gt in 2012–14 and another in 2019/20). This chart bears witness to the monumental struggle waged in China against coal dependence—a struggle that is in many ways much harder to exercise than the creation of new green sources of both power generation and transmission.

It is at the provincial levels that the drive by China to dismantle the coal-fired power grid comes into sharpest focus, as in the case of South Korea (see Chapter 6). Take the case of the southern province of Guangdong, which we have examined and analysed.[14] Overall in China, fossil fuel use in power generation has declined from 79 per cent in 2010 to about 70 per cent in 2019—or nearly a ten per cent decline in a decade. But in Guangdong, home to major cities like Guangzhou (formerly Canton), the share of fossil fuels in power generation has dropped from 77 per cent in 2010 to 48 per cent in 2019—or a 29 per cent decline in a decade (Tan et al. 2021). It is the provincial government that has taken the lead in driving this shift, through a mix of 'carrots'—incentives for introducing green power sources—and 'sticks'—penalties for continued FF usage (as discussed in Chapter 2).

In the same Guangdong study, we reported both push and pull market-based mechanisms deployed by the provincial government and Guangzhou city government. The push mechanisms included rezoning of land used for power generation and imposing structural caps on further coal-burning by power plant operators. The pull mechanisms included 'smart' strategies making use of the improved valuation of land occupied by power station operators, and offering to redevelop this land jointly with the operators, sharing the profits. These are sophisticated market-based mechanisms deployed in China that are virtually unknown elsewhere, and

---

[13] See '2021 National Coal Trade Fair: How to make a steady start?', *Xinjiang Coal Exchange Center*, 24 January 2021, https://www.xjcec.com/c/2020-12-24/523565.shtml

[14] See Tan et al. (2021).

which depend on close relations between state-owned and private companies—or hybrid institutions. We capture this term in our discussion of hybridized industrial ecosystems below.

While these exercises in the 'destructive' aspects of 'creative-destruction' of the Chinese power grid have come to occupy centre stage, the shift to UHV as a 'creative' initiative has continued at a rapid pace to make the grid 'strong' as well as enhancing its 'smart' or IT-enabled aspects. The extent of the UHV power grid by 2020 is shown in Figure 7.6.

State Grid switched on its first UHV-AC power line in 2009 (operating at million-plus volts) and its first 800 kV DC line in 2010. These were experimental projects, designed to prove to SGCC senior management and to the Chinese leadership that UHV was a viable technology. After a great deal of debate over the merits or otherwise of UHV technology (and associated suspicions of SGCC's ambitions) the State Council finally gave full approval for a UHV national grid in April 2014. The principal obstacle to such a development was the uncertainty over the capacity and reliability of Chinese developed UHV technology—an obstacle that only a state-owned corporation like SGCC could overcome through its investments and R&D and project development capacities. Implementation of the UHV grid shift proceeded rapidly after 2015.[15] There followed what chairman Liu Zhenya described as a 'golden era' for Chinese UHV technology development,

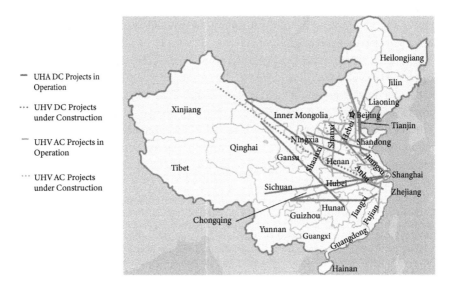

Figure 7.6 China's UHV-DC and UHV-AC power grid, 2020

Source: Authors (based on SGCC website)

---

[15] For discussion on this point, see Xu (2016; 2019).

with value chains being constructed for transmission and distribution of power equipment, power generators, and other technologies new to China.[16]

Parallel to China's national Five-Year Plans, SGCC itself also prepares FYPs. Its twelfth FYP (2011–2015) outlined the '3 + 3' N-S and E-W powerline grid, while the thirteenth FYP (2016–2020) outlined a serious extension of the UHV grid, and consolidation of the '3 + 3' grid plan plus 'ring', now with the full support of the Chinese government and State Council. In parallel with the national FYPs, the SGCC's own thirteenth FYP has the principal target of completing the backbone of the national UHV grid with three vertical and three horizontal corridors combined with a UHV-AC 'ring' that connects urban load centres.

By the end of 2020, no fewer than 26 UHV power lines had been completed, with five further lines under construction.[17] Even with a slow-down in construction (needed partly to allow transformer and equipment manufacturing to keep up) this still places China and State Grid well in advance of other countries and companies in operating UHV transmission systems.[18] According to the Chinese version of the SGCC website, by the end of 2020 SGCC had completed 14 UHV-AC and 12 UHV-DC projects with another two UHV-AC and three UHV-DC transmission projects under construction.[19] The UHV-AC lines are rated at 1.1 million volts, while the UHV-DC lines are rated at 800 kV. By the end of 2020, the total line length reached 35,868 km, and these lines had transmitted a total of 2,076 TWh of electric energy.[20] By this time, China was the clear world leader in installation of ultra-high-capacity power lines, drastically reducing its dependence on rail transport of coal as primary fuel and expanding the possibilities for feeding in green sources of electric generation.

In January 2019, State Grid publicly announced completion of the world's largest UHV-DC power line across China, stretching 3,293 km from Xinjiang in the north-west to Anhui in the east-central. This Changji to Guquan line (from Gansu province in the north-east, through Ningxia, Shaanxi, and Henan provinces) terminates in Anhui province in the city of Xuancheng. The RMB 40.7 billion (USD 5.9 billion) project was approved in December 2015 and construction started immediately, with the line coming into service three years later, at

[16] See the business assessment of China's strong and smart grid prospects from Credit Suisse: 'China power transmission and distribution equipment', *Credit Suisse*, 21 October 2014, https://research-doc.credit-suisse.com/docView?language=ENG&source=ulg&format=PDF&document_id=806437340&serialid=zMwQbGQdR3nFHk6NfnntZ5HuHchV64Vbc59M1QsAv0o%3D;
'A Primer on China's Seven Strategic Industries', *Bank of America Merrill Lynch*, 17 January 2011, (https://www.longfinance.net/media/documents/baml_china_stratindustries_2011.pdf)
[17] See: 'Ultra High Voltage Electricity Transmission', *State Grid Corporation of China*, 2021, http://www.sgcc.com.cn/html/sgcc_main/col2017041259/column_2017041259_1.shtml
[18] The slowdowns are documented in the article by Edmund Downie, 'Sparks fly over ultra-high voltage power lines', *ChinaDialogue*, 1 February 2018, at: https://chinadialogue.net/article/show/single/en/10376-Sparks-fly-over-ultra-high-voltage-power-lines
[19] See: 'Ultra High Voltage Electricity Transmission', *State Grid Corporation of China*, 2021, http://www.sgcc.com.cn/html/sgcc_main/col2017041259/column_2017041259_1.shtml
[20] Ibid.

the beginning of 2019. The new line can transmit power at 12 GW (equivalent to 24 large 500 MW power stations), and it operates at a voltage of 1.1 million volts (1,100 kV). It can shift 66 billion kWh (66 TWh) of electricity from the remote north-west to China's eastern seaboard each year, reducing coal use by 30 million tonnes. This new line, which was opened for full commercial operation in 2018, is sending 50 per cent more power 1,000 km further than any line built.[21]

The complexity of this undertaking is not to be underestimated. There is a non-linear build-up in complexity as a grid moves from 500 kV to 800 kV and then to 1,100 kV. In leapfrogging to the lead, China (and SGCC) has had to develop hundreds of standards and then provide the right incentives to enable Chinese companies to produce the equipment needed to build this transmission and distribution system.[22] It is a nation-building enterprise comparable to the building of the federal interstate highway system in the US in the mid-twentieth century and to China's building of a national high-speed rail in the later twentieth century and early twenty-first century (Chan 2018).

This nation-building effort by China promises to give the country pole position in setting standards for UHV grids over the course of the next several decades—as outlined by former SGCC chair and president, Liu Zhenya, in an address to the Harvard Law Society in April 2018.[23] In fact, these achievements put China well in front in building a new twenty-first century power grid, one which is capable of transmitting vast quantities of electric power over vast distances.

China's strategy for introducing the UHV power grid encompasses not just the turn to UHV power distribution technology, but an entire industry of power grid companies making up what we call a hybridized industrial ecosystem.

Creating a hybridized industrial ecosystem for the grid: The building of an electric power equipment industry in China

As China was embarking on the leapfrog strategy towards the UHV power grid in the first decade of the twenty-first century, the technology of power generation was

[21] J. Temple, 'China's giant transmission grid could be the key to cutting climate emissions', *MIT Review*, 8 November 2018, https://www.technologyreview.com/s/612390/chinas-giant-transmission-grid-could-be-the-key-to-cutting-climate-emissions/); See also 'World's biggest ultra-high voltage line powers up across China', *Bloomberg News*, 2 January 2019, https://www.bloomberg.com/news/articles/2019-01-02/world-s-biggest-ultra-high-voltage-line-powers-up-across-china

[22] See 'World's first 1100 kV DC line will be constructed in China', *Modern Power Systems*, 29 August 2016, https://www.modernpowersystems.com/features/featureworlds-first-1100-kv-dc-line-will-be-constructed-in-china-4991040/; On China's development of UHV standards for both UHVDC and UHVAC power lines, see the report by the Center for Energy, Environmental and Economic Systems Analysis at Argonne National Laboratory (CEESA 2015).

[23] See the quote at the beginning of the chapter. Liu Zhenya spoke at Harvard in April 2018: 'Harvard talk outlines plan for global energy sharing', *The Harvard Gazette*, 19 April 2021, https://news.harvard.edu/gazette/story/2018/04/harvard-talk-outlines-plan-for-global-energy-sharing/

dominated by a handful of multinationals—the Swiss-Swedish giant ABB, French Alstom, German Siemens, US General Electric and Cisco, and Japanese Toshiba and Mitsubishi. As they saw China embarking on UHV strategies, these companies envisaged a rapid expansion in their markets. But the SGCC was firmly focused on building a Chinese power equipment industry alongside the grid itself, as part of a nation building exercise.

In common with the parallel case of high-speed rail (HSR), the China State Council has allowed some of these foreign multinationals to share in the early bids to build the parts of the UHV grid, sometimes through joint ventures with Chinese partner firms where the inducement is 'trading market for technology'—a well tried and tested formula in the Chinese case.[24]

Chinese firms have benefited from these arrangements and are now coming to prominence in the domestic and international markets for transmission and distribution equipment industries, in accordance with the aims of the State Council, announced in 2004, to build a domestic Chinese power equipment industry. The firms include Shanghai Electric (now the world's largest producer of steam turbines); Dongfang Electrical Corporation (DEC), and Harbin Power Equipment, as well as later arrivals like TBEA Co., Baoding Tianwei Group, Xidian Group (XD), Xuji Electric (XJ), Pinggao and the NARI Group, the latter three of which have been incorporated in SGCC as the result of vertical integration initiatives and are now thriving as upstream suppliers to SGCC (Table 7.1).

The key point to notice with these corporate initiatives shown in Table 7.1 is that they create both capital equipment manufacturers as well as leading suppliers along the value chains that culminate in these capital equipment companies like Shanghai Electric. Indeed, Shanghai Electric has been looking to build a global brand (in the manner of GE or Mitsubishi) while creating the value chain supplying needed components. It is by now the world's largest manufacturer of steam turbines. It is diversifying into the building of wind turbines, thereby opening up a new market for renewable power generation equipment in parallel with the traditional thermal generator sector.[25] Meanwhile, companies like Xuji are becoming leading players in a new HIE focused on supplying UHV grid equipment. The 'hybrid' quality of SGCC's network of partners and suppliers lies in its quasi-governmental character (Kim 2019, cf. Weiss 2014)—a network which exhibits a blend of both public and private features focused on building domestic value chains for UHV technologies.

---

[24] See He and Mu (2012) for a discussion of how 'technology for market share' has worked for China in the automobile and telecoms sectors.
[25] See: 'Homepage', *Shanghai Electric*, 2021, https://www.shanghai-electric.com (shanghai-electric.com)

Table 7.1 China's creation of an electric power hybridized industrial ecosystem

TBEA	Has grown to become a leading producer of power transformers and heavy electrical equipment.[a]
Xuji	A leading Chinese producer of high-end UHV and UHV transmission equipment. It was acquired by SGCC through a complicated series of manoeuvres in 2008, having acquired initial technology from JVs with Mitsubishi.
Pinggao	Another Henan-based producer of grid power equipment, it was acquired by SGCC in 2008 with the promise of making a substantial investment in the company, allowing both companies to raise further capital themselves.
NARI Group	A company formed in 2008 by the merger of two leading research institutes, and as such it became another important supplier of electric equipment to SGCC. Now consolidated as the NR Electric group.[b]
XD Electric	Now grown to become a leading Chinese electric equipment producer.[c]

[a] See homepage and company history at: 'About Us', *TBEA*, 2021, https://www.tbea.com/cs/ Satellite?c=Page&cid=1467897312334&d=Touch&lib=2&pagename=TBEA_ EN%2FPage%2FENTemplate%2FAboutUS%2FcorpInfo
[b] See: 'About NR Electric', *NR Electric Co. Ltd*, 2020, https://www.nrec.com/en/index.php/about.html
[c] See homepage at: 'Homepage', *China XD Group Co. Ltd*, 2021, http://en.xd.com.cn/; 'China XD Group – Wikipedia', *Wikipedia*, 7 July 2021, https://en.wikipedia.org/wiki/China_XD_Group
Source: Authors' own elaboration

The full flowering of creative-destructive alignment: Internationalization of State Grid Corporation of China and the Chinese power industry

In keeping with its size and significance in the Chinese economy, State Grid Corporation of China has been pursuing an ambitious strategy of internationalization, backed by an even more ambitious strategy for interconnecting power grids across national boundaries. SGCC has been building its presence in owning and operating power grids around the world, as it makes strategic acquisitions whenever opportunities present themselves. In Brazil, for example, SGCC has invested more than USD 21 billion to become the largest power generating entity in the country, promising a further USD 38 billion in investments over the next five years. It has taken the opportunity to build the world's first UHV transmission line in the developing world, running 2,000 km from the Belo Monte hydroelectric dam in the Amazon region to cities like Rio de Janeiro in the country's southeast. Likewise in southern Europe, SGCC became the largest shareholder in the Portuguese power grid company REN in 2012 (in parallel with China's Three Gorges taking a 23 per cent stake in EDP, Portugal's largest power company) while China's SoEs own significant shares in the Italian and Greek power grids. These expansions abroad are affected in conjunction with China's state banks China Development Bank (CDB) and China Export-Import Bank.[26]

At the same time SGCC has been looking to build transnational power interconnections in a bid to enhance the security of China's power supplies. A Northeast Asian agreement between SGCC, Softbank from Japan, KEPCO from Korea, and corporate entities from Russia and Mongolia, has created a framework of cooperation for a long-discussed Asian Super Grid.[27] Such interconnections serve several purposes. They enable the abundant renewable supplies in Mongolia and Russia to be transported with low losses to load centres in Japan, China, and Korea. They promote free trade in renewable electric power between the NEA countries, setting an example for themselves and the world.[28]

SGCC former CEO and president Liu Zhenya has championed a global set of grid interconnections dubbed the 'Global Energy Interconnection' (GEI). This is a long-term strategy that would see completion some time before 2050—and place China at the core of such a globally interconnected power grid. The plans as announced include acquisitions of power grid companies around the world in the period leading up to 2020. Plans as published by GEI are shown in Figure 7.7. Liu

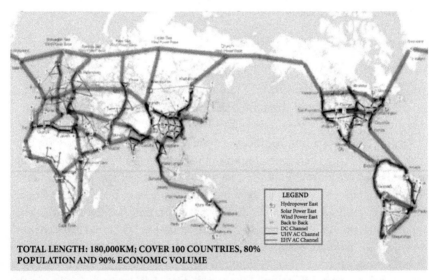

TOTAL LENGTH: 180,000KM; COVER 100 COUNTRIES, 80% POPULATION AND 90% ECONOMIC VOLUME

Figure 7.7 Internationalization of China's power grid: GEI Backbone Grid

Source: Adapted from Global Energy Interconnection Development and Cooperation Organization

---

[26] See the article by J. Kynge and L. Hornby, 'Truly wielding power: How China wants to create the world's first global electricity grid', *OZY*, 14 June 2018, at: https://www.ozy.com/fast-forward/truly-wielding-power-how-china-wants-to-create-the-worlds-first-global-electricity-grid/87270

[27] See for example the Korean reports, such as 'Northeast Asia supergrid to cost at least $6.2 billion: KEPCO', *Korea Times*, 11 December 2018, https://www.koreatimes.co.kr/www/tech/2018/12/325_260204.html

[28] See the discussion of the Asian Super Grid in Mathews (2015; 2017a).

Zhenya has championed UHV grids as an optimal technology for creating such a globally integrated grid.[29]

At the same time, it has to be acknowledged that governments are hitting back at attempts by China and SGCC to extend their influence globally. Attempts by SGCC to acquire a substantial stake in Germany's high-tech grid operator 50 Hertz were rebuffed by the German government when it took a 20 per cent stake in 50 Hertz in July 2018.[30] China's ambitions for a global grid that facilitates electrification in poor countries and promotes trade in renewable power everywhere has to be tempered by suspicion of China's motives in advancing such an ambitious scheme.

Concluding remarks

China occupies a unique position in discussion of the green energy shift in Northeast Asia in that the scale and urgency of industrialization creates a strategic necessity to move beyond the fossil fuel era. China is modernizing on the basis of electrification—and its degree of electrification has already taken it to a position of world leadership, both in terms of geopolitical strategy and the emergence of leading electrical multinational corporations. The UHV case study is a singular aspect of this overarching story of Chinese urbanization, industrialization, and the building of the world's largest manufacturing system.

Our argument in this case is that China has no option other than to move to green its energy system (and related systems like transport, through EVs, FCEVs, and HSR) based on its imperative to overcome geopolitical limits to its growth. We take the notion of 'limits to growth' as laid out in the famous *Limits to Growth* Report to the Club of Rome of 1973, but give the notion a fresh twist. The limits we see as guiding Chinese energy choices are not so much physical limits (important as these are) so much as geopolitical limits—as when a supply country can no longer provide supply due to war, civil war, or financial disruption. China has experienced many crises in its oil and gas supply lines due to such geopolitical disruptions. And China is uniquely vulnerable to such disruptions because of the enormous scale of its dependence on fossil fuel imports—with China now grown to become the largest importer of oil, gas, and coal in the world.

The Chinese leadership seems to have devised a solution to this problem in the form of an energy strategy based on electrification, and the greening of the electrical system by raising the proportion of power sourced from water, wind, and

[29] See C. Clini and A. Marieni, 'China plans UHV transmission lines that span continents', *Energy Post*, 22 March 2019, https://energypost.eu/china-plans-uhv-transmission-lines-that-span-continents/#:~:text=China%27s%20Global%20Energy%20Interconnection%20(GEI,can%20deliver%20electricity%20between%20continents.

[30] See V. Bryan and G. Heller, 'Germany moves to protect key companies from Chinese investors', *Reuters*, 27 July 2018, https://uk.reuters.com/article/us-50hertz-m-a-kfw/germany-moves-to-protect-key-companies-from-chinese-investors-idUKKBN1KH0RB

solar and utilizing domestically manufactured energy devices (solar cells, wind turbines, offshore wind platforms, batteries, fuel cells) as the core of its energy strategy. In this way China is able to short-circuit the geopolitical constraints that would otherwise cripple its industrialization strategy, and look to replace its dependence on fossil fuel imports (mined and drilled from the earth) with the manufacture of its energy security by the manufacture and widespread utilization of its energy devices. The UHV strategy and related strategies to introduce IT-enabled 'smart grids' are central to such an overarching strategy of manufacturing energy security—a different paradigm of modernization and industrialization from one that was centred on FFs.[31]

The fascinating feature of this strategy is that it translates into lower costs and prices for renewable power (because of the learning curves associated with manufactured products like solar cells and wind turbines), not just for China but for the world—making it more likely that other industrializing countries will follow the Chinese lead. China is pursuing an emergent global strategy where it dovetails policies of expanding trade and finance through the Belt and Road Initiative and exports products and processes through its commitments to renewable energy, energy storage, and 'strong and smart' grid upgrading, where UHV occupies a central position.

The other fascinating feature of the strategy is that it leads China and the world to lower carbon emissions, not as a central aim of the strategy but as a highly convenient side-effect. Our argument is that China is greening its energy system for its own domestic reasons—both economic and environmental—and utilizing the power of its state to drive the process as hard and as fast as possible. The outcome is energy security for China—as well as a global reduction in carbon emissions which can be attributed to China's state strategies.[32]

China's strategies to build a 'strong and smart' grid, along with the parallel series of initiatives to build the world's largest and most advanced high-speed rail system, are two of China's most ambitious twenty-first century infrastructure building projects. At this scale, it is not feasible to consider market forces on their own as being able to guide the investments and their necessary coordination. This is well understood in China, where governments at both national and provincial level set out the guiding goals, and state-owned companies like SGCC (and China Southern Power) perform their state entrepreneurial initiatives in seeing that the goals are accomplished. This is a canonical example of what we mean by 'developmental environmentalism'—where the state and private sector combine in setting

---

[31] John Mathews and Hao Tan spelt out this argument in their commentary article in *Nature*, see: J. Mathews and H. Tan, 'Manufacture renewables to build energy security', *Nature*, 10 September 2014, https://www.nature.com/articles/513166a

[32] This is not to deny that some aspects of China's Belt and Road Initiative can also have negative environmental consequences. For an insightful discussion of China's complex role in this regard see Yeophantong and Goh (2022).

forth a vision for a sustainable industrial development and combine their forces in seeing that the vision is accomplished.[33]

The case illustrates that for China it is not just a case of building a 'strong and smart' grid as part of a green energy system, but of building the value chains that can manufacture the energy and power devices needed. China has utilized strategies that impose local content requirements in building local manufacturing value chains and setting the standards that they must work towards as the 'strong and smart' grid is constructed. This is an example of what Kim (2019) has called a hybridized industrial ecosystem, in the sense that power equipment companies like Xuji, TBEA, Pinggao, and the NARI Group, that span public and private sectors, combine with the state-owned enterprises SGCC and SPG to design and build the UHV grid to standards developed in China, and work within guidelines laid down by the NDRC and State Council at the highest levels of the Chinese state system.

This total industrial ecosystem, ensuring that value chains culminating in power equipment producers that are internationally competitive are coaxed into existence through appropriate procurement and other policies, works with the state agencies in formulating strategic goals in a hybridized or blended approach to the development and implementation of policy. The case has sought to demonstrate that this approach to greening, through the building of a power grid capable of accepting and distributing green power from renewable sources, actually works in China. It delivers on the green goals today while building strategic export industries for tomorrow.

In this chapter we have explored how China has pursued a strategy of first building the world's largest fossil-fuelled power system to drive the world's largest manufacturing system, followed by the ruthless destruction of this system in favour of an emergent green power system with its superior energy security characteristics. The process of 'creative-destruction' encompasses both the building of an alternative green power generation system complemented by a 'strong and smart' grid, embodying hyper-modernisation with UHV carrying capacity, and ultimately a shift to a global interconnected grid that promises energy security for all participants. The 'creative' aspects of building a renewably powered grid with UHV distribution technology is increasingly complemented by state dismantling of the fossil fuel system, headed by the closure of coal mines, coal transport, and coal usage as input into industrial processes. We have sought to demonstrate how China's changing strategies in relation to its 'strong and smart' grid are consistent with its rising levels of innovation and its strategic goals as demonstrated in its turn to laying the foundations of a global IT-enhanced power grid as the ultimate source of domestic energy security.

[33] See Kim and Thurbon (2015).

8

Drivers and Dynamics of Northeast Asia's Green Energy Shift: A Comparative Strategic Analysis

Earlier chapters have laid out the details of the striking incursion by Northeast Asian (NEA) countries into the greening of business. From fossil-fuelled industrial success stories, we have shown that these countries are now emerging as the epicentre of the global green energy transition. Whether it be the shift to renewable forms of energy, or the rise of green electrical energy storage and distribution systems, or the shift to green transport, the NEA region encompassing Japan, Korea, Taiwan, and now most emphatically China, have made their presence felt in a sudden and dramatic manner. In this chapter we review these experiences, both the case studies highlighted in the previous four chapters, as well as other national experiences that extend beyond Korea and China to encompass Taiwan and Japan, and other industrial sectors beyond the grid and new electric vehicles (NEVs).

Our argument is that fundamentally, the dramatic appearance of the Northeast Asian economies in greening processes is a result of state-guided development and largely reflects the political choices of state agents. We argue that 'normal' evolutionary processes would not bring about such a sudden shift, and that the intervention of state agencies is needed to explain this otherwise puzzling development. We emphasize the fact that there are political-economic drivers of the greening process that state agencies could be expected to respond to, whereas private firms acting in their own interests might not see opportunities in the same way. In particular, we see countries like China and Korea, and their peers in NEA, responding to the exigencies of energy and resources security as well as pollution threats from over-reliance on fossil fuels (FFs), and seeking via a green shift to avoid the economic, environmental, and political problems that would otherwise be encountered. However, while state agents set the overall directions for development, it is companies that are the drivers and carriers of this green shift—companies responding to economic settings that are created by the state agencies involved. Moreover (we argue) this state involvement leaves its mark in the attention paid to both aspects of the Schumpeterian process of creative destruction, with state agencies looking to promote fresh and 'clean' developments (the creative side) while at the same time dismantling the structures that support the role of FFs in the economy (the destructive side).

Developmental Environmentalism. Elizabeth Thurbon et al., Oxford University Press. © Elizabeth Thurbon, Sung-Young Kim, Hao Tan, and John Mathews (2023). DOI: 10.1093/oso/9780192897794.003.0008

In this chapter we detail how the vision of developmental environmentalism (DE) translates into sets of policies directed towards different aspects of the green energy transition, notably with transport (electric vehicles) and industry (hyper-modernizing of the electric power grid). We review the cases elaborated in previous chapters, and analyse them in comparative strategic terms from three vantage points, viewing DE: 1) as a driving mindset or ambition for transformation; 2) as a legitimation strategy; and 3) as providing a particular approach to sequencing policies involved in the green energy transition (GET). Our aim is to demonstrate how the DE mindset enables Northeast Asian countries to address both environmental issues and business development prospects simultaneously; how the DE mindset provides the basis for regime legitimation by attending to evolving economic and geostrategic challenges while cleaning up the environmental problems arising from previous fossil-fuelled development strategies; and how DE, by virtue of the traditional developmental goals it embodies, necessarily translates into particular policy priorities—with an ambitious early 'creative' emphasis centred on securing local manufacturing capability, technological autonomy, and export competitiveness giving way over time to a dual focus on new green energy industry creation *and* fossil fuel industry destruction. Our ultimate goal is to depict the green energy shift in NEA as an industrial evolution that is guided by DE thinking and acting.

East Asian approaches to the green energy transition

We have examined in the previous four chapters two case studies of industrial sectors featuring a green energy shift—green transport (battery electric vehicles (EVs) and fuel cell electric vehicles (FCEVs) and green grid modernization—and two countries—China and Korea—as exemplars. In this chapter we highlight commonalities in their approaches as well as differences, with a view to identifying what is distinctive about the Northeast Asian approach to the green energy transition.

In each case we highlight the drivers, setting them in the context of techno-industrial transformation policies targeted at enhancing environmental conditions, or what we are calling developmental-environmental (DE) strategies. We identify the key innovations that help to account for the sudden appearance of Northeast Asia's electric vehicle and 'smart and strong' grid industries, with the state driving the transformation. We then compare the temporal pattern of development of these new sectors, which typically starts with rapid new green industry creation before finally reaching something akin to alignment between the new green industry creation and the dismantling of the incumbent fossil-fuelled industries (i.e., alignment between creation and destruction). In each case we have sought to highlight the role of the state (at both central and provincial government levels) in guiding this process via various direct and indirect means including the development of long-term, carefully targeted techno-industrial development plans and the strategic deployment of economic and environmental regulations, control over finance, and state-owned enterprise (SoE) activity. Our aim is to place these case studies of green industry development in a wider international political economy (IPE) setting of heightened geostrategic competition. In doing so, we show how China's and Korea's domestic green techno-industrial initiatives respond to external politico-economic challenges and evolve into global strategies aimed at outmanoeuvring competitors and securing leadership at the techno-industrial frontier. In this way, we seek to demonstrate how NEA's green energy transition strategies result in developmental-environmental transformation and a cleaner planet *without being focused exclusively on the goal of mitigating climate change.*

Grid hypermodernization

Taking the cases in reverse order, we see how both Korea and China have pursued a dual strategy of electric power transformation, both in terms of introducing green sources of electricity generation and in terms of transformation of the distributive electric power grid itself (as well as its expansion in keeping with growth in scale of manufacturing). China started out on its industrial transformation from the end of the 1980s with a huge build-up of manufacturing industry powered (as in each of the prior East Asian industrialization experiences) by coal and fossil fuels, particularly from 2001 when China joined the WTO. We can see from the relevant policy documents (from the NDRC, State Council et al.) that energy security was a principal driver of this process, with irregular blackouts and brownouts disrupting the whole industrialization trajectory. By the early years of the new century China was registering severe problems in pursuing this FF build-up, notably rising levels of particulate air pollution in cities as well as what we have called geopolitical 'limits to growth' such as wars, revolutions, and rebellions in supplier countries that would disrupt supplies of fuels and make dependence on FF imports increasingly problematic. By early in the second decade voices were being raised concerning the costs of this dependence on FFs, and calls were heard for an alternative strategy based on green (renewable) sources of energy and a transformed grid that could accommodate rising levels of green energy.

Likewise in Korea, the early years of industrialization were powered by a massive build-up in manufacturing capacity and a fossil-fuelled power system as the engine of development. Because in geopolitical terms Korea was closer to the US than China (hosting troops stationed in Korea ever since the armistice that marked the end of the Korean War), there was less emphasis in Korea on domestic energy security and more emphasis on keeping electricity costs low and building electrically-powered export industries, through the medium of an SoE—KEPCO—at the centre of the Korean electricity grid. Korea thus powered its industry for longer with fossil fuels, and to a greater level of dependence, than in the case of China. But Korea too was reaching the limits of its fossil fuel dependence in the 2000s, due to rising levels of particulate pollution (making the air in industrial cities like Ulsan unbreathable), and KEPCO was tasked with searching for alternatives in the form of renewables and in grid modernization projects. These latter included modular initiatives and the beginnings of a new export industry in the form of modular grid systems and battery-based energy storage systems (ESS).

China as an emerging superpower saw the seeding of new energy industries marked by independence from fossil fuels (particularly breaking with geopolitical dependence on oil) as being strategically advantageous, and it was an early mover in Northeast Asia in making a break towards the creation of new green energy industries, even as early as the 2000s. This involved creating new clean energy generation industries such as solar and wind power, which would help to provide independence from FFs, encompassing not just the generation of renewable electric power but the manufacturing value chains culminating in solar photovoltaic (PV) modules and wind turbines, which we dub as hybridized industrial ecosystems (HIEs).

Early experiences with renewables generation and its intermittent character, and with high levels of curtailment, were perceived as technical barriers calling for technical solutions, which in the case of China's grid called for higher levels of capacity in the grid, notably ultra-high voltage (UHV) transmission, as well as IT-enhancement of current flow, or 'smart-grid' innovation. These initiatives were explicitly viewed in China as the seeds of new export industries of the future. Likewise in Korea, the shift to renewables, while slower than in China and maintaining dependence on low-cost fossil-fuelled electricity generation as an industrial policy for longer, became the explicit strategy of the government after the arrival of the Moon Jae-In administration, when the Presidential Blue House asserted its political authority to coordinate a renewables-focused energy strategy and a grid modernization program, with KEPCO as the driver of the process.

Whereas in the US and the West generally, fossil-fuel incumbents and nuclear power operators held a tight grip on political and economic power, keeping renewables at arm's length, in China the state agencies adopted a more long-term, strategic perspective and were willing to promote renewable sources of electric power as (potentially) lower-cost and geopolitically favourable alternatives to FFs. Here again the broad strategic directions laid down by central state agencies (NDRC, State Council, National Energy Administration) were translated into economic and technological strategies by SoEs, with the SGCC driving the switch from very-high voltage (VHV) to UHV as the clearest such case. In Korea a comparable role was played by KEPCO, where its prior reliance on coal-fired and nuclear electric power was systematically dismantled by successive presidential administrations, culminating in the anti-nuclear and coal-dismantling programs of the Moon Jae-In administration. Through clear state involvement in both cases, China and Korea were enabled to put into effect a rapid phase-down of FFs (and nuclear electric power) and by promoting market forces to effect a rapid build-up in renewable power sources and their associated hybridized industrial ecosystems.

Greening of transport: The shift to electric vehicles

In the case of transport, we have comparable stories to tell as outlined in the relevant Chapters 4 and 5. Here we see rapid build-up of automotive industries in Korea and China, following on from the success of Japan in emulating and then surpassing the US and EU automotive industry success. In each case the prevailing internal combustion engine (ICE) paradigm, linked to oil as dominant fossil fuel, was unquestioned. If anything, Korea was more daring and hypercompetitive in building a domestic automotive industry and national champion like Hyundai, which was able to break into international markets based on its lower costs and competitive quality, becoming an innovator within the broad parameters of the ICE–oil industry paradigm. China as the latecomer had to be content with national automotive champions like SAIC Motor, Dongfeng, FAW, and Chang'an that were technologically tied to (mainly) Japanese incumbents, and national oil companies that likewise found it difficult to break free of geopolitical constraints.

In both countries electric vehicles were perceived as a means of breaking with the ICE–oil constraints and resetting the competitive parameters of the global automotive industry. State agencies and state policies in Korea drove the evolution of Hyundai as it became one of the top ten automotive companies in the world (noting that Samsung's efforts to enter the industry as a serious competitor were cut down by the 1997–98 Asian Financial Crisis). The case study notes that Hyundai's efforts to create a 'green car' as a latecomer competitive strategy go back to the 1990s, where the emphasis was on then-futuristic fuel cell-powered electric vehicles. After early setbacks, the Korean government swung into action and promoted not just FCEVs but also the more widely recognized battery-powered EVs (BEVs), with an ambitious drive to create a Korean battery industry that would serve as the foundation of the national BEV sector.

By contrast, China had to be content to pursue its automotive industry ambitions in clear recognition of the prevailing Japanese technological supremacy and the US and EU competitive dominance. In the Chinese case the goal to create a globally dominant automotive industry on the foundation of EVs, as a competitive fresh start that would level the playing field in favour of Chinese manufacturing supremacy, is clear and manifest. By 2020 the outlines of this global competitive strategy were becoming clear, with China occupying a dominant 43 per cent share of global EV sales; its battery producers occupying 70 per cent of global battery sales; and its upstream companies occupying 50–70 per cent of lithium and cobalt processing in the global value chain (IEA 2021). The Chinese strategy to move from being latecomer and technological laggard in ICE-oil vehicles, to global innovator and leader in EVs (termed new energy vehicles in China), is clear. Even so, as the case study emphasizes, NEVs only accounted for five per cent of global sales of vehicles by 2020, making it clear that it will be a long and difficult road to reach the point where China might anticipate becoming the world's leading automotive industry on the basis of its NEV dominance.

Both Korea and China viewed the early stages of a shift to EVs as a means of recalibrating the global competitive dynamics of the automotive industry, allowing both countries to break free of the competitive-cum-technological ordering imposed by Japanese, EU, and US leaders. There was barely a mention of environmental concerns in Korea's early government policies for the promotion of EVs, while there was not a strong environmental emphasis in the corresponding planning documents in China. But in the first decade of the twenty-first century, as urban pollution worsened, caused partly by the unrestrained growth of private oil-powered ICE vehicles (and diesel-powered vehicles in the EU), the potential role of Evs and NEVs as green alternatives to conventional transport, with its carbon emissions and particulate pollution, became clear.

In China, this fresh developmental-environmental perspective on green transport was captured in planning documents like the 2017 *Automotive Industry Medium- and Long-Term Development Plan* and the 2015 *Made in China* manufacturing plan, and the *New Energy Automobile Industry Development Plan (2021–2035)* issued most recently in October 2020. These documents clarify and elaborate on the Chinese state's clear ambitions to drive the 'creative' side of the 'creative-destruction' dynamic in transport (along with fast rail transport, the expansion of metro rail services and light rail services in new eco-cities) to the point where NEVs (HEVs, BEVs, FCEVs) are anticipated to occupy a dominant share of the world's automotive market. These central state initiatives are complemented by provincial state policies being announced where clear limits are being placed on continued growth of the conventional ICE–oil powered vehicle industry, with some cities already announcing caps on the sales of conventional vehicles and outright bans anticipated by the 2030s or even as early as 2025.

It is a characteristic of the Northeast Asian green energy transition that we see state power being deployed both to drive the 'creative' aspects of the creative-destructive transformation (seeding new industries and providing needed infrastructure) as well as the 'destructive' aspects (dismantling incumbents). This is a clear competitive advantage of the NEA nations over their Western counterparts.

It is worth noting that Northeast Asian strategies to promote EVs in their various forms focus not just on expanding the market for the vehicles (through both financial incentives and through curbs on conventional ICE-powered vehicles) but also on building relevant infrastructure such as charging stations and the value chains that culminate in manufacture of the NEVs themselves. In the intense geopolitical technoeconomic competition between the US and China in EVs, China has emerged as creating the world's largest EV-charging network, in collaboration with the SoE SGCC and associated companies.[1] Likewise in Korea, it is state agencies and SoEs that have coordinated the roll-out of a nationwide EV charging infrastructure. In July 2021, the country's largest oil refiner and distributor, SK Energy, and largest electric power and grid operator, KEPCO, announced their agreement to upgrade the Korean national EV-charging network.[2] Here is another demonstration of the role played by the state and state agencies in driving rapid emergence of the new green energy industries in Korea.

Dramatic incursion by Northeast Asian economies: Leapfrogging strategy

Ever since the rise of Japan, followed by Korea and Taiwan and Singapore—and now spectacularly China as well—there has been a clear understanding of how the state could be used to guide a process of industry renewal and modernization, usually with an advanced foreign industry as guide and precedent. There has been no shortage of state initiatives to choose from in a rich palette of strategies and policies that have been tried by these various governments—without any of the inhibitions that have held back the role of the state in Western economies, saddled as they are with 'neoliberal' constraints and hostility to state leadership. These initiatives encompass market creation policies (e.g., state procurement, consumer subsidies, standard setting); technology acquisition (e.g., state patent pools, state bank financing); state entrepreneurship (e.g., firm creation, tax breaks); forward-targeted education and training initiatives; as well as state sponsorship of clusters and consortia. In advanced countries these kinds of initiatives are recognized as being useful in industry renewal programs, but policy is confined to promoting private endeavours aimed at achieving their effects.

In Northeast Asia, by contrast, state guidance is viewed as desirable and even necessary in catching up efforts and in industrial renewal, where there is a target to be aimed at and achieved. The closer the country is to the technological frontier the less scope there is for simple 'catch-up' and greater the reliance on 'leapfrogging', where there is a targeted technology with state support for efforts by private firms and SoEs to reach the designated target. There are famous and spectacular cases

[1] See M. Griffin, 'China unveils the world's largest EV charging network', 311 Institute, 26 October 2017, https://www.311institute.com/china-unveils-the-worlds-largest-electric-vehicle-charging-network/

[2] See H. Rim, 'SK Energy, KEPCO team up to facilitate domestic EV supply', The Korea Herald, 5 July 2021, http://www.koreaherald.com/view.php?ud=20210702000764

like Korea's leapfrogging to CDMA technology for cellular networks, where firms like Samsung were encouraged to follow the state-guided strategy of advancing beyond current and incumbent technologies to the frontier (where royalty rates could be anticipated to be lower or zero) and where competitive dynamics would be moderated. All of this is abundantly illustrated in the historical record governing the rise of Japan, and then Korea and Taiwan, plus Singapore, and now certainly encompassing China as well.[3]

We can see the full panoply of these industrial strategy initiatives at work in contemporary cases of industry renewal and advance, such as China's all-out efforts to catch up and move ahead in the fundamental field of integrated circuits and semiconductors. Here the Chinese state leadership is utilizing every facet of state guidance and promotion to establish its own advanced semiconductor industry and decouple it from its prior dependence on American technology and companies such as Intel. China is the outstanding exponent of developmental *technology leverage* strategies in the field of semiconductors in the twenty-first century—and it is building on the prior experiences and strategies deployed by Japan, then Korea (Samsung, SK Hynix) and Taiwan (e.g., TSMC), and Singapore (Chartered).[4]

So, there is no doubt regarding the capacity of Northeast Asian countries, and China in particular, to deploy state-level developmental strategies in one sector after another—despite efforts by some scholars to claim that the 'developmental state' (meaning state agencies with quintessentially developmental functions) is dead or dying.[5] On the contrary, such state agencies are alive and well and working to great effect to drive NEA countries to more and more advanced levels of technological sophistication—in advanced sectors like IT, IoT, AI and machine learning (ML) and in new green sectors with their cluster-like development. Our argument in this book is that the same process is well under way in the fields of greening of industrial processes, where state agencies are taking the lead in promoting certain green technologies and the infrastructure supporting them as a way to reduce environmental levels of particulate pollution, as well as rising reliance/dependence on fossil fuels with all their geopolitical uncertainties.

---

[3] See the classic works on this theme, dating from Johnson (1982) on Japan and its creation of a DS; Amsden (1989), B. Kim (1992), Tan and Mathews (2015), and D. Kang and J. Cho, 'Korea's KEPCO, Russia's Rosseti to cooperate on power grid projects', *Pulse News*, 25 June 2018, https://pulsenews.co.kr/view.php?sc=30800028&year=2018&no=399796; 'Hyundai Motor, Korea East-West Power and Deokyang to build a 1-MW hydrogen FC power facility using NEXO technology', *GreenCarCongress*, 13 April 2019, https://www.greencarcongress.com/2019/04/20190413-nexo.html; 'China looks to repeat EV success with fuel cell vehicles', *Automotiveworld*, 8 March 2021, https://www.automotiveworld.com/articles/china-looks-to-repeat-ev-success-with-fuel-cell-vehicles/

[4] As outlined by one of the current authors in *Tiger Technology* (Mathews and Cho, 2000).

[5] A large body of literature is now devoted to reviewing and systematically countering claims of developmental state demise, and to specifying the ongoing utility of the developmental state idea. See for example Weiss (1998, 2003), Weiss and Thurbon (2004, 2020) Kim (2012, 2013, 2019, 2021) Klingler-Vidra and Pacheco Pardo (2020), Wade (2018), Thurbon (2014, 2016, 2020) Thurbon and Weiss (2016, 2019).

Consistent with these strategies, we argue that the Northeast Asian countries are engaged with devising and implementing greening strategies utilizing state guidance. As in the wider cases of semiconductors and IT generally, it is state agencies that are monitoring the global technological developments and fashioning means for securing access to these technologies (e.g., via licensing, or acquisition of the companies that have mastered the technologies). In the case of wind turbines, for example, Chinese state-owned firms like Goldwind were able to monitor technological developments and frame acquisition strategies to acquire novel wind power technologies such as permanent magnet direct drive (PMDD) as an alternative to conventional gearboxes. In the past decade this technology leverage strategy has helped to power Goldwind to world leadership in wind turbine production and global sales.[6]

While most literature on sustainable development recognizes the need for industrial policy to guide industry renewal, nevertheless the goal in most cases is deemed to be mitigation of climate change via dematerialization and decarbonization of economies. The difference with strategies that we identify as Northeast Asian in character is that the NEA countries view their industrial strategies in terms of their efficacy in renewing industries and targeting industries for their future wealth-generating potential. In this sense, while the greening repercussions in terms of decarbonization and dematerialization are an important goal, environmental considerations are by no means the exclusive or even primary goal.

Thus, we find that in the case of electric vehicles, Korea has opted in advance of other countries for a full industrial-scale development of FCEVs as part of a wider commitment to the green hydrogen economy. The Korean government is betting heavily on the likelihood of the world moving to hydrogen-powered transport and industry, via FCEVs and stationary fuel cells (FCs) for energy storage, and for wider applications in trucking, rail, and shipping. It is making the preliminary investments in projects involving production of green hydrogen from electrolysis of water and dissemination of hydrogen-fuelled FCs, as well as building state-owned infrastructure such as hydrogen refuelling stations along highways and in city centres. It is the sudden shift towards FCEVs in Korea, and the mobilization of finance and infrastructure consistent with this new direction—including the veritable leapfrogging involved—that calls for an explanation involving state agencies as drivers and guides of the process.

This is developmental environmentalism in action—now oriented not to fossil-fuelled development and large agencies like Korea's EPB as in the past, but to a novel green growth industrial economy that calls for sophisticated state agency partnerships and creation of hybridized industrial ecosystems. In the Korean case just discussed, it involves pursuit of a hydrogen powered green economy that

---

[6] For an examination the DE strategies of NEA countries in the offshore wind industry see Mathews et al. (2022).

promises to place the country in a world leadership position. Any doubt that attaches to such a strategy is precisely whether the world will indeed move towards such a hydrogen powered economy at the pace anticipated by the Koreans. From the perspective of the Korean leadership this is a very large bet—but a bet worth taking because of the huge economic benefits of being right—and the minimal costs of being wrong, since hydrogen will always be an excellent energy carrier.

It is not that Korea is a stranger to such bold leaps forward in its earlier catch-up efforts—encompassing the dramatic moves into shipbuilding and the automotive sector in the 1970s, into integrated circuits (ICs) and microchips in the 1980s, into CDMA and ICT in the 1990s—and moreover where Korean firms like Samsung, Hyundai, and SK Hynix held the positions so strenuously acquired.[7] Now we see Korean state agencies charting a way forward in green energy strategies, and a new round of intra-NEA competition as China looks to emulate Korea in such areas as batteries and FCEVs.

Indeed, we have seen how China is now moving from an exclusive reliance on BEVs to a joint strategy involving both BEVs and FCEVs (known in China as NEVs). China has clearly been waiting for the costs of green hydrogen and of fuel cell-powered electric motors to come down, as they are and can be anticipated to continue to fall through the associated learning curve effects. State-guided green development strategies can be complemented by state financial provision via state development banks. Thus, a government decision to pursue a green strategy of hydrogen-powered transport can be followed and complemented by a decision to pour investment capital into the firms looking to pursue such a strategy (e.g., Hyundai in FCEVs), and state promotion of both value chains leading to final producers as well as cluster-level developments.

Developmental environmentalism in action

We have offered a succinct yet novel account of the state-led strategies deployed in Northeast Asia to effect real change in transitioning away from fossil-fuelled energy systems. The core of our book consists of the four case studies described in Chapters 4 to 7 on electric vehicles and 'smart and strong' grid initiatives. These chapters reveal the ways in which developmental environmentalism has been interpreted and adopted by state agents as a guiding influence in driving the transition away from fossil fuel dependence in NEA.

When it comes to evaluating Northeast Asia's green transition, we do not claim 'mission accomplished' as yet; none of the countries that we have examined in

[7] For the classic studies of these experiences see Amsden (1989) and Kim (1992). For the classic statement on the role that can be played by the state in economic transformation, see Weiss and Hobson (1995).

detail in our case studies or touched on briefly in this chapter could be said to have achieved anything approaching a 'green economy' so far. Indeed, in our case studies we critically assess the ongoing processes in China and Korea and identify the major limitations of and challenges to the actions guided by developmental environmentalism in the sphere of energy transitions. We focus on how state-led strategies are enabling these countries to move their economies in a green direction, where the drivers are the concrete goals of national energy and economic, techno-industrial competitiveness, and particulate pollution reduction—rather than an abstract goal of mitigating climate change (although this goal has become more important over time). And yet we are not unmindful of the fact that the pursuit of the green energy transition driven by national security and political legitimacy goals results in a more climate friendly economy as a fortunate side-effect. This is indeed a convenient truth.

To drive home our argument, we now proceed to probe the workings of developmental environmentalism in Northeast Asia from three different aspects or vantage points. We start with the foundational mindset and ambitions that drive the whole process, then proceed to examine DE as a political legitimation strategy, and finally to evaluate DE as an approach to sequencing the policy shifts that the green energy transition evolves.

Aspect One: Developmental environmentalism as mindset and ambition driving the green energy transition

The four case studies all in their different ways highlight developmental environmentalism in terms of elite ambitions and motivations and identify the various pressures (domestic and international) feeding into those ambitions and motivations. Each industry case lends weight to our claim that DE emerged from and represents an extension of the traditional developmental mindset that had informed techno-industrial policymaking in Korea and China for a significant portion of the twentieth century. They do so by revealing the extent to which, in the early to mid-2000s, political leaders in both countries began to question the long-term viability of their countries' traditional, fossil-fuelled industrial developmental strategies, thanks largely to the intensifying energy, economic, and environmental security challenges arising from the same. At the same time, evolving geostrategic circumstances associated with China's rapid rise (in Korea's case) and the US's faltering as global hegemon in the wake of the 2008 global financial crisis (GFC) (in China's case) set these countries' political leaders on a quest to devise a new growth model—one capable not only of advancing their newly twinned energy/economic and environmental security goals, but also the pursuit of international competitiveness and potential leadership at the technological frontier. Thus, in both China and Korea we see the mindset of DE emerge and grow hand in hand with the phenomenon of domestically-oriented economic statecraft centred on both electric vehicles and 'strong and smart' grids, that is, local industrial development initiatives that reach for the tech frontier and that are aimed squarely at keeping pace with or outmanoeuvring a set of clearly defined rivals (*c.f.* Thurbon and Weiss 2019; Weiss and Thurbon 2020).

As we discuss further in Chapter 9, in recent years we have witnessed intensifying levels of geostrategic competition, from the great power rivalry between China and the US to the intra-Northeast Asian rivalry between Japan, Korea, and China. Our cases have shown that these growing rivalries and heightened elite ambitions are not just lending further momentum to the green energy transition, but are intensifying the embrace of economic statecraft as part of that shift—in both its domestically-oriented and traditional externally-oriented forms. In this context we note how the 'strong and smart' grid initiatives in both China and Korea now encompass international aspects, with both countries promoting fresh initiatives like the 'Northeast Asian Super Grid' in Korea's case and the 'Global Energy Interconnection' (GEI) in China's case. These initiatives are viewed by elites in both China and Korea as ways of enhancing the domestic initiatives described in our case studies—as a means of economic statecraft propelling the countries in new, green directions.

Moreover, our cases have further helped to specify the conditions under which developmental-environmental ideas might exert more (or less) influence over the trajectory of a nation's green energy transition. By adopting an agent-centred historical institutionalist approach to our analysis, we have been able to highlight the important role of political leadership (or leadership by DE-minded presidents) at particular moments in time. To explain the intensification of 'creative' initiatives (and of economic statecraft) in recent years, and the growing alignment between 'creative' and 'destructive' ambition and action, we have paid particular attention to two presidents—Xi and Moon—who may be viewed as highly DE-motivated and whose ambitions have loomed large not only generally but also in certain industry strategies. This is especially true of Korea's FCEV strategy (and green hydrogen more broadly) and China's UHV grid strategy where new grid technologies and companies like Shanghai Electric are being deployed. In pursuing these initiatives, Korea and China have both sought to and succeeded in establishing themselves as global technological frontrunners. Korea's ambitious FCEV efforts have earned it the position as the world's leading producer and exporter in this cutting-edge technological arena, allowing it to differentiate itself from China, which has made its massive push into the electric vehicle space on the back of more conventional battery EV technology. For its part, China has succeeded in actually building the world's first UHV grid—leapfrogging both the US and Europe—a development that would have seemed almost unthinkable just a decade ago.

At the same time, and to further nuance our argument about the importance of elite ambition and orientation, we have shown that political leadership and developmental motivations and ambitions also matter at the local level. Cases like China's Liuzhou City in its development of a local EV market intertwined with the building of local EV manufacturing capacity, and Korea's Chungnam province in its combination of ambitious coal phase-out commitments and enthusiastic promotion of new hydrogen-related industries, offer clear examples. These striking local-level developments should also remind us to be cautious about trying to discern the dynamics and future trajectory of Northeast Asia's green energy transition from the macro-level data alone (see Chapter 2). Insofar as the shift in question is made up of many micro-level transitions, many of which will initially manifest locally, any attempt to discern the drivers and dynamics of the GET must pay serious attention to local-level developments like the ones we have canvased in our cases.

To be clear, our argument that the developmental-environmental shift starts as a change in elite mindset and ambition (at both central and local levels) is more than a claim to do with ideas that 'come and go'. As our case studies have shown, once the initial investments in a new technological trajectory like FCEVs or UHV grids are taken, they have a self-perpetuating dynamic that can transcend particular political regimes. It thus becomes evident that political leadership and the DE ambition it embodies may matter more to the green energy transition at some moments than at others, and that the importance of one technology may rise or decline over time. This brings us back to the role of capitalist market dynamics as a crucial piece of the GET puzzle, and the fact that as cost reductions continue and market dynamics change, the GET can take on a life of its own. So, even when ambitious leaders are replaced, the green shift is likely to continue after a certain point because it takes on a self-sustaining momentum.

Thus in the Korean context, perhaps the most critical question to now emerge is: was President Moon's five-year term (2017–2022) sufficient to fully enliven market forces and to thereby frustrate any future attempts at policy reversal? The next five years will prove particularly enlightening in this regard, given the recent election of President Yoon Suk-yeol. Widely described as Korea's first populist president, Yoon's energy visions differ significantly from Moon's, especially in regards to nuclear's role in the clean energy transition. Recall that, as an ambitious advocate of a green energy shift, former president Moon pledged to phase out both coal and nuclear as his flagship policies (see Chapters 4 and 6). Moon also pumped massive volumes of funds into building a hydrogen industry—with a focus on green hydrogen—and to achieve net zero by 2050. At the same time, he promoted gas as a medium term 'bridging fuel' on the road to Korea's fully renewable future. By supporting a temporary gas expansion, Moon's aim was to mobilize existing gas assets and direct them towards the pursuit of the hydrogen shift, while at the same time securing relatively cheap and stable energy supply while coal and nuclear were phased out and renewables in.[8]

Thanks to Moon's 'bridging fuel' policy, over the 2017–2022 period Korea's gas reliance significantly increased—with all of it imported. This growing gas reliance increased Korea's exposure to fluctuations in global energy prices, not least those caused by geopolitical ruptures. In 2022, a massive new rupture came in the shape of Russia's brutal invasion of Ukraine—at a time largely coinciding with Korea's presidential election. The Russia crisis sent shockwaves through global energy markets, pushing the price of gas—one of Russia's key exports—to new highs. And thanks to Moon's bridging policy, by the time the crisis hit, Korea had emerged as the world's fourth largest importer of LNG—which had been relied on to reduce coal and nuclear. Korea therefore felt the pain of higher gas prices acutely.

The Russia crisis thus lent momentum to Korea's pro-nuclear voices, including then presidential hopeful Yoon Suk-yeol.[9] President Yoon came to power in 2022 pledging to expand the role of nuclear power in Korea's 'clean energy' mix. According to Yoon, meeting Korea's Net Zero by 2050 pledge via renewables alone—as Moon had pledged to do—would be too costly for the country, especially for industry. In stark contrast to Moon, Yoon thus promised to expand domestic investment in nuclear, and to develop the newest generation of small modular reactors as a strategic export industry.

President Yoon's major emphasis on nuclear sparked fears of a reduction of investment in renewables, and a reversal of Korea's Net Zero commitments. However, we see many reasons to question this outcome. First, Yoon will face many domestic obstacles to reviving nuclear locally, in light of the divisiveness of this issue following the 2011 Fukushima disaster in Japan. At the same time, despite the encouragement of the new president, there is no guarantee that Korean firms will be willing to take the risk to plough investments back into nuclear, having experienced five years of policy uncertainty under former president Moon. Given the contentious nature of nuclear in Korea, there is no guarantee that a future president won't reverse Yoon's pro-nuclear policy to secure political advantage. Business leaders will be acutely aware of this, and wary of pledging resources to an industry whose future remains so uncertain—especially when there are more certain options—like renewables.

At the same time, while President Yoon is clearly pro-nuclear, there is no sign that he is seriously against renewables, or a clean energy shift more broadly. In March 2022, Yoon reconfirmed the Moon government's plans to ban the sale

---

[8] It is worth noting here that as methane emissions from gas production are the worst culprit when it comes to climate change, the idea of gas as a bridging fuel cannot be justified on climate grounds. That said, and as Moon clearly understood, gas is preferable to coal when it comes to the challenge of particulate pollution, which poses a major environmental and health challenge for Koreans (and a political legitimacy challenge for the government, as discussed in previous chapters and elaborated below).

[9] The remainder of this section draws on Thurbon et al. 2022, with permission.

of new ICE vehicles by 2035. Yoon also remains firmly committed to Korea's 2030 carbon reduction targets. At the same time, any move to alter the country's 2050 obligations would meet fierce global criticism, not least from Korea's major strategic partner, the United States. Moreover, by amplifying Korea's longstanding energy security concerns, the Russia crisis appears to have lent even greater momentum to the country's push to reduce its reliance on fossil fuel imports via a more aggressive clean energy shift. Upon coming to power, the Yoon administration announced its intention to reduce the share of coal and gas in the energy mix to between 40 and 45 per cent by 2030, and to ramp up the country's efforts to transition to a hydrogen society—albeit with a significant role for nuclear in that picture.

Global market forces will also continue to lend major momentum to Korea's green shift. International investments in renewables will continue to drive costs down, and the Korean government and businesses remain steadfast in their desire to maintain and extend the country's competitiveness in the global renewables race, and to stay ahead of China in the green hydrogen race. To scale back investment would be to cede ground to China in this crucial advanced technology industry. Since the Russia crisis, China has been ramping up its renewables to offset associated price shocks. Most recently, China announced a major push into green hydrogen, which is expected to expand rapidly in the coming years. Like China, Korea will also be anxious to capitalize on the more vigorous pursuit of renewables, including green hydrogen—already underway in Europe, again as a consequence of the Russia crisis. In early March 2022, the EU announced a plan—REpowerEU—to become independent from Russian oil and gas by 2030, largely through the promotion of renewables. This plan will potentially increase already significant demand in the EU for renewable energy products from Northeast Asia's powerhouse economies (such as EVs, batteries, fuel cells). This in turn will further drive down the costs of renewables and green products, encouraging greater domestic uptake.

Moreover, regardless of Yoon's nuclear plans, Korea's electricity operators will still have to work within the ambitious renewable energy targets set by the Moon administration. As recently as October 2021, the Ministry of Trade Industry and Energy (MOTIE) revised the country's renewable energy portfolio standard, mandating that energy companies source at least 25 per cent of their energy from renewables by 2026, up from 9 per cent previously. This followed MOTIE's January 2021 announcement that it would finally allow renewable energy providers to sell electricity directly to industrial and retail consumers—reducing a longstanding obstacle to the widespread roll-out of renewables.

For all of these reasons, the revival of the nuclear debate in Korea under President Yoon is unlikely to come at the expense of the country's ambitious renewables push. Korea's green energy shift is likely to continue apace, thanks to the increasingly symbiotic relationship between political and capitalist market forces.

Aspect Two: Developmental environmentalism
as legitimation strategy

The second aspect worth highlighting is that developmental environmentalism serves as a political legitimation strategy—in both the context of our case studies, and also with an eye to the future in both Korea and China. As noted in Chapter 3, throughout the twentieth century, Northeast Asia's developmental regimes viewed the pursuit of rapid industrial development as the primary foundation of both their domestic political legitimacy and their international status and prestige. But at the dawn of the new century, these countries' traditional fossil-fuelled development strategies and their negative environmental consequences began to produce significant political blow-back, not just domestically but internationally as well. Thus, we find political leaders in NEA turning to developmental-environmental strategies as a new source of regime legitimation, as they seize the opportunity to tackle major environmental issues while simultaneously building the industries of tomorrow. In this context, what matters is the degree of ambition of the greening strategies and the technological choices involved (e.g., BEVs vs FCEVs in transport, or VHV vs UHV in power grids) and their capacity to further the political ambitions of the elites making these choices. While in past decades proud leaders like Park Chung-hee in Korea could call for dirty skies and industrial din to be recognized as the mark of industrial success in a city like Ulsan, now it is the very same cities that are emerging with clean chemical industries that are a badge of DE pride. Likewise in China, while it was fossil fuel-powered energy that built a modern city like Shenzhen on the Pearl River Delta, now it is initiatives like the building of an EV industrial park in Shenzhen, headed by EV producer BYD with its cross-linked supply chains, that captures attention and grants legitimacy to the local Communist Party officials.

In this context, it is worth emphasizing the extent to which political legitimacy concerns are also driving developmental-environmental ambition and action at the local government level, be it in provinces like Chungnam in Korea or Hefei in China that are taking the lead in driving the GET locally, in line with overall national policies and programs. As our case studies have revealed, the environmental and health challenges of particulate air pollution are geographically uneven—and typically worst in areas that have been home to coal-fired power plants and fossil-fuelled manufacturing industries (such as Chungnam and Ulsan in Korea), and to large concentrations of fossil-fuelled automobiles (such as the populous city of Seoul). It is typically local government officials who find themselves confronted with the ire of citizens who—thanks to disastrous levels of air pollution—might find themselves confined to their homes as the air in their town or city becomes unbreathable. It is thus not surprising that we find many of these local provincial governments setting the scene for a green transition, in terms of

their land allocation policies, their local taxation and financing, their job creating, and their training and industrial policies—all framed within overarching DE
ambitions.

Yet despite growing public demand for a green shift in Northeast Asia, it is also
worth noting that there remain major political obstacles to the greening shift in
China and Korea, as segments of the political elite and incumbent firms wedded
to the fossil fuel regime fight to protect their established interests, just as they do
in Western capitalist economies. Nevertheless, as our case studies have revealed,
FF incumbents also play complex roles in the green energy transition in NEA—as
both obstacles to and enablers of the shift in question. We have demonstrated that
the state-owned power grid companies SGCC in China and KEPCO in Korea have
emerged from the FF era as champions of grid modernization and of renewables,
through some complex political manoeuvres. The same can also be said of private
firms like Hyundai that have their origins in—and dominate—the fossil-fuelled
industries of the past, but that now straddle both the 'dirty' and 'clean' economies
and clearly intend to retain their dominance in the net zero emissions era of the
future.

Indeed, in the case of China, it is now not uncommon to find large energy
incumbents seeking to *resist* local government calls to expand their investments
in coal for short-term political reasons. Some context here is needed. Since President Xi announced his Net Zero pledge in 2020, many local governments have
raced to close coal-fired power stations to win central government approval, as we
have seen. However, in some provinces, this coal-exit race has led to severe power
shortages and blackouts, including during a bitterly cold winter.[10] These power
shortages have only been amplified by the Russia crisis (discussed in the section
above), which has pushed up the price of coal, worsening energy shortages in areas
under-resourced by renewables. The political blow-back has been severe at both
local and central government levels, leading many Chinese people to question the
pace of China's green shift and to demand greater attention to energy security. In
response to this snowballing political crisis, in March 2022 the Central Government published its '14th Five-Year Plan for a Modern Energy System', covering the
period from 2021 to 2025. Compared to the previous 12th and 13th plans (2011–
2015 and 2016–2022 respectively), this document comes with a notable change
in the title. Where previous documents emphasized 'A Plan for Energy Development', the 14th Five-Year Plan is 'A Plan for a Modern Energy System'. This change
hints a shift in policy focus from energy growth to the quality of the energy system

---

[10] Some commentators have likened local government reaction to Xi's net zero call to 'campaign
style' efforts to attract central government praise for their energy control and carbon emissions targets.
See, for example, the news report by Bloomberg at https://www.bloomberg.com/news/articles/2021-
07-30/china-softens-tone-on-climate-ambition-amid-power-shortages

from an energy transition perspective.[11] The Chinese leadership has also recently made clear that the country must 'establish [new energy supplies] before break [the old energy supplies] (先破后立)'.[12] So, unlike previous FYPs plans which set aggressive emissions targets, the 14th FYP adopts vaguer language and according to some sends 'mixed signals' in its energy targets.[13] By adopting vaguer language, the plan appears to leave more scope for local governments to temporarily expand their reliance on coal in the quest to balance energy security with greening goals.

Importantly for our purposes however, China's powerful energy incumbents are not thrilled about this change. Thanks to continuous reduction in renewable energy costs and resultant competitive advantages over fossil fuels in many areas, major energy companies in China reportedly no longer have an interest in investing in coal power projects—unless pushed hard by local governments.[14] This highlights just how far China's green shift has progressed since the mid 2010s. And Xi's announcement of his country's net zero pledge in 2020 has prompted new waves of policies and investments to facilitate the energy transition. According to the latest *Renewables Global Status Report*, China became the first country to have more than 1 terawatt of installed renewable energy capacity in 2021 amid the pandemic and led in all renewable technologies in terms of installed capacity in the year except concentrated solar power (CSP) (Ren21 2022). Thanks to the rapid growth in water, wind, and solar (WWS)-based power capacity and closures of power stations in large-scale in certain regions, coal-based power in China fell below 50% of the total electricity system in term of power generating capacity for the first time in 2020, dropping from a level of 67% ten years ago (Tan et al. 2021). These cost reductions are only likely to continue since China ramped up its renewables investment in the wake of the Russia crisis, to counter ongoing energy security concerns. In this context, the reluctance of incumbents to throw good money after bad—even at the urging of government officials—is understandable.

Here again, it is likely to be capitalist market dynamics (encompassing both industry creation and destruction) that determine for just how long those seeking to stall the energy shift—be they politicians, incumbent firms, or the wider public—might be able to succeed. At several points we have pointed to the learning

---

[11] Jiang, Y. and Gao, B. (2022). China's Five-Year Plan for energy: One eye on security today, one on a low-carbon future. *China Dialogue*, available at https://chinadialogue.net/en/climate/chinas-five-year-plan-for-energy-one-eye-on-security-today-one-on-a-low-carbon-future/

[12] See, for example, a briefing available at https://www.carbonbrief.org/china-issues-new-single-game-instructions-to-guide-its-climate-action/ .This term is a derivative of a slogan from Mao Zedong, the supreme leader of China before his death in 1976. Mao's original term, 'no breaking no establishing', reflects his view as a revolutionist that an old system must be removed to make room for a new one. Using the terminology in the creative-destruction literature, the new instruction requires the energy system to 'create before destruct' in the process of energy transition.

[13] Jiang, Y. and Gao, B. (2022). China's Five-Year Plan for energy: One eye on security today, one on a low-carbon future. *China Dialogue*, available at https://chinadialogue.net/en/climate/chinas-five-year-plan-for-energy-one-eye-on-security-today-one-on-a-low-carbon-future/

[14] See Jiang, Y. and Gao, B. (2022). China's Five-Year Plan for energy: One eye on security today, one on a low-carbon future. *China Dialogue*, available at https://chinadialogue.net/en/climate/chinas-five-year-plan-for-energy-one-eye-on-security-today-one-on-a-low-carbon-future/

curves leading to cost reductions in several green energy industries that provide the context for forward-looking industrial policies. It is these market dynamics that facilitate the green shift and that will inevitably resolve the political deadlocks that would otherwise threaten to derail the process—although whether this occurs in time to limit global warming to the 1.5 degrees required to avert climate catastrophe remains to be seen.

In this context, perhaps the key political legitimacy challenge remaining for Northeast Asian governments—both central and local—will be the growing problem of economic inequality, just as in the West. As we have shown in the case of Korea, while developmental-environmental strategies have largely delivered on their promise of renewed economic growth, they do not appear to have relieved the problem of growing inequality or the related problems of weak job creation and growing household indebtedness. At the same time, we have seen how concerns about living costs and job security in Korea have served to slow the green transition, for example, when it comes to green cars and concerns about related job losses in the automobile industry, or when it comes to ending subsidies for cheap, fossil-fuelled electricity. Evidently, the relationship between greening the economy, socio-economic prosperity, and political legitimacy in Korea (and beyond) is complex and deserves sustained scholarly and policy attention. In the meantime, Korea's deteriorating socio-economic conditions have now become—and are likely to remain—the focus of global attention, thanks to worldwide fascination with blockbuster Korean television series and films like Squid Game and Parasite that put the country's socio-economic problems front and centre. Given its global status-seeking ambitions, it is fair to say this is not the national image that the Korean government would wish to project abroad. In this sense, we are witnessing the clear limits to developmental environmentalism as a legitimation strategy both domestically and internationally.[15]

Similarly, despite the country's socialist proclamations, China's developmental-environmental strategies alone are unlikely to solve the country's growing income inequality and the political legitimacy challenges arising from the same. And while the world may find much to admire in the ambition and execution of China's DE strategies from a technical, economic, and environmental perspective, that admiration does not extend to China's increasingly repressive and exploitative actions towards its own population, and to some of its government's broader international actions—such as incursions into the South China Sea—which are widely viewed as aggressive and expansionist. Our argument seeks to separate what is positive and beneficial in these Northeast Asian nations' actions and behaviour from what is negative and retrograde. Suffice to say, the undeniable benefit of the approach we describe as developmental environmentalism is that it helps to overcome fossil-fuel resistance to and blockage of the green energy transition and frees up economic resources for future green industries.

---

[15] For an insightful commentary related to this topic see Lee (2021).

Aspect Three: Developmental environmentalism as an approach to sequencing the green energy transition

Thirdly and finally, we may view developmental environmentalism as a particular approach to sequencing the green energy transition—implying an emphasis on new industry creation and localization at the outset, and on infrastructure that encourages and nourishes fresh green industrial initiatives like FCEVs or smart grids. It is only when these new 'green shoots' of the economy have appeared that fossil fuel phase-out can begin in earnest. The cases demonstrate again how this works in practice—where both Korea and China started with early promotion of 'new energy vehicles' and are now moving to seriously dismantle the incumbent ICE vehicle industries that can be expected to give way to the new vehicle technologies.

It is in respect to the sequencing of the green energy transition that we again see the strong similarities between traditional developmentalism and developmental environmentalism; in both worldviews, the goals of building local manufacturing capacity, technological autonomy, and export competitiveness are understood as the essential foundation of national security and prosperity in an inherently hostile international arena. As such, in the DE mindset, there is little to be gained from replacing the country's dependence on fossil-fuelled imports with imports of renewable energies (REs)—especially when REs can form the foundation of a new suite of globally competitive, technology intensive, export-oriented manufacturing industries. In this sense, we see the mindset of DE as inextricably linked with the vision of 'manufacturing energy security' (*cf.* Mathews and Tan 2014). Thus, for DE-minded policymakers, new clean energy industry creation is viewed as the logical pre-requisite to fossil fuel sector destruction.

In this context it is worth reiterating that developmental-environmental strategies in Northeast Asia are not solely concerned with a change in market—say, green electricity consumption vs. coal-fired power—but with the value chains that culminate in the new capital equipment companies, such as Hyundai in the case of FCEVs in Korea, or Xuji electrical transformers in supplying UHV power grid components to SGCC in China. The interconnected value chains that we identify as hybridized industrial ecosystems are as much a part of the green energy transition in NEA as the final products being substituted—and which underlines the significance of viewing the GET as a full-blown industrial transformation and not just a set of substitutions like decarbonizing transport or an industry like steel or cement.[16] In this sense, our argument has focused on the dual aspects of the GET— the role of markets vs. state agencies; the role of industry creation vs. industry

---

[16] We also utilize the term HIEs as a means to understand the quasi-governmental entities exhibiting both public and private features as Kim (2019) defines. The examples of HIEs we have identified includes H2Korea in Korea's FCEV industry, EV100 in China's BEV industry, the role of SGCC in China's UHV industry network and the National Pilot Smart Cities program in Korea's smart grid industry.

destruction; and the final product substitution vs. the creation of HIEs. In our analysis, the GET is the most complex industrial, economic, and social transformation underway on the planet at this time, and it is driven by state agencies acting on environmental impulses—hence our description of the process in Northeast Asia as developmental environmentalism.

Concluding remarks: In Northeast Asia, there is no alternative to the green energy transition

What is it that compels China, Korea, and the other Northeast Asian countries to green their economies? Our take on these issues has been to depict China's green energy shift as a strategic response to the challenges as arising from the unprecedented scale of its industrialization strategy, requiring it to abandon fossil fuel reliance for reasons concerned with both domestic environmental degradation and 'geopolitical limits' to growth.[17] Viewed in this light, China is effectively compelled to make green choices as it moves to electrify its economy and replace its import-dependent, pollution-intensive, fossil-fuelled energy and resource flow systems with systems centred on locally produced, manufactured goods. Manufacturing choices are linked to innovation and learning curve-related cost reductions associated with each technology (such as wind turbines, solar PV cells and lithium-ion batteries). Manufacturing choices also reduce particulate pollution and import dependence, thus easing domestic political legitimacy challenges and geopolitical tensions associated with the relentless quest for fossil fuel resources. There is thus a plausible case that China is compelled to adopt a leading position as it greens its economy for largely nationalistic reasons. We have made a similar argument in relation to Korea—albeit with some modifications, insofar as Korea's challenges (at least in terms of population size and economic and educational diversity) appear less daunting than China's, and its global ambitions less hegemonic.

We argue that the way to understand the choices actually made in these countries more broadly is to view them as embodying wider politico-economic choices (e.g., support for manufacturing industry and export platforms for the future), as opposed to immediate interests in securing energy supplies from around the world. The choice on the part of both Korea and China to go with EVs and high-speed rail is based on future calculations of likely global demand for private transport, and the goal of having a well-established domestic industry to meet the demand as well as exports. That this will decarbonize both the Korean and Chinese automotive industries and industry generally is a highly fortunate side-effect of this strategy.

---

[17] See: J. Mathews and H. Tan, 'Manufacture renewables to build energy security', *Nature*, 10 September 2014, https://www.nature.com/articles/513166a

Similar arguments apply to Japan and Taiwan as they all in their different ways fashion a green shift in their economies that addresses their need for enhanced energy and resource security. Objective evaluation of the green growth strategies deployed by these countries frame them as a means to resolve intense pollution problems and energy/resources security problems. From the perspective of the mid-twenty-first century, it will doubtlessly be marvelled that countries were willing to hock their future to fossil fuels mined from the earth and distributed in such a way that access to them was constrained by geopolitical barriers.

We insist that this emphasis on nationalistic reasoning on the part of Northeast Asian countries is not in any way meant to diminish the importance of climate change concerns. They are and will remain central and critical issues. The point we are making is that climate change concerns do not exhaust the sources of compulsion felt by countries as they contemplate the green energy shift. In our argument it is NEA countries with their legacy of state-guided industrial development that find themselves in a peculiarly advantageous position as they embark on green choices, where state agencies play a central role. They can set the overall direction of change, the standards to be followed, and promotional efforts such as state procurement and market expansion to drive the adoption of the green technologies, as well as to curb the use of the incumbent fossil fuel technologies. So to what extent does this NEA approach of developmental environmentalism provide a model for other countries? And what does the intensification of geostrategic competition mean for the future of the global green shift? We tackle these questions in the concluding chapter.

9

The Global Green Shift in an Era of Geostrategic Rivalry

Our aim in this study has been to illuminate and explain Northeast Asia's distinctive pattern of performance in the green energy shift, with a particular focus on China and Korea. This pattern—which is difficult to discern from macro-level data alone (see Chapter 2)—has been characterized by a two-phased approach to the shift in question. Phase One began just after the turn of the twenty-first century and involved unprecedently ambitious efforts on the part of these states to rapidly build and scale the green energy industries of the future. By the mid-2010s, in the space of just over a decade, China and Korea had between them constructed the world's largest renewable energy system and assumed a leadership position in some of the key green technologies and industries of the future. Then began Phase Two of their shift, which since around 2015 has involved the increasingly ambitious embrace of fossil fuel phase-out—from the announcement of serious net-zero goals, to the closure of coal-fired power stations at home, and abroad to the phasing-out of financing for fossil-fuelled projects.

To summarize these developments in Schumpeterian terms, between the early 2000s and the mid-2010s, Northeast Asia's green shift was characterized by an overwhelming emphasis on the 'creative' side of the creative-destruction equation and the relative (though certainly not complete) neglect of the 'destructive' dimension. Since the mid-2010s however, we have witnessed a growing alignment between these states' creative and destructive ambitions and capabilities. Specifically, since around 2015 these states have not only ramped up their creative activities, but have also introduced significant destructive initiatives explicitly aimed at ending the era of dependence on fossil fuels. As a result, China and Korea are now arguably emerging as leaders rather than laggards in the global green shift—albeit with some important obstacles remaining.

Our explanation for this distinctive pattern of performance has focused squarely on elite orientation and ambition, which we have identified as the crucial factor both driving Northeast Asia's green energy shift and shaping its distinctive trajectory. Specifically, we have focused on the powerful legacy of these states' longstanding developmental traditions, and the relatively recent evolution of traditional developmental ways of thinking and acting into a newfound *developmental environmentalism* (DE). We have used the term developmental environmentalism in a very particular way: to capture an influential elite mindset

Developmental Environmentalism. Elizabeth Thurbon et al., Oxford University Press. © Elizabeth Thurbon, Sung-Young Kim, Hao Tan, and John Mathews (2023). DOI: 10.1093/oso/9780192897794.003.0009

combined with a related political legitimation strategy and a distinctive policy approach, by which we mean a particular approach to phasing and implementing the green shift.

We have shown that since the early 2000s, developmental environmentalism has exerted a profound influence on the direction of economic policymaking in China and Korea as these states have sought to overcome the acute environmental, economic, and political costs associated with their traditional fossil-fuelled growth strategies. Around the turn of the century, key policymakers in China and Korea came to realize that those traditional strategies could no longer deliver on their fundamental objectives of driving industrial development while achieving domestic political legitimacy and international security, status, and prestige. So, in light of their enduring developmental commitment and in order to address these new challenges, policymakers were forced to reimagine the relationship between their economic, environmental, and security goals. The result of this reimagining was what we are calling developmental environmentalism.

We provide a novel Schumpeterian perspective on this strategic orientation. When Schumpeter introduced his notion of *creative destruction* in the 1940s, as a means of accounting for the vibrancy and restlessness of capitalism, he had in mind a private sector where incumbent firms would be challenged by new entrants that could draw on the credit facilities of capitalist banks to finance production operations that matched the scale of those of incumbents, but with newer technologies or lower costs. This was a brilliant insight into the driving dynamics of capitalism that has stood the test of time. Because of creative destruction, incumbent firms cannot simply rest on their laurels, or benefit from monopoly rents, but instead have to continually revolutionize their operations to out-compete the new arrivals. But Schumpeter left out the role of the state. The East Asian 'tiger' economies have provided text-book cases of how to keep abreast of new technological developments, and catch-up with current technological leaders, through the institutional mechanisms of developmentalism. First Japan, then Korea and Taiwan (and Singapore) were able to close the gap between themselves and industrial leaders and become the prosperous entities that we recognize and admire today. In the twenty-first century, China has joined the ranks of these 'catch-up' economies, or fast-followers, emulating the prior successes of its Northeast Asian (NEA) neighbours but at ever greater scale. It was these late-comer exemplars, with China as the latest exponent, that showed how to add the missing ingredient of state agencies to the processes of creative-destruction.

But there was a major flaw in the Northeast Asian (NEA) strategy. At the scale of operations that has emerged in NEA, with China as the new lead exponent of fast-followership, the environmental costs of pursuing a traditional fossil-fuelled pathway became simply unbearable. The political elite in NEA, particularly in China and Korea, were forced to acknowledge this as the air in cities became unbreathable. And as the geopolitical costs of continuing to import fossil fuels from ever more dangerous parts of the planet were rising, so the notion of giving an environmental dimension to a traditional developmental trajectory became increasingly attractive. Instead of leaving this shift to a fickle private sector, in China and Korea the green shift was increasingly directed by state agencies acting to bolster the legitimacy of prevailing regimes. While 'developmental environmentalism' has never been articulated as such by political elites in these countries, we argue that this has in fact been the conceptual and political framework that has guided political thinking in China and Korea as these states confronted their existential environmental and geopolitical challenges.

Inspired by their newfound developmental-environmental orientation and ambition, since the early 2000s policymakers in East Asia have sought to simultaneously green and grow their economies in order to bolster their domestic political legitimacy and to shore up their nations' security, status, and prestige. In the earliest years, developmental environmentalism in Northeast Asia principally involved policymakers responding to pressing environmental problems with ambitious green industry building initiatives rather than 'destructive' initiatives aimed at fossil fuel (FF) phase-out.[1] This is because policymakers viewed green industry creation as the most politically viable means of addressing their sometimes (but certainly not always) conflicting environmental, economic, and security problems in one hit. By the mid-2010s, however, policymakers' early creative efforts were being lent serious momentum by broader capitalist market dynamics, especially those associated with manufacturing learning curves and related cost reductions. These dynamics helped to dramatically drive down the costs of renewable alternatives, and—coupled with intensifying environmental and geostrategic challenges—made 'destructive' policies aimed at FF phase-out more economically and politically viable. So, while elite orientation and ambition has been the primary driver of these states' ambitious greening strategies, we have argued that the material dynamics of industrial capitalism itself have played an equally important role. Finally in NEA, we now find state actors and market forces pushing in the same green direction—with serious implications for the future direction of the global green shift.

It is the scale of the market interventions in Northeast Asia, both to pave the way for new green industries to emerge (the creative side) and more recently to phase-out incumbent fossil-fuelled industries to make way for the green industries of the future (the destructive side) that is historically unprecedented. We argue that it is no accident that we find in NEA a green shift that is occurring at the largest scale on the planet (the shift to renewables as well as to a circular economy) that is complemented now by an equally large destructive push to phase-out incumbent fossil-fuelled industries, again at a scale that is the largest on the planet. The NEA

---

[1] See Chapter 3 for a discussion of the rationale that lies behind our deployment of the term 'destructive' in the context of the state's strategic role in driving and shaping Northeast Asia's green energy shift.

political elites understand that the destructive aspect releases resources needed for the creative initiatives to flourish—as we saw in the closure of coal-fired power operations in southern China to release land for new green initiatives in Guangdong. Thus, the creative and the destructive aspects of this green shift are taking place in NEA at a scale never before attempted—and at a scale that demands state guidance and coordination if it is not to result in total chaos and destruction. This is the challenge recognized and accepted by political elites in the region. It is a very different orientation from the familiar appeal to moral choice that is prevalent in discussions on environmental strategy and climate change mitigation in the West.

By placing elite orientation and ambition at the centre of our analysis, our approach differs fundamentally from existing interpretations and explanations of the green shift in Northeast Asia and beyond. A comparison between authoritarian China and democratic Korea has allowed us to challenge the conventional view that ambition and effectiveness in the green shift somehow hinges on regime type, be it authoritarianism (*cf.* Beeson 2010; Drahos 2021) or democracy (*cf.* Aghion et al. 2021). We have instead emphasized how the developmental-environmental orientation of the policymaking elite and their institutional underpinnings have helped drive a *collaborative* approach between state and business actors. Drawing upon concepts such as 'governed interdependence' (Weiss 1995) and its manifestation in green industries in East Asia through 'hybridized industrial ecosystems' (Kim 2019), our analysis highlights the Chinese and Korean states' role in *inducing* the cooperation of industrial actors in effecting developmental-environmental outcomes. This stands in stark contrast to the writers mentioned above who emphasize the state's ability to *overpower* or *coerce* industry to drive rapid environmental progress. To the extent that state orientation matters as the pillars upon which state capacity is built (as we have argued)—regime type should have little bearing on the emergence of developmental environmentalism in any given national context.

Our distinctive analytical approach centred on elite orientation and ambition also leads us to reject the view that there is nothing really new going on in East Asia, that the embrace of 'green growth' represents nothing more than greenwashed 'business as usual' for the region's growth-obsessed developmental states. In a serious departure from this conventional perspective, we argue that there is indeed something fundamentally transformative occurring in the region. Far from its being 'business as usual', East Asia's green shift represents a genuine effort to dismantle these states' entrenched fossil-fuelled, linear throughput model of industrial capitalism with a more sustainable model centred on renewable energies and circular economy principles—albeit at a scale hitherto unprecedented. While this newfound developmental environmentalism consists of a novel set of strategic prescriptions, we argue that it is deploying many of the same kinds of long-term strategic techno-industrial policies that characterized policymaking in the traditional developmental era. So, there is continuity and discontinuity in this green transformation in Northeast Asia. There is continuity in the sense that the environmentally-focused interventions draw on the well-established developmental traditions found in the region, and which provide the material basis for the wealth now found in countries like Korea and China. But there is discontinuity in the sense that a green industrial future calls for radical intervention on both the creative and destructive fronts, at a scale that far exceeds comparable policy-guided interventions in the West.

Importantly however, we have also observed techno-industrial policymaking taking on a distinctly new geostrategic flavour in Northeast Asia. In both China and Korea, the state's strategic activism in the green energy arena has now morphed into a kind of domestically-oriented economic statecraft (*cf.* Thurbon and Weiss 2019; Weiss and Thurbon 2020). In sharp contrast to the developmental period, industry creation initiatives are now aimed not simply at 'catching up with the west' in generic terms, but at keeping up with, ahead of, or outflanking clearly identifiable specific rivals: the US in the case of China, and China in the case of Korea. Indeed, more than anything else, it is this growing geostrategic competition that will henceforth shape the dynamic of the global green shift and determine its future trajectory. It is to the global implications of NEA's green shift that we now turn.

Geostrategic rivalry and the global green shift

It's difficult to imagine the United States winning the long-term strategic competition with China if we cannot lead the renewable energy revolution. Right now, we're falling behind. China is the largest producer and exporter of solar panels, wind turbines, batteries, EVs. It holds nearly a third of the world's renewable energy patents. If we don't catch up, America will miss the chance to shape the world's climate future in a way that reflects our interests and values, and we'll lose out on countless jobs for the American people.

(US Secretary of State Antony Blinken, 19 April 2021)[2]

We are in competition with China and other countries to win the 21st century. We are at a great inflection point in history. We have to do more than just build back better. ... We have to compete more strenuously.

(President Joe Biden, 28 April 2021)[3]

[2] 'Secretary Blinken: Tackling the Crisis and Seizing the Opportunity: America's Global Climate Leadership', *U.S. Embassy & Consulates in Brazil*, 19 April 2021, https://br.usembassy.gov/secretary-blinken-tackling-the-crisis-and-seizing-the-opportunity-americas-global-climate-leadership/

[3] 'Remarks by President Joe Biden in Address to a Joint Session of Congress', *The White House, Briefing Room Release*, 28 April 2021. https://www.whitehouse.gov/briefing-room/speeches-remarks/2021/04/29/remarks-by-president-biden-in-address-to-a-joint-session-of-congress/

The question is whether we'll lead or fall behind in the race for the future. It's whether we'll build [green] vehicles and ... batteries ... in the United States ... or [whether] we're going to have to rely on other countries ... Right now, China is leading the race, and is one of the largest and fastest-growing electric vehicle markets in the world ... And there's no reason why we can't reclaim that leadership and lead again. But we just have to move, and we have to move fast.

(President Joe Biden, 4 August 2021)[4]

It is widely accepted that geostrategic rivalry between China and the US has intensified greatly since the mid-2010s, and that this rivalry has been reflected in a long series of economic moves and counter-moves by both parties, from China's ambitious Belt and Road Initiative (BRI) to America's push for the Transpacific Partnership Agreement (TPPA) under President Obama and its China-focused 'trade war' under Trump. Now it is clear that a new frontline has emerged in this battle between the superpowers—one centred on the struggle for both technological and economic dominance in the green industries of the future.[5]

Yet somewhat ironically, in this sphere of crucial geostrategic importance, it is now the US playing catch-up with its Northeast Asian counterpart. In what can only be described as major strategic oversight, in the first two decades of the twentieth century, successive US administrations failed to grasp the economic, environmental, and geostrategic opportunities inherent in an ambitious national green energy shift. In addition to mitigating climate change, a sustained national greening effort might have helped stall or even reverse the decades-long decline of America's manufacturing base. And as a significant number of policy experts and scholars have now shown, America's manufacturing decline is not just a problem from an economic (i.e. jobs, income equality, and export) perspective. It is a problem from an innovation perspective as well, insofar as in many advanced technology industries, manufacturing and innovation are inextricably linked.[6] In other words, when you lose manufacturing capability, you can lose the capacity to innovate, especially at the technological frontier. As Linda Weiss has shown (2014, 2021) this point is now well understood by the US national security establishment, who are acutely aware that America's high-tech innovation engine is

[4] 'Remarks by President Joe Biden on Strengthening American Leadership on Clean Cars and Trucks' (5 August 2021). https://www.whitehouse.gov/briefing-room/speeches-remarks/2021/08/05/remarks-by-president-biden-on-strengthening-american-leadership-on-clean-cars-and-trucks/

[5] On the drivers and dynamics of the growing strategic rivalry between the US and China, and the conditions under which outright war between the superpowers might be avoided, see the insightful analysis by former Australian prime minister and China specialist Kevin Rudd (2022). From an International Relations perspective, his study is refreshing in the emphasis it places on the agency of national leaders and their ability to shape global dynamics.

[6] A growing body of scholarly and policy literature probes the essential relationship between production and innovation, as well as the complex drivers and implications (both economic and military) of America's techno-industrial hollowing-out, and possible pathways to techno-industrial re-building. See for example Berger (2013) Bonvillian (2017); Weiss (2014, 2021), Weiss and Thurbon (2018).

the foundation of its military primacy, and that this engine will struggle to survive in the absence of a vibrant domestic techno-industrial ecosystem. In this context, America's ongoing failure to establish a meaningful domestic production base in the green energy arena to complement (and help preserve) its innovation capabilities is deeply concerning.[7]

Meanwhile, China's approach to developing its green energy industries could not have been more different. Over the past two decades, while the US' political leaders stood idly by, China was able to seize leadership in a swathe of green technologies and industries (including but not limited to those we have canvassed in this book), and to establish a near monopoly over not just *access* to critical renewable energy inputs (such as rare earth minerals and metals) but the capability to *refine* those inputs at home.[8] By the time the US' national security establishment fully awoke and began to respond to China's techno-industrial challenge in 2017, the proverbial horse had bolted.[9] As such, and as the epigraphs at the start of this section indicate, the US now sees itself as engaged in an urgent battle to reclaim its position at the top of the global techno-industrial ladder—especially (but not only) in the green energy arena.[10]

The election of President Joe Biden in 2020 marked a new turning point in this growing struggle for supremacy, insofar as President Trump's climate denialism created a growing gulf between the US' domestic and foreign economic policy approaches to the green energy shift. Under Trump, fledgeling moves to revive the US' techno-industrial capabilities in the green energy arena[11] were effectively negated by the president's determination to withdraw the US from global climate initiatives—initiatives that could have dramatically expanded markets

---

[7] See Nahm (2021) for an insightful analysis of the divergent techno-industrial trajectories of US and Chinese renewable energy industries, with a focus on solar and wind. His analysis reveals that US energy start-ups have focused almost exclusively on the invention of new technologies, while largely neglecting commercialization and manufacturing. China's wind and solar firms on the other hand have pursued 'innovative manufacturing': i.e., the commercialization and scaling-up of novel technologies (2019: 60). Nahm provides a compelling explanation for these differences centred on the ways in which firms engage with legacy institutional arrangements in their respective domestic settings. While Nahm's study emphasizes the significant benefits associated with national specialization along these lines, it is less attentive to the potential risks involved (from an innovation perspective) in America's relinquishing manufacturing.

[8] See for example Hijazi and Kennedy (2020).

[9] See Weiss (2021) on the timing of America's awakening to China as a peer adversary in the techno-industrial arena.

[10] On the rise, consolidation and recent erosion of America's advanced technological and manufacturing capabilities and the geostrategic drivers of America's quest for technological supremacy for military primacy, see Weiss (2014, 2021).

[11] These included, for example, Trump's 2017 Presidential Executive order mandating the development of a Federal Strategy to Ensure Secure and Reliable Supplies of Critical Materials (see Humphries 2019), and the 2017 National Security Strategy that identified 'energy dominance' via the development of 'clean, affordable and reliable energy' as a primary national security goal (albeit with a dual emphasis on 'clean' and 'efficient' fossil fuels alongside renewables (National Security Strategy 2017, 22). That strategy also highlighted the risks arising from the erosion of America's manufacturing capabilities and identified the revival of those capabilities and the development of manufacturing self-sufficiency in critical industries (including energy) as a central security objective.

for US green technologies and products at home and abroad. Biden's election went some way towards resolving this contradiction. Almost immediately upon his inauguration in 2021, the new president moved to deliver on his pledge to re-engage with international climate change efforts while also turbo-charging efforts to re-establish US technological supremacy, manufacturing capability, and resource self-sufficiency in the green energy arena (and beyond). Thus through-out 2021, clean energy took centre stage in the global geostrategic battle between the superpowers.

So, what does this intensifying competition mean for the global green shift? Whether the Biden administration is up to the task of rebuilding the US' grossly depleted techno-industrial base is a complex question that deserves dedicated analysis and cannot detain us here.[12] What we can say is that the goal of promoting clean energies as the foundation of the US' domestic techno-industrial revival and to out-compete China has now achieved widespread consensus amongst US poli-cymakers and agencies concerned with the nation's environmental, economic, and military security.[13] As such—and in light of China's seemingly relentless ambitions (canvassed in Chapters 5 and 7) we see greening momentum in—and grow-ing competition between—the US and China as likely to further intensify. As a result, we are also likely to see an increasingly symbiotic relationship between state

[12] For a discussion see Weiss (2021).

[13] Over the course of 2021, the sentiments of Biden and Blinken captured in our epigraphs were echoed by agencies across the economic-military security spectrum including the Department of Defense and the Department of Energy. For example: 'We have to start, not just ... shifting to clean energy, but it has to be manufactured in the United States of America – you know, not in other countries.' (Comment made in reference to China, Gina McCarthy, US National Climate Advisor, 27 January 2021. 'Press Briefing by Press Secretary Jen Psaki, Special Presidential Envoy for Climate John Kerry, and National Climate Advisor Gina McCarthy', *The White House*, 27 January 2021, https://www.whitehouse.gov/briefing-room/press-briefings/2021/01/27/press-briefing-by-press-secretary-jen-psaki-special-presidential-envoy-for-climate-john-kerry-and-national-climate-advisor-gina-mccarthy-january-27-2021/); 'America is in a race against competitors like China to own the EV market – and the supply chains for critical materials like lithium and cobalt will determine whether we win or lose. If we want to achieve a 100% carbon-free economy by 2050, we have to create our own supply of these materials, including alternatives here at home in America' (Jennifer M. Granholm, US Secretary of Energy, 18 March 2021). 'DOE Announces $30 Million for Research to Secure Domestic Supply Chain of Critical Elements and Minerals', *US Department of Energy*, 18 March 2021, https://www.energy.gov/articles/doe-announces-30-million-research-secure-domestic-supply-chain-critical-elements-and); 'The Department of Defense (DOD) has announced an investment in the expansion of the largest rare earth element mining and processing company outside of China to provide the raw materials necessary to help combat the climate crisis ... China, using state-led, non-market interventions, captured large portions of value chains in several critical minerals and materials necessary for national and economic security. China accounts for an outsized share of the world's refining capacity, meaning that even if the United States were to diversify our sources of critical minerals or increase domestic extraction, we would still be reliant on China for processing before use in end-product manufacturing.' (The White House, Department of Defense. 'Fact Sheet: Biden–Harris Administration Announces Supply Chain Disruptions Task Force to Address Short-Term Supply Chain Discontinuities', *The White House*, 8 June 2021, https://www.whitehouse.gov/briefing-room/statements-releases/2021/06/08/fact-sheet-biden-harris-administration-announces-supply-chain-disruptions-task-force-to-address-short-term-supply-chain-discontinuities/

activism and market dynamics—not just in East Asia but increasingly in the US and its allies.

Ironically then, we might find that it is *national competition* (economic and geostrategic) rather than *international cooperation* that drives greatest action on climate change—confounding liberal assumptions that nationalism necessarily presents an obstacle to addressing collective global challenges. There are, however, also clear dangers associated with this growing competition, which could just as easily derail the action needed to contain climate change to the 1.5 degrees required to avoid global catastrophe. There is no question that a set of concrete and binding global emissions reduction targets are desirable and would help to drive more ambitious greening action in countries across the globe. But as we saw in the lead-up to COP-26 in 2021, the achievement of binding global targets hinges in no small part on cooperation between the US and China. While such cooperation is by no means unthinkable under the current leadership in both countries—even in the context of geostrategic rivalry—it is likely to remain highly unpredictable and is far from guaranteed.[14] And when it comes to the challenge of climate change, there is also the danger that growing geostrategic competition serves to split the world into different technological camps. This would make the global diffusion of green technologies difficult and slow the uptake of new green products and services, slowing decarbonization efforts. Competition could also slow the development of global standards, again stalling commercialization (see Chapter 6) and the emergence of new mass green markets.[15] In this sense, while we highlight the enormous transformative potential of great power competition in the green energy arena, we remain wary of its destructive potential as well. At this point, judging the most likely outcome remains premature, and rightly the focus of separate studies. However, if our analysis has revealed anything, it is the crucial role that elite orientation and ambition will undoubtedly play in shaping the future trajectory.

We face similar ambiguity when assessing the implications of US–China rivalry for global economic development efforts. We see it as likely that growing geostrategic competition will drive deeper engagement with developing countries as major powers look to extend their spheres of influence. So what are the implications of this growing engagement—and of Northeast Asia's green transition more generally—for global development efforts? To what extent are China's and Korea's experiences generalizable for a broader set of countries and at different levels of industrial progress?

---

[14] See Tan et al. 2021 'The US and China must find a way to cooperate at COP26 and beyond otherwise global climate action is impossible', *The Conversation*. 25 October. https://theconversation.com/the-us-and-china-must-find-a-way-to-cooperate-at-cop26-and-beyond-otherwise-global-climate-action-is-impossible-170094

[15] For an insightful examination of different productive and destructive scenarios emerging from US-China competition in the green tech arena, see Bazilian et al. (2020).

Implications of Northeast Asian experience
for developing countries

Our aim has been to demonstrate in this book how the Northeast Asian experience of greening the economy makes abundant sense—and in many ways is the only alternative—for the countries of the region, particularly China and Korea but also for others such as Japan, Taiwan, Singapore, Malaysia—countries that all in their different ways can look back at long developmental traditions. But to what extent does this NEA approach of developmental environmentalism provide a model for other countries? We tackle this question with regard to both developing and developed countries below.

The question as to whether Northeast Asia's approach to greening is a model that developing countries *should* now follow is redundant, largely because the temporalities have changed. The green energy shift was perhaps a difficult choice for Korea and China in the early 2000s because the technologies involved (solar, wind power, EVs, batteries) were so new. As a consequence, the costs of the transition stood much higher at the time when they started their green transitions, necessitating a short-term economic trade-off between (then) cheaper fossil fuels and the deployment of more expensive and uncertain green technologies. But now, thanks largely to the massive, long-term investment efforts of NEA governments, the cost and risks of transitioning to renewables for developing countries are much lower. In this sense, a renewable energy future is now a no-brainer. Given the availability of clean and green energy sources, at lower costs than for incumbent FFs, why would any country—developing or developed—wish to tie itself to the uncertainties and higher costs of a fossil-fuelled future? Why tie yourself to the geopolitical uncertainties of FFs, and the oil, gas, and coal wars of the future, when you have clean and green alternatives available at lower cost which will contribute to your manufacturing revival and—precisely because they are products of manufacturing under domestic control—to your energy and resource security?

Perhaps not surprisingly, we already see emulation of the Northeast Asian experience in tomorrow's industrial giants like Brazil, India, and Indonesia. These countries and those like them wish to capitalize on the chance to manufacture their own energy, economic, and environmental security. The switch away from fossil fuels not only reduces their energy insecurity, but the focus on manufacturing their own energy future also contributes to their manufacturing-led industrialization. The costs are already below those of incumbent FFs, and continue to fall through the operation of the learning curve (experience curve) that is associated with manufacturing operations. The clean energy alternatives are safe and clean compared with the sorry history of environmental disasters associated with mining/drilling and transport of oil, gas, and coal.[16] And as manufactured alternatives, the clean and green energy systems promise competitive advantages based on innovation in place of the monopoly rents relied on in the world of FFs. Under these circumstances, why would any country wish to continue with the 'fossil fools' option?

Based on the factors incentivizing a developmental-environmental project given above, one can reasonably expect many policymakers in the developing world to seek to emulate the Northeast Asian experience. However, there are also obstacles to the wider embrace of a developmental-environmental approach in the developing world. While a manufacturing-led development strategy is undoubtedly a desirable option for a developing country, it also poses challenges that are *sui generis*. The first challenge relates to the central importance of elite orientation and ambition when it comes to the sustained pursuit of a rapid industrialization drive, and thus to the question of how to build and sustain a degree of cohesion among the political, policy, and business elite around a national DE project. The second challenge relates to the equally important issue of state capacity, and thus to the question of how to build the institutional architecture and strategic policy capability required to translate DE ambition into sustained and effective action.

In this sense, the debate about the transferability of Northeast Asia's developmental environmentalism model will necessarily come down to the same kinds of questions that have informed the longstanding debate about the region's traditional developmental model and its wider applicability.[17] To wit: In today's world, what conditions (both domestic and international) might contribute to the emergence of a DE-mindset among the political and policy elite in developing country contexts? How might political leaders in these contexts forge a consensus (or something approximating a consensus) around the pursuit of developmental-environmental goals among their diverse economic and social constituencies? And how might DE-minded policymakers in these contexts navigate, manipulate or otherwise transform their institutional environments in ways that enhance state capacity and enable them to advance DE objectives over the long term? Evidently then, while NEA's DE model might provide a *desirable* development pathway for developing countries, emulating that model—while by no means impossible— remains an enormously complex endeavour that demands transformation not simply at *policy* level, but at the more fundamental level of political-economic

---

[16] This is notwithstanding the fact that to a large extent, the renewable energy economy is still dependent upon the extraction of natural resources—including rare earth minerals and metals—a process that entails many of the geostrategic, environmental and social risks and challenges involved in traditional fossil fuel extraction—a point we discuss in more detail below.

[17] For a mindset-sensitive approach to this question see Thurbon (2016, 2017) and Thurbon and Weiss (2016, 2019).

ideas and *institutions.* We thus see it as imperative that debates about green development pathways move beyond *policy prescriptions* (as important and helpful as these might be) to address the more challenging questions of the ideational and institutional transformations needed to support the green shift, and how best to enable these transformations.

However, it is also important to note that no matter how strong their developmental-environmental commitment or institutional capabilities, today's developing countries will still face major *external* obstacles to their pursuit of an Northeast Asian-style green growth strategy. Chief among these obstacles are international trade and investment rules that make it difficult—if not impossible—for developing countries to deploy the kinds of strategic industrial policies required to support an ambitious national industrialization strategy—green or otherwise. A voluminous body of literature now documents the ways in which various trade and investment rules (under both the WTO and various preferential trade agreements) limit developing countries' policy space, especially (but not only) on the techno-industrial front, and conflict with greening goals promoted by other international agencies like the UN Framework Convention on Climate Change (UNFCCC).[18] Yet over the past two decades, calls to reform these rules and to establish a more development-friendly trade and investment regime have fallen on deaf ears.

To be sure, the 2008 global financial crisis (GFC), the 2020 global pandemic, and growing concerns about climate change have all served in different ways to shake faith in the existing global order, and to focus debate on the kinds of trade and investment rules that might allow developing countries to build local manufacturing capability and self-sufficiency in some critical health- and energy-related industries. In fact, the 2021 UN *Trade and Development Report* highlights the importance of a 'developmental mindset' to the green transition in developing countries, and the urgent need to adapt trade and investment rules to allow developing countries the space to experiment with a Northeast Asian-inspired approach to greening and growing their economies.[19] Nevertheless, despite the fracturing neoliberal consensus since 2008, it is fair to say that little concrete progress has been made when it comes to reforming the problematic trade and investment rules in question.

Another potential obstacle to the green transition in developing countries is that despite the falling costs of renewables, other countries may continue to promote a 'brown growth' model abroad—against market logic—in order to maintain economic returns on legacy fossil fuel investments as long as possible. Many African

---

[18] On the later point see Mathews (2019). On the ways in which trade and investment rules tend to 'kick away the ladder' for developing countries see for example Chang (2002), Stiglitz and Charlton (2005), and Wilkinson (2014).

[19] See UNCTAD *Trade and Development Report 2021*. https://unctad.org/system/files/official-document/tdr2021_en.pdf

countries find themselves in this position, such as oil exporters like Nigeria or Namibia. Countries like Australia, for example, continue to finance FF projects abroad, although the pressure is now mounting for this to change, as international financial organizations turn their backs on FF financing. China and Korea are also playing their part in coal-exit in developing countries.[20] And while not necessarily an obstacle to the green transition itself, there is the important issue of managing the potentially negative environmental and social consequences of the extractives side of the renewable equation, namely, the mining of minerals, including rare earths, that are central to the production of clean energy-related equipment such as batteries, like lithium, cobalt, nickel and manganese. Here we see evidence of—and ongoing potential for—the exploitation of developing countries by governments and firms involved in mining activities related to the global green shift. Ensuring the environmentally and socially responsible extraction of resources thus looms as a major challenge for developed and developing countries alike, especially in the absence of effective international governance and accountability mechanisms.[21] Again, geostrategic logic comes in here because— as noted previously—China and the US (and their allies) will be competing to become 'development partners of choice' for less developed countries. In this sense, continuing to promote a 'brown growth' model or to engage in socially and environmentally harmful mining practices could undermine broader strategic objectives.

Finally, there may be some countries which have little appetite and/or institutional scope for developmental-environmental strategies, engulfed by the more basic challenge of *state-building* (e.g., war-torn states such as Afghanistan). On this front, our argument is clearly limited to developing countries exhibiting features of *modern states* although in some instances (such as the Gaza strip), the instability caused by state-building efforts on access to basic services such as electricity has been shown to drive wide-scale deployments into green technologies (*cf.* Fischhendler et al. 2021). The green shift is not a panacea and cannot work where states are broken.

Lessons for advanced countries

Finally, on the question of lesson learning, which is often discussed in relation to developing countries but should not be confined to this single category, we see important issues raised as well. We see Northeast Asia as holding potential lessons not just for developing countries but for developed countries too, in the sense

[20] See for example Tan et al., 'China closes the door to coal', *East Asia Forum*, 9 November 2021, at: https://www.eastasiaforum.org/2021/11/09/china-closes-the-door-to-coal/
[21] On this important topic, see the work of scholars such as Susan Park and Teresa Kramarz (Park and Kramarz 2019)

that developmental-environmental strategies and solutions have now globalized. Historically there has been a reluctance to 'learn lessons from' NEA—a Western arrogance perhaps. We see this in the willingness to downplay NEA's achievements in the global green shift, the tendency to underestimate the complex challenges they are negotiating, and how much they have achieved.

The advanced countries have much to learn from the Northeast Asian model of developmental environmentalism in its foregrounding of the need to strike a balance between the creative and destructive aspects of a green transformation. Advanced countries tend to see incumbent industries as sources of political conservatism and barriers to change, whereas their dismantling in NEA provides a textbook case of how to deal with large incumbents that must give way to new, clean and green sources of growth. Here again the Schumpeterian perspective provides telling insights. The Norwegian scholar Erik Reinert has contrasted the Schumpeterian institutions of a dynamic economy, fostering growth and development, with what he calls the Hayekian institutions that are focused on maintaining equilibrium or the *status quo* (Reinert 2006). Schumpeterian institutions like a development bank offer long lines of credit to aspiring challengers of the status quo. The China Development Bank acts in China as such an institution in sponsoring solar and wind power newcomers utilizing new, clean and green technologies at greater scale than envisaged in the West, while denying credit lines to incumbent coal-fired power generators. By contrast, Hayekian institutions look instead at seeking to restore a balance across the static characteristics of the economy, as when Western banks and economists promote carbon taxes as a way of restoring 'balance' between new green industries and their fossil fuel incumbent competitors. We build on this contrast in our argument that Schumpeterian institutions, grounded in strategic industrial governance, have much to recommend them in an advanced economy looking to its future prosperity as much as in a developing economy looking through industrialization to join the ranks of wealthy countries.

But how realistic is it that East Asia's lessons might resonate beyond the region— especially in countries where liberal economic thinking has long reigned supreme, turning hearts and minds against a more strategic role for the state in economic management, from the United States to the UK and Australia? Here we would note that even in East Asia, the inclination towards a stronger state and strategic techno-industrial governance is neither an inherent nor fixed feature of the socio-political landscape. Rather, developmental ideas emerged and gained prominence in East Asia at particular moments in history, typically as geostrategic conditions changed for the worse, creating the domestic political space required for a reset in the national economic policymaking approach. Under such conditions, the agents of change are often small groups of freer-thinking officials who do not share the dominant mindset, and who are able to seize the moment to start navigating, manipulating, and eventually remaking their existing institutional environments to advance a more long-term, strategic policy agenda. This much we know from the insights gleaned through an agent-centred, historical institutionalist approach, of the kind we have adopted in this study.[22] Do such conditions for change exist in the West today?

In recent times, the challenges of the Covid-19 crisis have seen economic policymakers in even the most neoliberal environments embrace polices that were unthinkable just months prior, in a pre-pandemic world—including full border closures. At the same time, at the height of the Covid pandemic, innovative policymakers in neoliberal contexts sought to bypass institutional constraints to meet pressing national challenges. For example, in both the UK and Australia, policymakers rapidly mobilized local firms to at least partially address pressing supply problems that threatened to undermine their pandemic response.[23] In times of crisis, the unthinkable becomes possible. So, as the twin challenges of the climate crisis and global geo-strategic competition intensify, it is not inconceivable that policymakers in liberal regimes may begin to embrace a more strategic approach to the green shift, as some scholars, including some of us, have anticipated (see for example Aghion et al. 2021, Kim 2021). From precisely where in the state apparatus such change might emerge will vary from country to country. In the US, change may emanate from the longstanding efforts of strategic thinkers within America's National Security State (Weiss 2014, 2021). In Australia, we have already seen 'green shoots' emerge from various federal and state government initiatives aimed at the development, storage, and shipping of renewables-derived 'green' hydrogen (*cf.* COAG Energy Council Hydrogen Working Group 2019). As this book went to press and in light of growing strategic tensions with China, Australia's new Labor government was seeking to turn those 'green shoots' into a proverbial forest, making cooperation with the country's Pacific neighbours on a rapid green energy shift its top policy priority. Australia's experience is hardly generalizable—and the success of its strategy yet to be determined. The broader point is that the global green shift (Mathews 2017) creates the conditions for a developmental-environmental response amongst national authorities.

Finally, we reiterate the point that this book is not a work in normative theorizing, but an exercise in describing and interpreting state policies in Northeast Asia. There is a moral challenge of course in terms of climate change, and there are lessons to be learned from NEA for developed and developing countries alike, but the key aim of this book has been to explain what is actually occurring in Northeast Asia—not to judge it as right or wrong, good or bad. In this we draw inspiration from the great social scientist of the twentieth century, Max Weber, who foresaw a

---

[22] Pioneering agent-centred HI studies include Bell (2011) and Bell and Feng (2013). For a systematic application of this approach to the East Asian context see Thurbon (2016, 2019).

[23] See Weiss and Thurbon (2021) for an examination of strategic state responses to the Covid crisis in neoliberal contexts.

program for the social sciences in terms of building empirical foundations (collecting 'facts') before seeking to account for these data through applying theoretical models. *First come the facts, then build theory to account for the facts and test competing theories against the facts.* This is Weberian social science in action, and we have been guided by these insights in our approach to the clean energy transition in East Asia.[24]

First, we have established the facts of the transition, as outlined in Chapter 2, demonstrating how the East Asian nations, led by China and Korea, have not only built the largest green energy and circular economy industries on the planet, but have complemented these state-guided initiatives with interventions to dismantle the huge fossil-fuelled industries that form the incumbent core of these countries' energy and resources industries. We argue that these facts call for a convincing theoretical explanation. And the explanation we offer is that in the NEA countries, the developmental traditions that propelled these countries to their present wealth and power have been merged with environmental strategies. As a result, these countries have forged a strategic framework of developmental environmentalism that is focused on solving environmental problems through economic and industrial initiatives. Is there a better explanation for the empirical facts that we have presented concerning NEA's clean and green transition? And is there a better strategy for both developing and developed countries to pursue as they confront existential environmental problems and the imperative of transforming outmoded fossil-fuelled industries?

---

[24] For the Weberian perspective on social science, see his magisterial *Economy and Society* (originally published in German in 1921 as *Wirtschaft und Gesellschaft*) and now available in numerous English translations such as a new 2019 translation by Keith Tribe.

Bibliography

ABB Hitachi. 2014. 'Enabling a stronger, smarter and greener grid: Opportunities and challenges for the evolving world of power'. Baden: Hitachi ABB Power Grids.

Abramovitz, Moses. 1986. 'Catching up, forging ahead, and falling behind', *The Journal of Economic History* 46 (2): 385–406.

Aghion, Philippe, Céline Antonin, and Simon Bunel. 2021. *The Power of Creative Destruction: Economic Upheaval and the Wealth of Nations.* Cambridge: Harvard University Press.

Amsden, Alice. 1989. *Asia's Next Giant: South Korea and Late Industrialisation.* New York: Oxford University Press.

Amsden, Alice and Takashi Hikino. 1994. 'Staying Behind, Stumbling Back, Sneaking Up, Soaring Ahead: Late Industrialisation in Historical Perspective', in William J. Baumol, Richard R. Nelson, and Edward N. Wolff (eds.), *Convergence of Productivity: Cross National Studies and Historical Evidence.* New York: Oxford University Press, pp. 285–316.

ASTE-NAEK. 2020. 'Hydrogen futures: Summary report', Melbourne and Seoul: Australian Academy of Technology and Engineering and the National Academy of Engineering Korea.

Bank of America Merrill Lynch. 2011. 'A primer on China's seven strategic industries'. New York: Bank of America Merrill Lynch.

Bazilian, Morgan, Michael Bradshaw, Johannes Gabriel, Andreas Goldthau, and Kirsten Westphal. 2020. 'Four scenarios of the energy transition: Drivers, consequences, and implications for geopolitics', *Wiley Interdisciplinary Reviews: Climate Change* 11(2): e625.

Beeson, Mark. 2010. 'The coming of environmental authoritarianism', *Environmental Politics* 19 (2): 276–294.

Beeson, Mark. 2018. 'Coming to terms with the authoritarian alternative: The implications and motivations of China's environmental policies: Environmental authoritarianism in China', *Asia & the Pacific Policy Studies* 5(1): 34–46.

Bell, Stephen. 2011. 'Do we really need a new "constructivist institutionalism" to explain institutional change?', *British Journal of Political Science* 41(4): 883–906.

Bell, Stephen. 2020. 'The renewable energy transition energy path divergence, increasing returns and mutually reinforcing leads in the state-market symbiosis', *New Political Economy* 25(1): 57–71.

Bell, Stephen and Hui Feng. 2013. 'How proximate and "meta-institutional" contexts shape institutional change: Explaining the rise of the People's Bank of China', *Political Studies* 62(1): 197–215.

Berger, Suzanne. 2013. *Making in America: From Innovation to Market.* Cambridge: MIT Press.

Best, Jacqueline, Colin Hay, Genevieve LeBaron, and Daniel Mügge. 2020. 'Seeing and not-seeing like a political economist: The historicity of contemporary political economy and its blind spots', *New Political Economy* 26(2): 217–228.

BNEF. 2021. Electric Vehicle Outlook 2021, available at: https://bnef.turtl.co/story/evo-2021/page/4/2

Bonvillian, William B. 2017. *Advanced Manufacturing: A New Policy Challenge*. Hanover: Now Publishers.

Booz & Co. 2014. 'China's next revolution: Leading the transition to electric cars', Presentation at *World Ecological Forum*. Online Accessed on 1 June 2019.

BNEF. 2021. 'Electric Vehicle Outlook 2021'. *BloombergNEF*, November. Available at: https://bnef.turtl.co/story/evo-2021/page/4/2

BP. 2021. *Statistical Review of World Energy*, available at https://www.bp.com/en/global/corporate/energy-economics/statistical-review-of-world-energy.html

Bremmer, Ian. 2009. 'State capitalism comes of age: The end of the free market?', *Foreign Affairs* May/June: 40–55.

Breznitz, Dan and Michael Murphree. 2013. 'The rise of China in technology standards: New norms in old institutions'. Washington D.C.: US–China Economic and Security Review Commission.

Brunekreeft, Gert, Marius Buchmann, Christian Dänekas, Xin Guo, Christoph Mayer, Marcus Merkel, Christian Rehtanz, André Göring, Andre Herrmann, Ray Kodali, Michael Stadler, Mathias Uslar, Nils Vogel, Till Luhmann, Tobias Menz, Sven-Uwe Müller, and Paul Recknagel. 2015. 'China's way from conventional power grids towards smart grids', in Gert Brunekreeft, Till Luhmann, Tobias Menz, Sven-Uwe Müller and Paul Recknagel (eds.), *Regulatory Pathways For Smart Grid Development in China*. Wiesbaden: Springer Fachmedien Wiesbaden, pp. 19–43.

Burton Bob. 2016. 'Hunger strike pushes South Korea to defer coal plant plan'. *Renew Economy*. https://reneweconomy.com.au/hunger-strike-pushes-south-korea-defer-coal-plant-plan-34148/

CAAM (China Association of Automobile Maufacturers). 2020. 'Annual sales of automobiles in China'. Beijing: China Association of Automobile Manufacturers.

Cao, Cong, Richard Suttmeier, and Denis Fred. 2006. 'China's 15-year science and technology plan', *Physics Today* 59: 38–43.

CEESA (Center for Energy, Environmental, and Economic System Analysis) and Paulson Institute. 2015. *Power Play: China's Ultra-high Voltage Technology and Global Standards*. Chicago: Paulson Institute.

Chan, Gerald. 2018. *Understanding China's New Diplomacy: Silk Roads and Bullet Trains*. Cheltenham: Edward Elgar.

Chang, Ha-Joon. 2002. *Kicking Away the Ladder: Development Strategy in Historical Perspective*. London: Anthem Press.

Chang, Kyung-Sup. 2011. 'Developmental Citizenship in Perspective: The South Korean Case and Beyond', in Kyung-Sup Chang and Bryan S. Turner (eds.), *Contested Citizenship in East Asia: Developmental Politics, National Unity, and Globalisation*. New York and London: Routledge, pp. 182–203.

Chang, Seungchan. 2018. 'Republic of Korea—2018 update: Bioenergy policies and status of implementation', in Luc Pelkmans (ed.), *IEA Bioenergy Country Reports*. Paris: IEA Bioenergy, pp. 1–14.

Chen, Geoffrey C. and Charles Lees. 2019. 'Political recentralisation and the diffusion of solar energy in China', *Europe-Asia Studies* 71(7): 1162–1182.

Chen, Xu, Kevin P. Gallagher, and Denise L. Mauzerall. (2020). 'Chinese overseas development financing of electric power generation: A comparative analysis', *One Earth* 3(4): 491–503.

Chen Yuan, C. Y., Cynthia Lin Lawell, and Yunshi Wang. 2020. 'The Chinese automobile industry and government policy', *Research in Transportation Economics* 84: 100849.

ChinaEV100. 2020. 'Comprehensive evaluation and promotion recommendations for the timetable for full electrification of vehicles in China'. Beijing: China EV100, Natural Resources Defense Council, and Institute for Transportation & Development Policy.

Choi, Byung-Sun. 1988. *Economic Policymaking in Korea: Institutional Analysis of Economic Policy Changes in the 1970s and 1980s*. Seoul: Chomyung Press.

Choi, Hyundo, Sangook Park, and Jeong-dong Lee. 2011. 'Government-driven knowledge networks as precursors to emerging sectors: A case of the hydrogen energy sector in Korea', *Industrial and Corporate Change* 20(3): 751–787.

Choi, Junyoung and Hyung Min Kim. 2020. 'State-of-the-Art Korean Smart Cities: A Critical Review of the Sejong Smart City Plan' in Hyungmin Kim, Soheil Sabri, and Anthony Kent (eds.), *Smart Cities for Technological and Social Innovation: Case Studies, Current Trends, and Future Steps*. Cambridge: Academic Press, pp. 51–72.

Chu, Wan-Wen. 2011. 'How the Chinese government promoted a global automobile industry', *Industrial and Corporate Change* 20(5): 1235–1276.

Chu, Wan-Wen. 2017. 'Inductive method and development perspective: Alice Amsden on Taiwan and beyond', *Cambridge Journal of Regions, Economy and Society* 10(1): 15–34.

COAG Energy Council Hydrogen Working Group. 2019. 'Australia's National Hydrogen Strategy'. Canberra: Australian Department of Industry, Innovation and Science.

Committee on Green Growth (CGG). 2019a. 'Jae 3 Cha Noksaek Seongjang 5 Gaenyeon Gyaehoek' [Third Five-Year Plan for Green Growth]. Seoul: CGG.

CGG. 2019b. *Jae 3 Cha Noksaek Seongjang 5 Gaenyeon Gyaehoek* (Third Five-Year-Plan for Green Growth) (Summary). Seoul: CGG.

Yan, Gloria and Dave Dal. 2014. 'China Power Transmission and Distribution Equipment'. Credit Suisse, 3 July. Available at https://plus.credit-suisse.com/r/V6TnLr2AF-WEqyjw

Cui, Hongyang and Hui He. 2019. 'Liuzhou: A new model for the transition to electric vehicles?', blog at The International Council on Clean Transportation, 18 December. Available at https://theicct.org/blog/staff/liuzhou-new-model-transition-electric-vehicles

Curry, Claire. 2017. Lithium-ion battery costs and markets, Bloomberg New Energy Finance, 5 July. Available at https://data.bloomberglp.com/bnef/sites/14/2017/07/BNEF-Lithium-ion-battery-costs-and-market.pdf

De Wit, Andrew. 2015. 'Japan's bid to become a world leader in renewable energy', *The Asia-Pacific Journal: Japan Focus* 13(40): 1–19.

De Wit, Andrew. 2020. 'Is Japan a Climate Leader? Synergistic Integration of the 2030 Agenda', *The Asia-Pacific Journal: Japan Focus* 18(3): 1–22.

Dent, Christopher M. 2014. *Renewable Energy in East Asia: Towards a New Developmentalism*. London: Routledge.

Dent, Christopher M. 2018. 'East Asia's new developmentalism: State capacity, climate change and low-carbon development', *Third World Quarterly* 39(6): 1191–1210.

Doner, Richard F., Gregory W. Noble, and John Ravenhill. 2021. *The Political Economy of Automotive Industrialization in East Asia*. Oxford: Oxford University Press.

Downie, Edmund. 2018. 'Sparks fly over ultra-high voltage power lines', *China Dialogue*, 29 January. Available at https://chinadialogue.net/en/energy/10376-sparks-fly-over-ultra-high-voltage-power-lines/

Drahos, Peter. 2021. *Survival Governance: Energy and Climate in the Chinese Century*. New York: Oxford University Press.

Eckersley, Robyn. 2018. 'The green state in transition: Reply to Bailey, Barry and Craig', *New Political Economy* 25(1): 46–56.

Eckersley, Robyn. 2004. *The Green State: Rethinking Democracy and Sovereignty*. Cambridge: MIT Press.

Economy, Elizabeth C. 2010. *The River Runs Black: The Environmental Challenge to China's Future* (2nd edn.). Ithica, New York: Cornell University Press.

Erickson, Andrew and Gabriel Collins. 2021. 'Competition with China to save the planet: Pressure, not partnership, will spur progress on climate change', *Foreign Affairs* 100(3): 136–149.

Evans, Peter. 1995. *Embedded Autonomy: States and Industrial Transformation*. Princeton: Princeton University Press.

Finamore, Barbara. 2018. *Will China Save the Planet?* Cambridge: Polity Press.

Fischhendler, Itay, Lior Herman, and Lioz David. 2021. 'Light at the end of the panel: The Gaza strip and the interplay between geopolitical conflict and renewable energy transition', *New Political Economy* 27(1): 1–18.

Fu, Xiaolan and Jing Zhang. 2011. 'Technology transfer, indigenous innovation and leapfrogging in green technology: The solar-PV industry in China and India', *Journal of Chinese Economic and Business Studies* 9(4): 329–347.

Gao, Xudong. 2013. 'A latecomer's strategy to promote a technology standard: The case of Datang and TD-SCDMA', *Research Policy* 43: 597–607.

Gao, Xudong. 2019. 'Approaching the technological innovation frontier: Evidence from Chinese SOEs', *Industry and Innovation* 26(1): 100–120.

Garnaut, Ross. 2019. *Superpower: Australia's Low-carbon Opportunity*. Melbourne: Black Inc.

Geall, Sam and Adrian Ely. 2018. 'Narratives and pathways towards an ecological civilisation in contemporary China', *The China Quarterly* 236: 1175–1196.

Gilley, Bruce. 2012. 'Authoritarian environmentalism and China's response to climate change', *Environmental Politics* 21(2): 287–307.

Global Green Growth Institute. 2015. *Korea's Green Growth Experience: Process, Outcomes and Lessons Learned*. Seoul: GGGI.

Global Green Growth Institute (GGGI). 2011. 'Green Growth in Motion: Sharing Korea's Experience'. Seoul: GGGI.

Goh, Evelyn (ed.). 2016. *Rising China's Influence in Developing Asia*. Oxford: Oxford University Press.

Gong, Huiming, Michael Q. Wang, and Hewu Wang. 2013. 'New energy vehicles in China: Policies, demonstration, and progress', *Mitigation and Adaptation Strategies for Global Change* 18(2): 207–228.

Greenhouse Gas Inventory and Research Centre of Korea (GIR). 2019. 'National Greenhouse Gas Inventory (1990–2017)'. Cheongju City: GIR.

Ha, Yoon-Hee and John Byrne. 2019. 'The rise and fall of green growth: Korea's energy sector experiment and its lessons for sustainable energy policy', *WIREs Energy and Environment* 8(4): e335.

Hallegatte, Stephane, Marianne Fay, and Adrien Vogt-Schilb. 2013. 'Green industrial policies: When and how'. *Policy Research Working Paper* No. 6677. Washington, D.C.: World Bank.

Han, Heejin. 2015. 'Authoritarian environmentalism under democracy: Korea's river restoration project', *Environmental Politics* 24(5): 810–829.

Han, Heejin. 2017. 'Singapore, a garden city: Authoritarian environmentalism in a developmental state', *The Journal of Environment & Development* 26(1): 3–24.

Hansen, Mette Halskov, Hongtao Li, and Rune Svarverud. 2018. 'Ecological civilisation: Interpreting the Chinese past, projecting the global future', *Global Environmental Change* 53: 195–203.

Harrell, Stevan, Joanna I. Lewis, Mary Alice Haddad, and Ashley Esarey. 2020. *Greening East Asia: The Rise of the Eco-developmental State.* Seattle: University of Washington Press.

Haslam, Gareth E., Joni Jupesta, and Govindan Parayil. 2012. 'Assessing fuel cell vehicle innovation and the role of policy in Japan, Korea, and China', *International Journal of Hydrogen Energy* 37(19): 14612–14623.

He, Xiyou and Qing Mu. 2012. 'How Chinese firms learn technology from transnational corporations: A comparison of the telecommunication and automobile industries', *Journal of Asian Economics* 23(3): 270–287.

Heilbroner, Robert L. 1974. *An Inquiry into the Human Prospect.* 1st edn. New York: Norton.

Helleiner, Eric. 2021. 'Neglected Chinese origins of East Asian developmentalism', *New Political Economy*, DOI: 10.1080/13563467.2021.1961217

Helleiner, Eric and Jonathan Kirshner. 2014. *The Great Wall of Money: Power and Politics in China's International Monetary Relations.* Ithaca: Cornell University Press.

Hertzke, Patrick, Nicolai Müller, and Stephanie Schenk. 2017. 'Dynamics in the global electric-vehicle market', McKinsey & Company, 6 July, Available at https://www.mckinsey.com/industries/automotive-and-assembly/our-insights/dynamics-in-the-global-electric-vehicle-market

Hickel, Jason and Giorgos Kallis. 2020. 'Is Green Growth Possible?', *New Political Economy*, 25(4): 469–486. DOI: 10.1080/13563467.2019.1598964

Hijazi, Jamil and James Kennedy. 2020. 'How the United States handed China its rare-earth monopoly and how Washington could get it back', *Foreign Policy*, 27 October. Available at https://foreignpolicy.com/2020/10/27/how-the-united-states-handed-china-its-rare-earth-monopoly/

Hove, Anders and David Sandalow. 2019. 'Electric vehicle charging in China and the United States'. New York: Columbia University Centre on Global Energy Policy.

Huang, Ping and Ping Li. 2020. 'Politics of urban energy transitions: New energy vehicle (NEV) development in Shenzhen, China', *Environmental Politics* 29(3): 524–545.

Huang, Qing, Yuan Zeng, and Qin Jiang. 2015. 'Progress and prospect of the study on "making great efforts to promote ecological civilisation construction"', *China Population, Resources and Environment* 25(2): 111–120.

Humphries, Marc. 2019. 'Critical minerals and US public policy', *Congressional Research Service*, 28 June. Available at https://crsreports.congress.gov/product/pdf/R/R45810

IEA (International Energy Agency) 2017a. 'Korea, Policies, Green Car Roadmap'. Paris: International Energy Agency.

IEA. 2017b. 'World Energy Outlook'. Paris: International Energy Agency.

IEA. 2018. 'Republic of Korea: 2018 Update'. In *IEA Bioenergy Country Report.* Paris: International Energy Agency.

IEA. 2019. 'The Future of Hydrogen'. Paris: International Energy Agency.

IEA. 2020. 'Global EV Outlook'. Paris: International Energy Agency.

IEA. 2021. 'The Role of Critical World Energy Outlook Special Report Minerals In Clean Energy Transitions'. International Energy Agency. Available at https://www.iea.org/reports/the-role-of-critical-minerals-in-clean-energy-transitions

IHA. 2021. 'Hydropower Status Report'. London: International Hydropower Association.

Innovation Center for Energy and Transportation (ICET). 2019. 'A study on China's timetable for phasing-out traditional ICE vehicles'. Beijing and California: Innovation Center for Energy and Transportation.

The International Council on Clean Transportation (ICCT). 2018. *Assessment of Incentive Policies for New Energy Vehicles in Chinese Cities*. The International Council on Clean Transportation. Available at https://theicct.org/publications/evaluation-incentive-policies-China-urban-NEVs

Intralink Limited. 2019. 'Smart Cities South Korea: Market Intelligence Report'. London: Department for International Trade.

Jaffe, Amy Myers. 2018. 'Green giant: Renewable energy and Chinese power', *Foreign Affairs* 97(2): 83.

Jason Hickel & Giorgos Kallis (2020) Is Green Growth Possible?, *New Political Economy*, 25:4, 469–486, DOI: 10.1080/13563467.2019.1598964

Jha, Shikha, Sonia Chand Sandhu, and Radtasiri Wachirapunyanot. 2018. 'Inclusive green growth Index: A new benchmark for quality of growth'. Manila: Asian Development Bank (ADB).

Jiang, Hong and Feng Lu. 2018. 'To be friends, not competitors: A story different from Tesla driving the Chinese automobile industry', *Management and Organisation Review* 14(3): 491–499.

Johnson, Chalmers. 1982. *MITI and the Japanese Miracle: The Growth of Industrial Policy, 1925–1975*. Standford: Stanford University Press.

Kahn, Mohsin. 2009. 'The 2008 Oil Price "Bubble"'. Peterson Institute for International Economics Policy Brief'. Washington D.C.: Peterson Institute for International Economics.

Kalinowski, Thomas. 2020. 'The politics of climate change in a neo-developmental state: The case of South Korea', *International Political Science Review* 42(1): 48–63.

Kan, Sichao. 2020. 'South Korea's Hydrogen Strategy and Industrial Perspectives'. Paris: French Institute of International Relations (ifri).

Kang David. 2018. 'South Korea's environmental ambition tackles the coal challenge', *Powering Past Coal Alliance*. https://poweringpastcoal.org/insights/policy-and-regulation/south-koreas-environmental-ambition-tackles-coal-challenge

Kim, Byung-Kook. 1992. 'Economic policy and the Economic Planning Board (EPB) in Korea', *Asian Affairs* 18(4): 197–213.

Kim, Hyung-Kook. 2010. 'Presentation slides of Keynote speech delivered at "Workshop on Delivering Green Growth"—Seizing New Opportunities for Industries hosted by the OECD and Korean Ministry of Knowledge Economy'. Seoul, Korea, 4–5 March 2010.

Kim, Linsu. 1997. *Imitation to Innovation: The Dynamics of Korea's Technological Learning*. Cambridge: Harvard Business Review Press.

Kim, Sang-Hyup and Choi Hyeon-Jung. 2013. 'Green Growth for a Greater Korea: White Book on Korean Green Growth Policy, 2008–2012'. Seoul: Korea Environment Institute.

Kim, Sung-Young. 2012. 'Transitioning from fast-follower to innovator: The institutional foundations of the Korean telecommunications sector', *Review of International Political Economy* 19(1): 140–168.

Kim, Sung-Young. 2013. 'The rise of East Asia's Global Companies'. *Global Policy* 4(2): 184–193.

Kim, Sung-Young. 2019. 'Hybridised industrial ecosystems and the makings of a new developmental infrastructure in East Asia's green energy sector', *Review of International Political Economy* 26(1): 158–182.

Kim, Sung-Young. 2021. 'National competitive advantage and energy transitions in Korea and Taiwan', *New Political Economy* 26(3): 359–375.

Kim, Sung-Young and John A. Mathews. 2016. 'Korea's greening strategy: The role of smart microgrids', *The Asia-Pacific Journal: Japan Focus* 14: 1–25.

Kim, Sung-Young and Elizabeth Thurbon. 2015. 'Developmental environmentalism: Explaining South Korea's ambitious pursuit of green growth', *Politics & Society* 43(2): 213–240.

Kim, Sung-Young, Elizabeth Thurbon, John Mathews, and Hao Tan. 2019. 'China succeeds in greening its economy not because but in spite of its authoritarian government', *The Conversation*, last modified 28 May. Available at https://theconversation.com/china-succeeds-in-greening-its-economy-not-because-but-in-spite-of-its-authoritarian-government–115568

Klingler-Vidra, Robyn and Ramon Pacheco Pardo. 2020. 'Legitimate social purpose and South Korea's support for entrepreneurial finance since the Asian financial crisis', *New Political Economy* 25(3): 337–353.

Koo, Hagen. 2021. 'Rising inequality and shifting class boundaries in South Korea in the neo-liberal era', *Journal of Contemporary Asia* 51(1): 1–19.

Korea Electric Power Corporation (KEPCO). 2017. 'Annual Report 2017'. Naju, Jellon-amdo.

Korea Smart Grid Institute (KSGI). 2015. 'Smart grid, an energy revolution in our daily lives'. Seoul: KSGI.

Korolev, Alexander. 2015. 'The PRC political regime's reaction to the basic needs of the population'. *Far Eastern Affairs* 2(43): 97–117.

Kramarz, Teresa, Susan Park, and Craig Johnson. 2021. 'Governing the dark side of renewable energy: A typology of global displacements', *Energy Research & Social Science* 74: 101902.

Lampton, David M. 2008. *The Three Faces of Chinese Power: Might, Money, and Minds.* Berkeley: University of California Press.

LeBaron, Genevieve, Daniel Mügge, Jacqueline Best, and Colin Hay. 2020. 'Blind spots in IPE: Marginalised perspectives and neglected trends in contemporary capitalism', *Review of International Political Economy* 28(2): 283–294.

Lee, Hyun-Soon. 2020. *Buckle Down: How I Invented South Korea's First Automobile Engine.* Singapore: Harriet Press.

Lee, Keun. 2013. *Schumpeterian Analysis of Economic Catch-up: Knowledge, Path-Creation, and the Middle-Income Trap.* Cambridge: Cambridge University Press.

Lee, Keun. 2019. *The Art of Economic Catch-Up: Barriers, Detours and Leapfrogging in Innovation Systems.* Cambridge: Cambridge University Press.

Lee, Keun. 2021. 'East Asia's Squid Game Economies', *Project Syndicate*. 20 December. Available at: https://www.project-syndicate.org/commentary/east-asia-squid-game-economies-inequality-by-keun-lee-2021-12

Lee, Keun and Chaisung Lim. 2001. 'Technological regimes, catching-up and leapfrogging: Findings from the Korean industries', *Research Policy* 30(3): 459–483.

Lee, Sanghun. 2015. 'Assessing South Korea's green growth strategy', in Raymond L. Bryant (ed)., *The International Handbook of Political Ecology*. Cheltenham, UK: Edward Elgar Publishing, pp. 345–358.

Lee, Sanghun. 2014. 'Electricity in Korea', in Christopher Findlay (ed.): *Priorities and Pathways in Services Reform. Part II, Political Economy Studies*. New Jersey: World Scientific, pp. 111–127.

Li, Mingjiang (ed.). 2017. *China's Economic Statecraft: Co-optation, Cooperation and Coercion*. Vol. 39. Singapore: World Scientific Publishing.

Li, Wenbo, Muyi Yang, and Suwin Sandu. 2018. 'Electric vehicles in China: A review of current policies', *Energy & Environment* 29(8): 1512–1524.

Lim, Yirang, Jurian Edelenbos, and Alberto Gianoli. 2019. 'Smart energy transition: An evaluation of cities in South Korea', *Informatics* 6(4): 1–20.

Liu, Zhenya. 2013. *Electric Power and Energy in China*. Singapore: John Wiley & Sons, Inc.

Liu, Zhenya (ed.). 2016. *Global Energy Interconnection*. London: IFC: Academic Press.

Malcomson, Scott. 2020. 'How China became the world's leader in green energy', *Foreign Affairs*, 28 February. https://www.foreignaffairs.com/articles/china/2020-02-28/how-china-became-worlds-leader-green-energy (22 November 2022).

Malyshev, Nick, Guillermo Hernández, Ruben Maximiano, and Leni Papa. 2021. 'Regulatory Quality and Competition Policy in Korea', in OECD, '12 Ways Korea is Changing the World' Paris: OECD, pp. 146–164.

Marketline. 2020. 'Autonomotive Manufacturing in China', Retrieved from Marketline Advantage Database, 1 March 2021.

Marquis, Christopher, Hongyu Zhang, and Lixuan Zhou. 2013. 'China's quest to adopt electric vehicles', *Stanford Social Innovation Review* 11(2): 52–57.

Mathews, John A. 2012. 'The Asian Super Grid', *The Asia-Pacific Journal: Japan Focus* 10(48): 1–6.

Mathews, John A. 2013. 'The renewable energies technology surge: A new techno-economic paradigm in the making?', *Futures* 46: 10–22.

Mathews, John A. 2015. *The Greening of Capitalism: How Asia Is Driving the Next Great Transformation*. 1st edn. Redwood City: Stanford University Press.

Mathews, John A. 2017a. 'China's electric power: Results for first half 2017 demonstrate continuing green shift', *The Asia-Pacific Journal: Japan Focus* 15(18): 1–20.

Mathews, John A. 2017b. *Global Green Shift: When Ceres Meets Gaia*. New York: Anthem Press.

Mathews, John A. 2018. 'Schumpeter in the twenty-first century: Creative destruction and the global green shift', in Leonardo Burlamaqui and Rainer Kattel (eds.), *Schumpeter's Capitalism, Socialism and Democracy: A Twenty-First Century Agenda*. Abingdon, Oxon. and New York: Routledge, pp. 233–254.

Mathews, John A. 2019. 'The green growth economy as an engine of development: The case of China', in Roger Fouquet (ed.), *Handbook on Green Growth*. Cheltenham: Edward Elgar, pp. 325–342.

Mathews, John A. 2020. 'Schumpeterian economic dynamics of greening: propagation of green eco-platforms', *Journal of Evolutionary Economics* 30(4): 929–948.

Mathews, John A. and Dong-Sung Cho. 2000. *Tiger Technology: The Creation of a Semiconductor Industry in East Asia*. Cambridge: Cambridge University Press.

Mathews, John A. and Carol X. Huang. 2020. 'Greening trends within China's energy system: A 2019 update', *The Asia-Pacific Journal: Japan Focus* 18(17: 3): 1–1apa2.

Mathews, John A. and Hao Tan. 2013. 'The transformation of the electric power sector in China', *Energy Policy* 52: 170–180.

Mathews, John A. and Hao Tan. 2014. 'Economics: Manufacture renewables to build energy security', *Nature* 513(7517): 166–168.

Mathews, John A. and Hao Tan. 2015. *China's Renewable Energy Revolution. Building a Sustainable Political Economy – SPERI Research & Policy Series*. Basingstoke: Palgrave Macmillan.

Mathews, John A. and Hao Tan. 2016. 'Circular economy: Lessons from China', *Nature* 531: 440–442.

Mathews, John A., Elizabeth Thurbon, Sung-Young Kim, and Hao Tan. 2022. 'Gone with the wind: How state power and industrial policy in the offshore wind power sector are blowing away the obstacles to East Asia's green energy transition', *Review of Evolutionary Political Economy* 3(2), https://doi.org/10.1007/s43253-022-00082-7

Matsuo, Tyeler and Tobias S. Schmidt. 2019. 'Managing tradeoffs in green industrial policies: The role of renewable energy policy design', *World Development* 122: 11–26.

Mazzucato, Mariana. 2015. 'The green entrepreneurial state', in Ian Scoones, Melissa Leach, and Peter Newell (eds)., *The Politics of Green Transformations*. London and New York: Routledge, pp. 134–152.

Metzler, Mark. 2013. Capital as Will and Imagination: Schumpeter's Guide to the Postwar Japanese Miracle. Ithaca, New York: Cornell University Press.

Meng, Si. 2012. 'An insight into the green vocabulary of the Chinese communist party', *China Dialogue*, 15 November. Available at https://chinadialogue.net/en/pollution/5339-an-insight-into-the-green-vocabulary-of-the-chinese-communist-party/

Ministry of Economy and Finance (MOEF). 2020. 'National Strategy for a Great Transformation: Korean New Deal'. Sejong: Ministry of Economy and Finance.

Ministry of Science and Technology (MoST). 2001. 'The Ministry of Science and Technology's Briefing on implementation of the Ninth Five-Year National Science and Technology Plan and the Plan for the Work in the Science and Technology Area during the Tenth Five-Year'. Ministry of Science and Technology of the People's Republic of China. Available at http://www.scio.gov.cn/xwfbh/xwbfbh/wqfbh/2001/0424/Document/327727/327727.htm (accessed on 1 June 2019)

Ministry of Trade, Industry and Energy (MOTIE). 2017. 'The 8th Basic Plan for Long-Term Electricity Supply and Demand (2017–2031)'. Republic of Korea Ministry of Trade, Industry and Energy.

MOTIE. 2018. *Jae2cha Jineunghyeong Jeongryeokmang Gibon Gyehoek (2018–2022)* [Second Five-Year Master Plan for the Intelligent Grid (2018–2022)]. Seoul: MOTIE.

Moon, Jae-In. 2019. 'Remarks by the President at Presentation for Hydrogen Economy Roadmap and Ulsan's Future Energy Strategy'. Cheongwadae: The Republic of Korea. Last Modified 17 January 2019. Available at http://english1.president.go.kr/briefingspeeches/speeches/110.

Moore, Scott M. 2014. 'Modernisation, authoritarianism, and the environment: The politics of China's South–North Water Transfer Project', *Environmental Politics* 23(6): 947–964.

Nagashima, Monica. 2018. 'Japan's Hydrogen Strategy and Its Economic and Geopolitical Implications'. *French Institute of International Relations (ifri)*, October. Available at: https://www.ifri.org/sites/default/files/atoms/files/nagashima_japan_hydrogen_2018_.pdf

Nahm, Jonas. 2021. *Collaborative Advantage: Forging Green Industries in the New Global Economy*. Oxford: Oxford University Press.

Nam, Kyung-Min. 2011. 'Learning through the international joint venture: Lessons from the experience of China's automotive sector', *Industrial and Corporate Change* 20(3): 855–907.

National Security Strategy. 2017. 'National Security Strategy of the United States', December, Washington DC. https://trumpwhitehouse.archives.gov/wp-content/uploads/2017/12/NSS-Final-12-18-2017-0905.pdf

Newell, Peter and Andrew Simms. 2021. 'How did we do that? Histories and political economies of rapid and just transitions', *New Political Economy* 26(6): 907–922.

Nicholas, Simon and Tim Buckley. 2019. 'Briefing Note: South Korea shifting further away from coal', *Institute for Energy Economics and Financial Analysis (IEEFA)*. April. Available at: https://ieefa.org/wp-content/uploads/2019/04/South-Korea-Shifting-Further-Away-from-Coal_April-2019.pdf

Norris, William J. 2016. *Chinese Economic Statecraft: Commercial Actors, Grand Strategy, and State Control.* Ithaca and London: Cornell University Press.

OECD (Organisation for Economic Co-operation and Development). 2012. 'Inclusive Green Growth: For the Future We Want'. Paris: OECD.

OECD. 2020. 'Greenhouse Gas Emissions'. *OECD Statistical Database.* Available at: https://stats.oecd.org/Index.aspx?DataSetCode=air_ghg

Oh, Myŏng and James F. Larson. 2020. *Digital Development in Korea: Lessons for a Sustainable World (Second Edition).* Abingdon and New York: Routledge.

Ohta, Hiroshi. 2021. 'Why Japan is No-Longer a Front-Runner: Domestic Politics, Renewable Energy, and Climate Change Policy', in P. Midford and E. Moe (eds.), *New Challenges and Solutions for Renewable Energy.* International Political Economy Series. Switzerland: Palgrave Macmillan, pp. 51–77.

Oswald, James Peter Francis. 2017. 'Environmental governance in China: Creating ecologically civilised environmental subjects.' PhD Thesis, School of Social Sciences: Asian Studies, University of Adelaide.

Park, Hun-Joo. 2007. 'Small business' place in South Korean state–society relations', Asian Journal of Political Science, 15(2), 195–218. doi:10.1080/02185370701511560

Park, Sangook. 2013. 'The country-dependent shaping of "hydrogen niche" formation: A comparative case study of the UK and South Korea from the innovation system perspective', *International Journal of Hydrogen Energy* 38(16): 6557–6568.

Park, Susan and Tamara Kramarz. 2019. *Global Environmental Governance and the Accountability Trap.* Cambridge, MA: MIT Press.

Paterson, Matthew. 2020. 'Climate change and international political economy: Between collapse and transformation', *Review of International Political Economy* 28(2): 394–405.

Paterson, Matthew. 2021. '"The end of the fossil fuel age"? Discourse politics and climate change political economy', *New Political Economy*: 923–936.

Paterson, Matthew and Xavier P-Laberge. 2018. 'Political economies of climate change', *WIREs Climate Change* 9(2): 1–16.

PCGG (Presidential Committee on Green Growth). 2009a. 'Progress Report 2008–2009 on Low Carbon, Green Growth of the Republic of Korea'. Seoul: PCGG.

PCGG. 2009b. 'Road to Our Future: Green Growth, National Strategy and the Five-Year Plan (2009–2013)'. Seoul: PCGG.

Pierri, Erika, Ole Binder, Nasser G. A. Hemdan, and Michael Kurrat. 2017. 'Challenges and opportunities for a European HVDC grid', *Renewable and Sustainable Energy Reviews* 70: 427–456.

Qiu, Wenqian, Ke Sun, and Hao Zhou. 2018. 'Development of UHV power transmission in China', in Zhou Hao (ed.), *Ultra-high Voltage AC/DC Power Transmission.* Hangzhou: Zhejiang University Press, pp. 23–37.e

Reilly, James. 2021. *Orchestration.* Oxford and New York: Oxford University Press.

Reinert, Erik S. 2006. Institutionalism ancient, old and new: A historical perspective on institutions and uneven development'. *Paper 2006/77.* Tokyo: UN University World Institute for Development and Economics Research.

Ren, Zeping. 2020. 'New Energy Vehicle Report'. Evergrande Research Institute.

REN21. 2022. *Renewables 2022 Global Status Report.* Paris: REN21 Secretariat.

Rengarajan, Srinath. 2019. 'Letter to the editor: Complementing the Tesla forum EV discussion with a view upstream', *Management and Organisation Review* 15(1): 201–205.

Ritchie, Hannah and Max Roser. 2017. 'CO₂ and greenhouse gas emissions', *Our World in Data* [online], Last Modified August. Available at https://ourworldindata.org/co2-and-other-greenhouse-gas-emissions#citation

Ritchie, Hannah, Max Roser, and Pablo Rosado. 2020. 'CO$_2$ and Greenhouse Gas Emissions'. Published online at OurWorldInData.org. Retrieved from: 'https://ourworldindata.org/co2-and-other-greenhouse-gas-emissions' [Online Resource]

Rodrik, Dani. 2014. 'Green industrial policy', *Oxford Review of Economic Policy* 30(3): 469–491.

Rudd, Kevin. 2022. *The Avoidable War: The Dangers of a Catastrophic Conflict Between the US and Xi Jinping's China*. Sydney: Hachette Australia.

Samuels, Richard. 1994. '*Rich Nation Strong Army': National Security and the Technological Transformation of Japan*. Ithaca, New York: Cornell University Press.

Schumpeter, Joseph A. 2003. *Capitalism, Socialism and Democracy*. New York: Taylor and Francis.

Shan, Juan and Dominique R. Jolly. 2011. 'Patterns of technological learning and catch-up strategies in latecomer firms: Case study in China's telecom-equipment industry', *Journal of Technology Management in China* 6(2): 153–170.

Shapiro, Judith. 2016. *China's Environmental Challenges*. Cambridge: Polity Press.

Shih, Willy. 2018. 'Why high-tech commoditisation is accelerating', *MIT Sloan Management Review* 59(4): 53–58.

Shirk, Susan L. 2008. *China: Fragile Superpower*. Oxford: Oxford University Press.

Sigurdson, Jon. 2004. 'Industry and policy perspectives: Technological superpower China?', *R & D Management* 34(4): 345–347.

Smil, Vaclav. 2010. *Energy Myths and Realities: Bringing Science to the Energy Policy Debate*. Washington DC: AEI Press.

Soete, Luc and Carlota Perez. 1988. 'Catching up in technology: Entry barriers and windows of opportunity', in Giovanni Dosi, Christopher Freeman, Richard R. Nelson, Gerald Silverberg, and Lec Soete (eds.), *Technical Change and Economic Theory* London: Pinter Publishers, pp. 458–479.

Song, Yaowu and Mingqi Chen. no date. 'Comparative study on hydrogen economy policy of China and Korea'. Washington University Working Paper.

Sonnenschein, Jonas and Luis Mundaca. 2016. 'Decarbonisation under green growth strategies? The case of South Korea', *Journal of Cleaner Production* 123: 180–193.

Sovacool, Benjamin K. 2016. 'How long will it take? Conceptualising the temporal dynamics of energy transitions', *Energy Research & Social Science* 13: 202–215.

Sovacool, Benjamin K. 2019. 'The history and politics of energy transitions: Comparing contested views and finding common ground', in Douglas Arent, Channing Arndt, Mackay Miller, Finn Tarp, and Owen Zinaman (eds.), *The Political Economy of Clean Energy Transitions*. Oxford: Oxford University Press, pp.16–36.

Sovacool, Benjamin K. and Frank Geels. 2016. 'Further reflections on the temporality of energy transitions: A response to critics', *Energy Research & Social Science* 22: 232–237.

Stangarone, Troy. 2020. 'South Korea's green new deal', *The Diplomat*, 29 May. Available at https://thediplomat.com/2020/05/south-koreas-green-new-deal/

State Council. 2001. 'Notice on the Management of the National High-Tech Research and Development Plan (the 863 Program)'. People's Republic of China. Available at http://www.gov.cn/gongbao/content/2002/content_61702.htm (accessed on 15 March 2021)

Stiglitz, Joseph E. and Andrew Charlton. 2005. *Fair Trade for All: How Trade can Promote Development*. Oxford: Oxford University Press on Demand.

Swedberg, Richard. 1991. *Joseph A. Schumpeter : His Life and Work*. Oxford: Polity Press.

Sun, Zhe. 2015. 'Technology innovation and entrepreneurial state: The development of China's high-speed rail industry', *Technology Analysis & Strategic Management* 27(6): 646–659.

Taguchi, Hiroyuki 2001. 'Do developing countries enjoy latecomers' advantages in environmental management and technology?: Analysis of the environmental Kuznets curve', *International Review for Environmental Strategies* 2(2): 1–15.

Tan, Hao. 2018. 'A global industrial rebalance: China, the U.S. and energy-intensive manufacturing', *The Asia-Pacific Journal: Japan Focus* 16(10): 1–9.

Tan, Hao and John A. Mathews. 2015. 'Accelerated internationalisation and resource leverage strategising: The case of Chinese wind turbine manufacturers', *Journal of World Business* 50(3): 417–427.

Tan, Hao, Elizabeth Thurbon, Sung-Young Kim, and John A. Mathews. 2021. 'Overcoming incumbent resistance to the clean energy shift: How local governments act as change agents in coal power station closures in China', *Energy Policy* 149: 112058.

Tan, Hao, Elizabeth Thurbon, John Matthews, and Sung-Young Kim. 2021. 'China closes the door to coal', *East Asia Forum*, 9 November. Available at https://www.eastasiaforum.org/2021/11/09/china-closes-the-door-to-coal/

Tan, Hao, Elizabeth Thurbon, John Matthews, and Sung-Young Kim. 2021. 'The US and China must find a way to cooperate at COP26 and beyond: Otherwise, global climate action is impossible', *The Conversation*, 25 October. Available at https://theconversation.com/the-us-and-china-must-find-a-way-to-cooperate-at-cop26-and-beyond-otherwise-global-climate-action-is-impossible–170094

Tan, Hao and Mengying Yang. 2021. 'The New Liability of Origin in Global Decoupling', *Management and Organization Review* 17: 624–629.

Temple, James. 2018. 'China's giant transmission grid could be the key to cutting climate emissions', *MIT Technology Review*, 8 November. Available at: https://www.technologyreview.com/2018/11/08/138280/chinas-giant-transmission-grid-could-be-the-key-to-cutting-climate-emissions/

Thurbon, Elizabeth 2014. 'The resurgence of the developmental state: A conceptual defence', *Critique Internationale* 2: 59–75.

Thurbon, Elizabeth. 2016. *Developmental Mindset: Revival of Financial Activism in South Korea*. Ithaca: Cornell University Press.

Thurbon, Elizabeth. 2017. 'Lessons from South Korea: A developmental mindset makes a difference when governing the financial economy', in Juan Pablo Bohoslavsky and K. Raffer (eds.), *Sovereign Debt Crises: What Have We Learned?*. Cambridge: Cambridge University Press, pp. 236–253.

Thurbon, Elizabeth. 2019. 'The future of financial activism in Taiwan? The utility of a mindset-centred analysis of developmental states and their evolution', *New Political Economy* 25(3): 320–336.

Thurbon, Elizabeth, Sung-Young Kim, Hao Tan, and John A. Mathews. 2022. 'Korea's green new deal: A very big deal for Australia', *The Asia Society Policy Brief. 15 June.* https://asiasociety.org/australia/south-koreas-green-new-deal-very-big-deal-australia

Thurbon, Elizabeth, Sung-Young Kim, John A. Mathews, and Hao Tan. 2021. 'More "creative" than "destructive"?: Synthesising Schumpeterian and developmental state perspectives to explain mixed results in Korea's clean energy shift', *The Journal of Environment & Development* 30(3): 265–290.

Thurbon, Elizabeth and Linda Weiss. 2016. 'The developmental state in the late twentieth century', in Erik S. Reinert, Jayati Ghosh and Rainer Kattel (eds.), *Handbook of Alternative Theories of Economic Development*. Cheltenham: Edward Elgar Publishing, pp. 637–650.

Thurbon, Elizabeth and Linda Weiss. 2019. 'Economic statecraft at the frontier: Korea's drive for intelligent robotics', *Review of International Political Economy* 28(1): 103–127.

Trnka, Daniel 2020. 'Policies, regulatory framework and enforcement for air quality management: The case of Korea'. *OECD Environment Working Paper* No. 158. Paris: OECD.

United Nations Environmental Program (UNEP). 2010. 'Overview of the Republic of Korea's Green Growth National Strategy for Green Growth'. United Nations Environmental Program.

Vagliasindi, Maria and John Besant-Jones. 2013. *Power Market Structure: Revisiting Policy Options*. Washington D.C.: The World Bank.

Vogel, Steven K. 2018. *Marketcraft: How Governments make Markets Work*. Oxford: Oxford University Press.

Wade, Robert. 1990. *Governing the Market: Economic Theory and the Role of Government in East Asian Industrialisation*. Princeton: Princeton University Press.

Wade, Robert. 2018. 'The developmental state: dead or alive?', *Development and Change* 49(2): 518–546.

Wang, Dianming. 2019. 'The impacts of NEV development on energy structure and energy security', *Energy Review* 6: 56–60.

Wang, Yongpei, Weilong Yan, Shangwen Zhuang, and Jun Li. 2018. 'Does grid-connected clean power promote regional energy efficiency? An empirical analysis based on the upgrading grid infrastructure across China', *Journal of Cleaner Production* 186: 736–747.

Weber, Max. 2019. *Economy and Society. I: A New Translation*. Edited by Keith Tribe. Cambridge: Harvard University Press.

Weidmer, Helmut and Mez Lutz. 2008. 'German climate change policy: A success story with some flaws', *The Journal of Environment & Development* 17(4): 356–378.

Weiss, Linda. 1995. 'Governed interdependence: Rethinking the government–business relationship in East Asia', *The Pacific Review* 8(4): 589–616.

Weiss, Linda. 1998. *The Myth of the Powerless State: Governing the Economy in a Global Era*. Cambridge: Polity Press.

Weiss, Linda. 2003. 'Guiding globalisation in East Asia: New roles for old developmental states', in Linda Weiss (ed.), *States in the Global Economy: Bringing Domestic Institutions Back In*. Cambridge & New York: Cambridge University Press, pp. 245–270.

Weiss, Linda. 2014. *America Inc?: Innovation and Enterprise in the National Security State*. Ithaca: Cornell University Press.

Weiss, Linda. 2021. 'Re-emergence of great power conflict and US economic statecraft', *World Trade Review* 20(2): 152–168.

Weiss, Linda and John Hobson. 1995. *States and Economic Development: A Comparative Historical Analysis*. Cambridge: Polity Press.

Weiss, Linda, and Elizabeth Thurbon. 2004. 'Where there's a will there's a way: Governing the Market in Times of Uncertainty'. *Issues and Studies* 40(1): 61–72.

Weiss, Linda and Elizabeth Thurbon. 2018. 'Power paradox: How the extension of US infrastructural power abroad diminishes state capacity at home', *Review of International Political Economy* 25(6): 779–810.

Weiss, Linda and Elizabeth Thurbon. 2020. 'Developmental state or economic statecraft? Where, why and how the difference matters', *New Political Economy* 26(3): 472–489.

Weiss, Linda and Elizabeth Thurbon. 2021. 'Explaining divergent national responses to Covid-19: An enhanced state capacity framework', *New Political Economy* 27(4), 697–712.

Whang, Jaehong, Woohyun Hwang, Yeuntae Yoo, and Gilsoo Jang. 2018. 'Introduction of smart grid station configuration and application in Guri branch office of KEPCO', *Sustainability* 10(10): 3512.

Wilkinson, Rorden. 2014. *What's Wrong with the WTO and How to Fix It*. Cambridge: John Wiley & Son.

Woo-Cumings, Meredith. 1991. *Race to the Swift: State and Finance in Korean Industrialisation*. New York: Columbia University Press.

Wu, Fengshi and Ellie Martus. 2020. 'Contested environmentalism: The politics of waste in China and Russia', *Environmental Politics* 30(4): 493–512.

Wu, Xiaobo and Wei Zhang. 2010. 'Seizing the opportunity of paradigm shifts: Catch-up of Chinese ICT firm', *International Journal of Innovation Management* 14(1): 57–91.

Xu, Binjing and Ming Ouyang. 2017. *History of Chinese Automobiles*. Beijing: China Machine Press.

Xu, Yichong. 2016. *Sinews of Power: The Politics of the State Grid Corporation of China*. New York: Oxford University Press.

Xu, Yichong. 2019. 'The search for high power in China', in Loren Brandt and Rawski Rawski (eds.), *Policy, Regulation and Innovation in China's Electricity and Telecom and Industries*. Cambridge: Cambridge University Press, pp. 221–261.

Yang, Jeyun, Youngsang Kwon, and Kim Daehwan. 2021. 'Regional smart city development focus: The South Korean national strategic smart city program', *IEEE Access* 9: 7193–7210.

Yellen, David. 2020. 'How China came to dominate clean energy technologies, and how the US can catch up', *Green Tech Media*, 3 November. Available at https://www.greentechmedia.com/articles/read/how-the-us-can-better-compete-with-china-in-the-clean-energy-technology-cold-war

Yeophantong, Pichamon and Evelyn Goh. 2022. 'China as a "Partial" Environmental Great Power', in Robert Falkner and Barry Buzan (eds.), *Great Powers, Climate Change, and Global Environmental Responsibilities*. Oxford: Oxford University Press, pp. 70–94.

Young, Soogil. 2013a. 'Korea's green growth: Looking back, looking forward', in *Global Green Growth Summit*, Songdo Convensia, Incheon City, Korea, 10–11 June.

Young, Soogil. 2013b. *Noksaek Seongjang 1.0e Seonggwa – Noksaek Seongjang 2.0eul Wihan Gwaje (Outcomes of Green Growth 1.0 – Issues for Green Growth 2.0)* in Soogil Young (ed.), *Noksaek Seongjang 1.0: Noksaek Seongjang 2.0eul Wihan Pyeonggawha Jeon (Korea's Green Growth 1.0: A Critical Assessment and Recommendations for Green Growth 2.0)*. Gyeonggi-do, Paju-si: Kyobo Bookstore, pp. 529–619.

Yu, Keping. 2005. 'Notion of scientific development and ecological civilisation', *Marxism & Reality* 4(4): 4–5.

Zeng, Ming, Li Peng, Qiannan Fan, and Yingjie Zhang. 2016. 'Trans-regional electricity transmission in China: Status, issues and strategies', *Renewable and Sustainable Energy Reviews* 66: 572–583.

Index